Practical R<

The Problems of Philosophy:
Their Past and Present

General Editor: Ted Honderich
Grote Professor of the Philosophy of Mind and Logic
University College
London

Other books in the series

Practical
Reasoning

Robert Audi

London and New York

First published 1989
First published in paperback in 1991
by Routledge
11 New Fetter Lane, London EC4P 4EE

Simultaneously published in
the USA and Canada by
Routledge, Chapman and Hall, Inc.
29 West 35th Street, New York, NY 10001

© *1989, 1991 Robert Audi*

Phototypeset by Input Typesetting Ltd, London
Printed in Great Britain
by T. J. Press (Padstow) Ltd, Padstow, Cornwall

British Library Cataloguing in Publication Data
Audi, Robert
Practical reasoning – (The problems of philosophy)
1. Reasoning
I. Title   II. Series
160

Library of Congress Cataloging in Publication Data
Audi, Robert
Practical reasoning.
(Problems of philosophy)
Bibliography: p.
Includes index.
1. Act (Philosophy) 2. Will. 3. Ethics. 4. Reasoning.
I. Title.   II. Series: Problems of philosophy
0 415 07046 5

Contents

Contents

To my parents

Acknowledgments

This book has benefited much from the detailed comments given me by a number of philosophers who read earlier versions. It has been impossible to take full account of all their points, particularly given the intended brevity and deliberately limited scope of the book, but within these constraints I have tried to respond to them as best I could. For comments on earlier drafts I am deeply grateful to Richard N. Lee, Raimo Tuomela, Michael Zimmerman and, especially, Hugh J. McCann and Alfred R. Mele, who each commented on more than one version of some of the material. I also want to thank Nelson T. Potter for comments on the first three chapters, Ralf Meerbote for helpful remarks on chapter 3, and Robert H. Hurlbutt III for detailed discussion of chapter 3. I have benefited much from conversations with Karl Ameriks on chapter 3, David K. O'Connor on chapter 1, and W. David Solomon on chapter 2. For editorial work, I am indebted to Elizabeth Bilynskyj, Nancy Slonneger, and, in particular, Allison Lea Nespor, who also prepared most of the index.

A number of other philosophers have been of help to me through our discussions of some of the issues treated in the book or in related works of mine or theirs. Among these are members of the National Endowment for the Humanities Institute on Human Action which I directed in 1984 and participants in the epistemology seminars which I also directed under grants from NEH during recent summers. I particularly want to acknowledge the value of conversations I have had, over a number of years, on practical reasoning and related topics, with William P. Alston, Michael E. Bratman, Hector-Neri Castañeda, Alan Donagan, Carl Ginet, Robert M. Gordon, Hugh J. McCann, Alfred R.

Mele, the late Irving Thalberg, and Raimo Tuomela. I regret that space constraints made it impossible to take adequate account of their work. On one or another topic in the book, I have profited from discussions or correspondence with Frederick R. Adams, Lewis White Beck, Myles Brand, Richard B. Brandt, Paul M. Churchland, Norman Dahl, Stephen Darwall, Richard Foley, William K. Frankena, Brian McLaughlin, Alvin Plantinga, Amélie Oksenberg Rorty, John Searle, James P. Sterba, and Judith Jarvis Thomson. Numerous discussions with my students, particularly in graduate seminars, have also contributed much to my thinking on topics addressed in the book.

Much of the writing was completed while I held a Distinguished Scholar Fellowship in the Center for the Philosophy of Religion at the University of Notre Dame, and I benefited from the opportunity to carry on my research in an environment so conducive both to intellectual conversation and to philosophical work. Research support from the University of Nebraska, and discussions with my colleagues there over many years, have also helped me, particularly in the formative stages of the writing.

Introduction

Human life is pervaded by problems. Reasoning is a common response to problems we care about. We do it more than we notice; it is natural, often automatic, and need not call attention to itself. Reasoning is often associated with intellectual problems, such as what constitutes a just state, or whether a system of axioms is free of contradiction. But we also reason in response to everyday problems about how to get on with ordinary business. Confronted with a request for help at a time when we have planned something else, we must decide whether to decline or to adjust our schedule; given a roadblock, we must choose among possible detours. Reasoning appropriate to problems of the first kind has often been called theoretical; reasoning appropriate to problems of the second kind has often been called practical. These terms are not meant to suggest that every theoretical problem is connected with an actual theory, such as a philosophical or scientific one, or that every practical problem is unrelated to theories. Indeed, a theoretical problem may be as routine as determining the cause of a fire, and a practical problem may be as scientific as constructing a safe tunnel. Historically, the main point of the terminology is to suggest that practical problems are addressed to us as agents and concern what one is to do, whereas theoretical problems are addressed to us as knowers, or potential knowers, and concern questions of what is or is not true. The former are solved by one's practice, say by taking the right detour; the latter are solved by one's forming, or bringing to bear, the right belief, say by working out a sound proof that an axiom system is consistent.

1

Another way to draw the contrast is through distinguishing between practical and theoretical reasons. Practical reasons might be said to be reasons for acting; theoretical reasons might be described as reasons for believing. If, for instance, I want to attend a certain conference in London, then I have, and my want expresses, a prima facie practical reason for going to London. If I go there in order to attend it, my going will be done at least partly for that reason: to attend. On the other hand, suppose I believe that the topic is Hume's ethics. I have, and my belief expresses, a prima facie theoretical reason for believing that some people will discuss the idea of reason as the slave of the passions. If I believe the latter proposition on the basis of the former, I believe it at least partly for the reason in question: that the topic is Hume's ethics.

Perhaps we might say that whereas theoretical reasons in some sense point toward truth, practical reasons in some sense point toward action. The idea, in part, is that a good theoretical reason supports, though it need not entail, the rationality of believing the proposition(s) for which it is a good reason; a good practical reason supports, though it need not entail, the rationality of the action(s) for which it is a good reason. But if we hold this, we must *not* infer that beliefs cannot express practical reasons, in the sense of reasons for action, as well as theoretical reasons. Consider the belief that one would enjoy and learn from hearing more about Hume's views on reason and passion. Whether such beliefs express practical reasons is controversial, and it is among the important questions on which this book bears. The issue will not, however, be a central topic; for my main concern is practical *reasoning* rather than practical reasons.

A related problem on which the book bears (though it too will be discussed only in relation to practical reasoning) is whether practical and theoretical reasons may be objective, in the sense that they are reasons for *anyone* to act or believe accordingly, or just subjective, in the sense that they are reasons only *for* a particular person. That a conference on Hume's ethics will be in London may be a (prima facie) reason for me to go there; it is not a reason for just anyone to do so. But perhaps an action's being cruel *is* a (prima facie) reason for anyone to abstain from it; and that a conference is on Hume's ethics may be a reason for anyone, or at least anyone generally informed about Hume, to believe that reason and passion will be discussed, though of course one could have such an objective reason without realizing one does.

Practical and theoretical reasoning have both been much discussed by philosophers, but the latter has had a larger share of their attention. It is usually treated at least implicitly in the course of teaching logic; it is stressed in many epistemological works; and it figures centrally in numerous discussions in the philosophy of science, metaphysics, and other areas of philosophic inquiry. This book mainly concerns practical reasoning, but that can be adequately understood only in relation to theoretical reasoning. Indeed, a satisfactory account of practical reasoning must enable us to see both why it is appropriately called *reasoning* and how it is related to theoretical reasoning. At many points in the book, then, I discuss similarities and differences between these two kinds of reasoning.

A special problem we face in discussing practical reasoning is that there is no everyday expression whose use can guide us in clarifying it, in the way the use of terms like 'explanation', 'knowledge', and 'justice' can guide us in understanding the concepts they express. As philosophers use 'practical reasoning', it is – like 'practical reason' and 'theoretical reason' – a term of art. It has little life in ordinary parlance and a multiple personality in philosophical literature. Fortunately, there *are* terms crucial for understanding practical reasoning, such as 'reasoning', 'inferring', and 'concluding', which do have sufficiently settled uses to help us focus certain of our ideas. Furthermore, there are several problems which, in discussing the nature and role of practical reasoning, philosophers have wanted to solve. We can also use these problems in guiding our inquiry, and I shall discuss them in detail.

To get a better sense of the problems to be examined in developing an account of practical reasoning, consider an example. Suppose I enter my living room and find that two guests, a husband and wife, are quarreling. I am disturbed. I like them both, and I want them to get along. I have a problem: how to reconcile them, or at least temporarily make peace between them. I listen to see if there is simply a misunderstanding. I find the matter more complex: she, Janet, has criticized him, William, for not making time to do something with their children on the weekend, and they are beginning to argue about who is responsible for various aspects of the children's activities on the coming weekend. It seems that they each made weekend plans on the assumption that the other would take over the children, and both are trying to make minimal adjustments. It now occurs to me that I could myself do something with their children and mine, thereby helping with the problem. I think about this prospect a moment and become convinced that I can manage all the children. I come to believe that offering to do something with all the children this weekend would help end the quarrel, and I conclude that I should offer this. Though slightly restrained by my awareness of all the extra effort, I quickly decide to propose my plan. I wait a bit for a good time to interrupt them, and I then suggest that I might help this weekend by getting all the children together at my home. Making this suggestion is my (attempted) solution: I am trying to resolve the reconciliation problem by removing an obstacle to their harmony.

The example shows a number of important elements in what we might broadly call *practical thinking*, using this term to encompass not only practical reasoning, but also less structured reflection on the same problem to whose solution the practical reasoning is directed. First, I am confronted by a problem of what to do; and it is a problem *for me* because of what I care about: very roughly, there is something I want, here harmony between friends, and I take it that I cannot have it unless I do something appropriate, or at least I suppose that I may be able to get it by doing the right thing. Second, I deliberate about how to achieve what I want, a process which includes such things as reflecting on apparent options, recalling facts, and reasoning theoretically, for instance from the supposition that I take their children over on the weekend to the conclusion that telling William and Janet that I will do so would likely remove an obstacle to their harmony. Third – but perhaps simultaneously – I form the belief that offering to take the children over would help end the quarrel. Fourth, I judge, partly on the basis of that belief, that I should offer. And finally, after waiting for a good opportunity, I act on this judgment: I suggest to Janet and William that I get all our children together.

If, in a stretch of such practical thinking, we try to isolate something that it is natural to call practical reasoning, there need be no one piece of reasoning which uncontroversially fills this role. Suppose, however, we are guided by the thought that we should identify a piece of reasoning that is a response to a practical problem and concludes with an answer to the problem – in the sense of an answer to the associated question, which is here roughly 'How can I reconcile Janet and William?' The best candidate is probably my reasoning from the premise that I want to (or perhaps must) reconcile them, together with the related premise (itself arrived at by theoretical reasoning) that suggesting I take over all our children this weekend will reconcile them, to the conclusion that I should suggest it. I have reasoned to an answer to my problem; the answer is practical in the sense that it indicates an action of mine which it represents as a means of solving my practical problem; and my acting in accordance with that answer is my attempted solution. In different terminology, my reasoning both *arises* from a practical reason, namely, my wanting to reconcile my friends, and *generates* such a reason, by concluding with the judgment that I should suggest taking over the children; and my acting on that reason – by making this suggestion – is what I take to be my solution to my problem.

There are, however, many other strategies for identifying practical reasoning, and in examining some of what philosophers have said about such reasoning I want to compare other strategies with the one just illustrated. If 'practical reasoning' had a sufficiently settled use, then one good way of choosing among the various accounts of such reasoning might be to appeal to intuitions about the application of the term. In the absence of such a use, we need a different way to ascertain what constitutes practical reasoning. As it happens, there are certain major problems that give the topic of practical reasoning its special interest. These are philosophically important in their own right; but one or another of them has also been a main concern of philosophers writing on practical reasoning, and all seem discernible in Aristotle, who is, historically, the most important writer on the topic. This book aims above all at developing at least partial solutions to these problems. If this end is achieved, then even if the specific account of practical reasoning that is offered does not capture all the plausible conceptions of it to be found in the philosophical literature, we shall at least have a framework for understanding those conceptions.

The problems that seem central to the topic of practical

reasoning can all be illustrated with respect to our reconciliation example. Let me briefly sketch each one, leaving detailed discussion for the main body of the book.

The first problem is to connect practical reasoning with the kinds of questions that provide the occasion for it. Above all, *how is a practical question rationally answered?* The problem is to give at least a partial account of how a rational person – say, the kind Aristotle called a person of practical wisdom – answers a practical question, such as 'What am I to do to reconcile Janet and William?' Clearly, practical reasoning, as described above, constitutes one way that a rational person produces an answer. I take it that such a question can *arise* for an agent without being *asked*, by that agent or anyone else. Simply through confronting a practical problem, one can feel the need to answer a practical question. Thus, the occasions that call for practical reasoning go far beyond cases in which a practical question is explicitly asked. The context may be social, as in our example, or personal, as where one is planning a quiet afternoon. The question may be instrumental, say about how best to make up for time lost in a detour; or it may concern intrinsic ends, for instance when, with only enjoyment in view, one considers which of several books to read. And one's options may, like alternative vacation trips, call for complex planning, or they may arise spontaneously, as where one is offered a choice of desserts, or comes upon two equally appealing paths on a woodland walk.

The second problem centers on the question *What is it for an agent to act for a reason?* Since reasons on which one acts are (in some sense) practical, and any practical reason *can* in some way be acted on, this is roughly the question of how a practical reason grounds an action based upon it. Clearly, I act for a reason when, *in order to* help reconcile Janet and William, I suggest my taking over all the children on the weekend. Acting on the basis of practical reasoning is a paradigm of acting for a reason. It may indeed turn out that either actions so based are the only ones performed for a reason, or, at least, in giving an account of action based on practical reasoning, we can exhibit the crucial elements in acting simply *for* a reason. The central issue here, then, is whether, to some extent at least, action for a reason can be explicated as action based on practical reasoning. More broadly still, to what degree do reasons for which we act operate through reasoning?

The third problem is structural. *Is there a pattern of reasoning by which all intentional actions can be explained, including actions exhibiting weakness of will?* (I take actions exhibiting weakness of will to be – roughly – uncompelled, and normally intentional, actions against one's better judgment.) Here there are two main difficulties. One is to ascertain how reasoning *processes* might figure in producing our actions. Call this the *explanatory problem*. The other is to determine whether all intentional action is intelligible in terms of a pattern that applies to the agent's psychological state at the crucial time, whether or not this pattern is actively expressed in a reasoning process. Call this the *intelligibility problem*. Suppose, for instance, that my desire to avoid extra work had prevailed over my judgment that I should suggest taking over all of the children on the weekend. By keeping silent and thereby failing to act on that judgment, I might have exhibited weakness of will, and we should need an account of how the motivational pattern causing me to keep silent interacted with the pattern of motivation and judgment corresponding to my practical reasoning. On the other hand, suppose that I had not reasoned my way to the judgment that I should take over all the children, yet simply made it as an immediate 'intuitive' response to my problem. Both the judgment and my action based on it might still be intelligible in relation to the motivational and cognitive (roughly, belief) elements that are represented in practical reasoning. The same kind of intelligibility apparently characterizes what underlies the imagined weak-willed failure to act on my judgment: the relevant omission is intentional and seems attributable to a similar (prevailing) pattern. As these cases suggest, our structural problem is both to ascertain the explanatory role of practical reasoning and to determine how the patterns it exhibits make intentional actions intelligible.

By contrast with the third problem, the fourth concerns the *dynamics* of action: the events or processes or whatever that produce an intentional action, given the agent's reasons for it. Specifically, *what is it that causally mediates between reasons and actions?* The issue here, more precisely stated, is what it is that causally links one's motives, intentions, beliefs, and other psychological elements that provide one's reasons *to* act, and, on the other hand, the actions one performs *for* those reasons. Consider my wanting to reconcile Janet and William, and thereby having a reason to act toward that end. This motivational state does not automatically yield such action; I may, for instance, have no thought that points toward an available means to accomplish my end. Practical reasoning that concludes in favor of a specific action seems to fill the bill perfectly: it is a process with both the right sorts of constituents to motivate and direct the action, and the right kind of content and conscious manifestations to trigger the action. For instance, in some way it embodies adequate motivation, and it concludes with a judgment that I should (now) suggest taking over all the children.

The fifth problem concerns the *rationality* of action. *Can we so specify the structure of acting for a reason that actions for a reason can be seen, in the light of that reason, as not only intelligible but also prima facie rational?* If actions for a reason are always based on practical reasoning, or are even somehow undergirded by a motivational and cognitive pattern of the *kind* that yields practical reasoning, then it seems plain why they should be prima facie rational: they are grounded in reasoning and to that extent guided by reason. This is especially likely to seem a plausible explanation of their prima facie rationality if we presuppose a notion of practical reasoning which, as in our example, makes it minimally acceptable by appropriate standards for evaluating the cogency of reasoning. Suppose my reasoning is from my positing an end not overridden by any competing end of mine, and from my reasonable belief that doing a certain thing will easily accomplish that end, to the conclusion that I should do it. If, for instance, I presently want to reconcile Janet and William more than to do anything that might compete with this aim, and I believe (for adequate reason) that offering to take over the children will accomplish my end, then judging that I should offer is a prima facie quite reasonable inference to draw, making the offer is a prima facie quite reasonable thing to do, and actually offering to do this is a prima facie rational concrete action.

The last problem I want to stress concerns the *degree of unity* of the notion of reasoning in general. Specifically, *How can we account for both the similarities and the differences between practical and theoretical reasoning?* In virtue of what, for instance, are they both reasoning? Do they differ in relation to the standards appropriate to their evaluation, or even in respect to what sorts of items constitute their premises and conclusions? Or do they differ mainly in the kinds of reasons they give us, or perhaps simply in the sorts of problems that motivate our engaging in them? Here, too, there is a considerable diversity of views in the philosophical literature.

If I were to add another problem giving special interest to the topic of practical reasoning, it might be to understand Aristotle's views on practical thinking and the nature of human action. Aristotle appears again and again in discussions of practical reasoning, and neither the history of the topic nor the current literature can be understood in abstraction from his work. It is quite appropriate, then, to begin a study of practical reasoning with him. It is also appropriate here to explore other important historical figures, though this book is by no means primarily historical and is concerned chiefly with the six general questions just raised. In the literature that addresses or bears on practical reasoning, Hume and Kant are, after Aristotle, perhaps the most important. But even if this is not so, they are major figures in this literature; each contrasts sharply with the other; and each has significant similarities to Aristotle, though they both depart from him in major ways. There are, of course, other important historical figures I shall simply not have space to take up. My hope is that if they are as important for the topic as Hume or Kant, their positions can either be seen as, in good part, combinations of elements of those of Aristotle, Hume, and Kant, or at least as understandable largely on the basis of the treatment of the topic which, beginning with those three philosophers, this book will give.

PART 1

Historical Background: Practical Reasoning in Aristotle, Hume, and Kant

CHAPTER 1

Aristotle on Practical Reasoning and the Structure of Action

Aristotle's principal writings on practical thinking are in the *Nicomachean Ethics* (*NE*), and this will be my main Aristotelian text, though some references will be made to others of his works. The *Ethics* is a densely packed and very rich text, and I cannot hope to formulate *the* Aristotelian position on practical reasoning, if there is just one such position in his works. Nor can I even begin to do justice to the large body of valuable literature on Aristotle's account of practical reasoning. My aim is simply to formulate and interpret one plausible Aristotelian conception (or range of conceptions) of practical reasoning, particularly as it appears in the *Ethics*, and to identify, through exploring Aristotle, some major concepts and problems crucial for understanding practical reasoning.

Aristotle did not use any term that can be literally translated as 'practical reasoning',[1] and what he called practical syllogisms may represent a narrower category than what I have so far called practical reasoning. In his treatment of practical thinking in general, however, he did say a great deal about deliberation, which some commentators have taken him to equate with practical reasoning.[2] Moreover, deliberation is plainly a kind of practical thinking; and, as illustrated by the reconciliation example in the Introduction, deliberation may embody what I have called practical reasoning. It may be wise, then, to begin with Aristotle's views about deliberation and work from there toward an understanding of his views of practical reasoning.

Practical Reasoning

I Deliberation

Regarding the objects of deliberation, Aristotle makes both positive and negative points:

> we deliberate about what results through our own agency, but in different ways on different occasions, e.g. about questions of medicine and money-making . . . . We deliberate not about ends, but about what promotes ends; a doctor, e.g., does not deliberate about whether he will cure, or an orator about whether he will persuade, or a politician about whether he will produce good order, or any other [expert] about the end [that his science aims at]. Rather, we first lay down the end, and then examine the ways and means to achieve it. If it appears that any of several [possible] means will reach it, we consider which of them will reach it most easily and most finely; and if only one [possible] means reaches it, we consider how that means will reach it, and how the means itself is reached, until we come to the first cause, the last thing to be discovered.[3]

To illustrate with one of Aristotle's examples, if I am a physician treating a patient, my governing end *as* a physician (leaving aside the issue of euthanasia) is to cure, and I do not deliberate about whether I will (or should) cure the patient. I do, however, deliberate about means, say about whether I should give medicine or simply recommend rest.

There are at least two cases consistent with the passage. In one, the deliberative chain contains a series of decisions leading to the final decision which is, or is at least closely tied to, the first thing in the order of causation. In this first instance, the deliberative chain is *decisional*: if I decide to prescribe medicine, doing so becomes a subsidiary end, and I may then deliberate about what medicine I should give. If I decide on penicillin as a means of cure, I have another subsidiary end and may deliberate about how I should carry that out, say by tablet or injection. If I now decide on tablets, I may realize that they are in the cabinet to my left. Suppose I do decide to give some of those very tablets; then, aware that I need only reach for them, I do it. In the second case consistent with the passage, while I make the same final decision, the deliberative chain is *cognitive*: instrumental beliefs (or other cognitive elements, such as judgments) express the subsidiary ends; for instance, I do not decide to prescribe medicine, but do judge prescribing it best and thereby proceed to identify the best medicine, and then the best vehicle for giving it. I finally decide to do the thing which is warranted by the entire sequence: reaching for the tablets.

Schematically, the difference between the two kinds of chain is the kind that exists between (1) deciding to A, which one believes one can well achieve by B, deciding to B, which one believes one can well achieve by C, and so on until one decides on something here and now, such as reaching for the tablets, and (2) forming the beliefs that A can be well achieved by B, that B can be well achieved by C, and so on until one reaches something one can do here and now, which one decides to do. In both kinds of chain there will be appropriate instrumental beliefs; they are in fact required to explain the subsidiary decisions. But in one there are subsidiary decisions, in the other not.

The decisional interpretation of the chain may be more often what Aristotle had in mind. Moreover, it is quite consistent with his overall views to allow cases in which the decisions are conditional. There, when one reaches the end, action will follow only on a further condition; for instance, if one decides to give tablets provided there are enough, then one would check before giving them, and give them only if one's checking indicates enough. I prefer the decisional interpretation for most of the relevant passages; but the more economical, cognitive reading may better fit others. In any case, no major point in our discussion will turn on which interpretation is taken.

The descriptions just given seem to encompass the completion of the process of deliberation, but they do not indicate what, exactly, is the first link in the chain of causation. If that is the last step in the order of discovery, one would think it is my final means to realizing my end: reaching for the tablets. For this is the final means I take to be necessary, and it seems to originate the causal chain leading (if I succeed) to cure. But the text is not without vagueness on this matter:

> What we deliberate about is the same as what we decide to do, except that by the time we decide to do it, it is definite; for what we decide to do is what we have judged [to be right]

as a result of deliberation. For each of us stops inquiring how to act as soon as he traces the origin to himself, and within himself to the dominant part; for this is the part that decides. . . . We have found, then, that what we decide to do is whatever action among those up to us we deliberate about and desire to do. Hence also decision will be deliberative desire to do an action that is up to us; for when we have judged [that it is right] as a result of deliberation, our desire to do it expresses our wish.

(NE: 1113a2–12)

If decision is 'deliberative desire', how can it be identical with something that is, in an active way, made, as decisions are? A decision is, if not an action, at least an event, whereas desires are not events (in the usual sense entailing change). One possible answer may be that 'deliberative desire' should be taken to be (in English) a technical term, and the weight should be put on 'decision', which does appear to designate action or at least behavior (the Greek term in question, *prohairesis*, is also commonly translated 'choice', which confirms this actional reading[4]). The decision would be deliberative by virtue of its origin in a deliberative process; it would be conative by virtue of expressing 'our wish'. If we add that it is an active expression of that wish, we may think of it as action-like.

There are at least two directions in which such an interpretation may be developed. First, it might be that in cases like this, in which one deliberatively reaches, and immediately performs, a bodily action in one's power as the final means to one's overall end, Aristotle thought of the decision to do the thing in question and the doing of it as the same action under two different descriptions. One need not decide to reach for the tablets *and then* do so; one's deciding to give them to the patient coincides with reaching for them; it occurs straightaway upon one's realizing that the tablets are in the cabinet on one's left. If this is correct, then a patient who was aware of the chain of deliberation and thus said, observing one's taking them from the cabinet, 'I see you decided to give me the tablets', would be saying nothing beyond what the passage licenses, and would preserve the vagueness of the reference of 'decide'. On the other hand, one might instead suppose that decision is, or is a precursor of, volition, understood as an act of will. To be sure, one might treat volition as ordinary action under a special kind of description, and in that case this interpretation would be quite similar to the first. But volition is more commonly taken to be a kind of doing that is not action, or as a sort of active intending to do something here and now.[5] In what follows, it will not be essential that we choose either interpretation; indeed my main points about Aristotle concern what happens prior to decision and will in any event be consistent with both interpretations, and indeed with taking decision to be a volitional state as opposed to an event of any kind.

II   The practical syllogism

If we can locate what Aristotle called the practical syllogism in relation to his deliberative chains, this may give us a better idea of the sort of reasoning he conceived as practical in the sense sketched in the Introduction. In discussing weakness of will (which will be considered shortly) Aristotle said a good deal about the practical syllogism. Here is an important passage about such syllogisms in general:

> One belief (a) is universal; the other (b) is about particulars, and because they are particulars perception controls them. And in the cases where these two beliefs result in (c) one belief, it is necessary in purely theoretical beliefs for the soul to affirm what has been concluded, and in beliefs about production (d) to act at once on what has been concluded.
>   If, e.g., (a) everything sweet must be tasted, and (b) this, some one particular thing, is sweet, it is necessary (d) for someone who is able and unhindered also to act on this at the same time
>
> (*NE*: 1147a25–31)

where (c), which is the 'one belief' that is a 'result' of (a) and (b) is presumably that this must be tasted. If we now recall the deliberative chain leading to reaching for tablets to cure the patient, we might take, as a clue in locating a practical syllogism like this one in the chain, the closeness of the syllogism to action – a feature of such syllogisms which Aristotle emphasizes elsewhere too.[6] Perhaps such a practical syllogism begins when I reach the conclusion (from previous reasoning) that diseases of the sort this patient has are to be treated with penicillin tablets. With this goal in view, I realize, perceptually, that they are in the cabinet to my left and judge that I must give them. I am bound to 'act on this at the same time.'[7]

It is noteworthy that Aristotle speaks in this passage both of the soul's being bound to affirm the conclusion – which in the example we are considering would be that this must be tasted [by me] – and of the agent's being bound to perform this act at once. If the act is tasting, we need a behavioral referent; if it is the soul's affirming the conclusion, we need a mental referent. The view that the crucial action is a decision (or a choice) conceived as *also* capable of bearing a physical behavioral description gives us precisely what we need. But Aristotle rightly refers to each category in distinct terms, since the crucial decision *need* not bear a physical act description, say where – as Aristotle realizes is quite possible – the agent is prevented from tasting the food.

To be sure, affirming the conclusion seems an essentially cognitive act, roughly an endorsing of a proposition, whereas decision, by virtue of being a deliberative desire and apparently entailing an intention to do the thing decided on, is essentially motivational. Nevertheless, clearly Aristotle is thinking of the relevant kind of judgment – roughly, that one must (or ought all things considered) do something – as normally implying a decision to do it. In part the connection might be expressed in terms of a relation between cognitive and behavioral decisions: *decision that*, of the kind one might identify with the concluding judgment, tends to produce a *decision to do*, particularly insofar as the latter is understood as a deliberative desire. This is not to say that Aristotle employed the relevant term in these two ways; but it is noteworthy that it has both functions. The cognitive function is appropriate to its playing the role of emerging from (and even expressing the conclusion of) reasoning; the behavioral function makes it practical, either in the direct sense that it is itself action or in the sense that it provides at once a reason for acting and some degree of motivation to act.

If this reading is correct, then the kind of reasoning that normally instantiates a practical syllogism is practical reasoning in the broad sense of reasoning that concludes with an answer to a practical question, such as, paradigmatically, 'What am I to do?', asked in the context of a felt problem. If my problem is to cure the patient and I deliberate toward that end, then upon concluding (cognitively deciding, one might say) that I should reach for the tablets in the cabinet to my left, I have arrived at an answer to my problem. I then *solve* the problem by reaching for the tablets and giving them to the patient. Since Aristotle took the action constituting a solution to occur at once given the agent's unimpeded ability to do the crucial thing, he sometimes talked as if the action itself were the conclusion. But I do not believe the text asserts precisely this.[8] It is noteworthy that he speaks of the physician's deliberating about 'what he will' do rather than simply about what *to* do. This may suggest that the concluding element in the reasoning is a cognitive item, say a resolution (or judgment or perhaps cognitive decision), to the effect that one will (or should) do something. The decision *to* do it, which may or may not be behaviorally instantiated by the immediate performance of the action, might then be seen as the appropriate action to be performed in response to the drawing of this conclusion.

III Weakness of will

If Aristotle took concluding in favor of an action normally to imply deciding to perform it, then we must ask how he allowed for weakness of will, in the sense of acting (normally intentionally) against one's better judgment, where this is precisely the *sort* of judgment which, like 'This must be tasted', concludes a practical syllogism.[9] We might call actions of this kind *incontinent* for short. In discussing them, I cannot present his overall account of weakness of will, if indeed he offered a fully unified account. Since my concern is with his view of practical reasoning, I simply want to indicate how he saw practical reasoning as allowing for incontinent action.

From this point of view, the following passage is especially important:

> Suppose, then, that someone has (a) the universal belief [say, that sweets are to be avoided], and it hinders him from tasting; he has (b) the second belief, that everything sweet is pleasant and this is sweet, and this belief (b) is active; and

he also has appetite. Hence the belief (c) tells him to avoid this, but appetite leads him on, since it is capable of moving each of the [bodily] parts.

The result, then, is that in a way reason and belief make him act incontinently. The belief (b) is contrary to correct reason (a), but only coincidentally, not in itself.

(*NE*: 1147a31–1147b2)

It looks as if one piece of reasoning presupposed here is prohibitional: from a universal premise, say that (a) sweets are to be avoided, to a negative judgment, say that (c) this is to be avoided, which 'hinders' but does not prevent the tasting. Its minor premise is presumably a perceptual one to the effect that this is sweet.

Moreover, while we need not suppose that there is a second piece of practical reasoning, there may also be competing, appetitional reasoning: from the premises that (1) everything sweet is pleasant and (2) this is sweet, to the conclusion that (3) this must be tasted. But then there would be an opinion, namely, (3), opposed to right reason, since reason dictates that things of this kind are *not* to be tasted. Furthermore, Aristotle specifically tells us that it is appetite, for instance a ravenous desire for sweets, that opposes right reason. Even if we take this opinion to represent appetite, we still have a problem: how can appetite prevail if a properly drawn practical conclusion, such as that this is to be avoided, at least normally implies acting accordingly when one can? The incontinent agent here is not, after all, *unable* to act rightly. He is simply weak-willed, and he appears to have *also* reasoned in accordance with the first syllogism, from (say) the premises that sweets are not to be tasted and this is such a sweet, to the conclusion that this is not to be tasted. But even assuming the passage should be read as implying competing syllogisms like the pair I have formulated, there remains the question why the syllogism on the side of right reason does not prevail in action. Indeed, the problem is pressing even if an incontinent action is imagined as going against a judgment not arising from practical reasoning: how can right reason not prevail even if it is represented only by a judgment which is not (at least at the time) based on any practical reasoning?

Aristotle's treatment of the problem draws on a distinction between kinds of knowledge:

> And since the last premise (b) is about something perceptible, and controls action, this must be what the incontinent person does not have when he is being affected. Or rather the way he has it is not knowledge of it, but, as we saw, [merely] saying the words as the drunk says the words of Empedocles . . . the knowledge that is present when someone is affected by incontinence, and that is dragged about because he is affected, is not the sort that seems to be knowledge to the full extent [in (c)], but only perceptual knowledge [in (b)].
>
> (*NE*: 1147b9–17)

Appetite can overcome one's (partly) perceptual knowledge that this is sweet and not to be tasted, but it cannot overcome what constitutes one's 'knowledge to the full extent': that things of this sort are not to be tasted. It is as if appetite detached the perceptual knowledge that this is sweet – which Irwin suggests (p. 352) may be what Aristotle referred to as the belief which is 'active' – from the universal known through right reason, and instead attached it to the object of desire. If there is competing reasoning, that object may be expressed in a universal, say that sweet things must be tasted; if there is not, then appetite may affect action more directly. But in either case, how is it possible for the knowledge that should direct action to be relegated to this ineffectual position?

Here it is essential to consider what Aristotle says about such knowledge. One important point is that

> Saying the words that come from knowledge is no sign [of fully having it] . . . . Further, those who have just learnt something do not yet know it, though they string the words together; for it must grow into them, and this needs time.
>
> Hence we must suppose that incontinents say the words in the way actors do.
>
> (*NE*: 1147a18–24)

In these and other passages, Aristotle is distinguishing both different kinds of knowledge and different ways of having it. One reading of his suggested distinction between kinds of knowledge

– or perhaps one of the two or more distinctions of kind he had in mind – is that it holds between a form of *recognition* – knowing *what*, for instance what one is eating – and a kind of *conviction* – knowing *that*, for example that things of a certain kind are to be avoided. The former, recognitional knowledge', represented in the minor premise, is overcome, and it operates under the control of appetite; the latter, the conviction of right reason, represented in the major, is not. One can act against one's better judgment precisely because one does not clearly grasp what one is doing, or at least does not grasp it in the right way. One may realize one is eating cake, or even a sweet, but one at best imperfectly knows one is eating something not to be tasted. This may occur even if one initially in some sense decided to act on the judgment that one is to avoid tasting this; that point might account for one's being initially hindered in acting. It may also be true that even the 'knowledge' representing right reason can in *some* sense be overcome, since it is not unqualifiedly present in the first place, in the sense that the knowledge is not, at the time, fully had.

On this reading, one kind of weakness of will is possible because agents can act against their better judgment (incontinently) when that judgment, or some other factor crucial in the genesis of the action, is obscured by appetite or other elements in the situation and so, in some way, inadequately known. Call this an *obscured knowledge reading*. One possible case here is inadequate knowledge of the major premise, as some of Aristotle's examples suggest; and one might speculate that if one's knowledge of that, or of other relevant principles of conduct, were fully adequate, one's knowledge of the minor would not be inadequate.

Once we reflect on Aristotle's remarks about knowledge of the major, we can see another plausible reading of his position on incontinence, which yields a different interpretation: even if the major is in one way unqualifiedly known, it is not fully integrated into one's character. The latter possibility, at least, is illustrated by Aristotle's comments, quoted above, about beginning students, who may have just learned something, yet do not (fully) know it, since it 'must grow into them.'[10] Thus, incontinent agents may know the major, yet not have integrated that knowledge into their motivational systems, say because they lack the required motivation to act on the knowledge, or lack certain habits, or both. The explanation need not be that they are like novices in the subject matter. Aristotle seems to leave open how deep knowledge can be in us intellectually without being integrated into our motivational systems. It may be that even if incontinent agents do fully know both premises, they can still act incontinently; for their knowledge of the major (and perhaps also of the minor) is not integrated into their character, and they do not use it.

This interpretation is particularly plausible so far as Aristotle stresses *using* knowledge, as when he says that

> we speak of knowing in two ways, and ascribe it to someone who has it without using it and to someone who is using it. Hence it will matter whether someone has the knowledge that his action is wrong, without attending to his knowledge, or both has and attends to it . . . wrong action when he does not attend to his knowledge does not seem extraordinary. (*NE*: 1146b31–5)

Unused knowledge is (at least at the time) unintegrated; on the other hand, knowledge not attended to is especially likely to be unused. When incontinence does occur in cases of unused knowledge, however, it is still intelligible. For since 'reason and belief make the agent act,' there is some kind of reasoning and opinion, a kind that matches practical reasoning in its means-end structure, yet represents only emotion (or appetite), rather than right reason, in its major premise. Indeed, this same passage suggests that obscured knowledge, at least of the particular judgment against which one is acting, can itself account for some kinds of incontinence, even if lack of integration – which Aristotle implicitly distinguishes from obscured knowledge – does not occur.

On the *insufficient integration reading*, weakness of will can apparently occur despite an awareness of an inconsistency (or incongruity) between one's (incontinent) action and one's practical judgment, since the failure is not in the clarity of one's knowledge but in its integration. Doubtless Aristotle emphasized lack of integration as a factor in at least some cases of incontinence; and the view in question helps to explain why incontinence is naturally called weakness of *will*, since failures of will are clearest where the agent definitely realizes what reason directs. But – particularly if we do not take him to be making a radical break with Socrates on this issue – it is doubtful whether he would countenance the possibility of such 'clear-eyed' weakness of will.[11] Possibly he took failure of integration to occur only when the relevant knowledge is either not fully had or not adequately attended to. In any event, each reading may give us part of the truth: *both* a deficiency in the quality of the agent's knowledge and an inadequacy of its motivational integration can provide Aristotelian explanations of how weakness of will is possible.

IV   Practical and theoretical reasoning

On one interpretation of Aristotle, practical and theoretical reasoning contrast sharply in virtue of having different sorts of conclusions: an action in the first case and something quite different (presumably a proposition) in the second. Anscombe has plausibly argued for this view. She maintains that

> we may accept from Aristotle that practical reasoning is essentially concerned with 'what is capable of turning out variously,' without thinking that this subject matter is enough to make reasoning about it practical. There is a difference of form between reasoning leading to action and reasoning for the truth of a conclusion. Aristotle however liked to stress the similarity between the kinds of reasoning, saying [*De Motu Animalium* VII] that what 'happens' is the same in both. There are indeed three types of case . . . the theoretical syllogism and also the idle practical syllogism [*NE*: 1147a27–8] which is just a classroom example. In both of these the conclusion is 'said' by the mind which infers it. And there is the practical syllogism proper. Here the conclusion is an action whose point is shewn by the premises, which are now, so to speak, on active service.[12]

One may wonder, of course, how *reasoning*, which is normally conceived as having as its conclusion something capable of truth or falsity, can have an action as its conclusion. On the other hand, though actions cannot be true or false, they can be *supported* by premises, particularly premises that show their point. Let us pursue the action-as-conclusion view further.[13]

The passage that perhaps most strongly supports the action-as-conclusion interpretation is *De Motu Animalium* 701a4–25. Consider this part of it first:

> What happens seems parallel to the case of thinking and inferring about the immovable objects of science. There the end is the truth seen (for, when one conceives the two premises, one at once conceives and comprehends the conclusion), but here the two premises result in an action – for example, one conceives that every man ought to walk, one is a man oneself; straightaway one walks.
>
> (701a8–14)

Aristotle is here drawing an analogy between what results from conceiving the (accepted) premises of a theoretical argument and what results from conceiving those of a practical one; and clearly he puts acting parallel to conceiving the conclusion of one's theoretical premises. But he does not here say that the action *is* the conclusion. Indeed, he leaves open the possibility that the action is the indirect result of conceiving the premises, where the direct result is the same sort of thing we have in the theoretical case – namely, drawing (in a sense normally implying accepting) the practical proposition, say that I ought to walk.

If this seems to make the parallel inexact, note that on the assumption that Aristotle distinguished conceiving from believing, he might be read as having left room for *incontinent belief*, as where one conceives a conclusion which, in the light of one's premises, one judges one ought to believe, or judges to be true, but, because it is highly distasteful, one does not believe it. Granted, in 19–20 he goes on to say that 'the conclusion, the "I have to make a cloak," is an action' (Nussbaum's translation). But it is important that here the conclusion, though *called* an action, is not *described* as something done – unless he is thinking of the *drawing* of it as the action here referred to. Certainly that would fit the parallel he is making, for the drawing of a conclusion, if taken to be like making a judgment or forming a belief, is no less behavioral in theoretical reasoning than in practical reasoning.

This reading is supported by a number of points. One is that it makes good sense of the way Aristotle emphasizes the parallel between the practical and theoretical cases; if the contrast is as strong as the action-as-conclusion view has it, one would expect him to stress the differences more than the similarities, and more than he does. Second, I have already quoted him as saying, of the case where two premises are combined as they are when a universal rule is realized in a particular case, that 'it is necessary in purely theoretical beliefs for the soul to affirm what has been concluded, and in beliefs about production to act at once on what has been concluded' (*NE*: 1147a27–8). Here he apparently *distinguishes* between the drawing (or affirming) of the conclusion and the action that results from drawing it, specifically, is taken 'on what has been concluded.' Since it is self-evident what the conclusion is in the simple instances imagined, in which a universal role is realized in a particular case, he has no need to mention the drawing of the conclusion as a separate act. But that the conclusion is distinct from the action seems implicit in his maintaining that the action occurs at once *for* someone who 'is able and unhindered' (1147a30–1). When inability or prevention occurs, apparently the conclusion has been drawn, but is not acted on.[14]

Indeed, if it is not possible for the agent to conclude the reasoning without acting on it, then it becomes at least more difficult to account for some of Aristotle's points about weakness of will. For there it certainly appears that emotion overcomes practical reasoning precisely in the sense that one completes it – if without appropriate knowledge of its constituents, particularly its major premise – and fails to act on it. One might argue that in cases of incontinence it is only the premises the agent fails to act on; but Aristotle does not say this and speaks of the 'reasoning' as if it were completed.[15] Often, at least, incontinent action represents not uncompleted practical reasoning, but unsuccessful practical reasoning.

There are, to be sure, problems for the suggested interpretation of Aristotle's conception of practical reasoning. One is that, as Anscombe is quite right to bring out, from Aristotle's point that practical reasoning concerns what can turn out variously, we must not infer that this restriction of subject matter was his criterion for what constitutes practical reasoning. One can surely do theoretical reasoning about any subject (though where the reasoning is scientific – as at least the paradigm cases are – it must concern matters that admit of the appropriate necessary connections). Another problem is how to take Aristotle's point that 'the last premise is a belief about something perceptible, and *controls* action' (*NE*: 1147b9–10, emphasis added). This point makes it appear that nothing else, such as drawing a conclusion, controls action (though some commentators have taken *he teleutaia protasis* here to mean 'conclusion' rather than 'last premise' – a reading which, though I am not adopting it, would certainly support my interpretation as against the action-as-conclusion view). Aristotle's point here may also seem to leave action as the only candidate for the conclusion. Let us consider these problems in turn.

On the interpretation I have suggested, it is not merely subject matter that accounts for the practicality of practical reasoning. If the reasoning occurs in the context of pursuing an end, and if this pursuit includes commitment to a judgment of what one ought to do, then its conclusion may indeed be expected to lead to one's acting 'at once' *provided* one is able and unhindered. Thus, practical reasoning may be seen as undertaken for a practical purpose, namely achieving some end, and normally as issuing in action. Furthermore, its conclusion is not just any judgment, but a *practical* one, to the effect that one must do something. On this view of Aristotle's conception of practical reasoning, then, we have both a significant contrast between practical and theoretical reasoning and an account of his emphasis on the parallels between them.

The other difficulty – that, since the acceptance of the minor premise controls the action, the action is the only conclusion for which there is room – can be resolved by three points. First, acceptance of the minor premise can determine our action even if it does not do so singly or, more important, directly, that is, without the mediation of some other psychological element. Second, even if the minor (or our conceiving and accepting it) should directly determine action, it does not follow that we do not *also* in some way draw a propositional conclusion, perhaps as a result of conceiving *both* premises. Drawing this conclusion might have a *guiding* role with respect to how the action is carried out even if the minor in some sense plays the *genetic* determining role. Third, and more positively, since perception is crucial in fully conceiving of the minor premise, which characteristically concerns a means one perceptually grasps here and now, it is appropriate that the premise play a crucial role in determining the action: the chain from one's ultimate goal back to oneself is completed at the point at which one accepts that premise (at which point one also normally judges in favor of the means it identifies);

and given the background motivation that underlies one's reasoning, say the desire to heal one's patient, one now acts if one can and is not prevented.

In my view, then, Aristotle may be emphasizing the determination relation he describes in accounting for incontinence, precisely because, when incontinence occurs, a conclusion *is* drawn – in accord with right reason – on which the agent fails to act, and the failure seems explainable by appeal to a similar determination. One main case is appetite's simply overriding the practical judgment, as where one's realization of the minor premise – that this is a sweet – does not integrate with one's belief of the major; such incontinence may or may not bespeak impetuosity. Another kind of incontinence involves a competing practical syllogism, say with a major premise to the effect that sweets are delectable, which *does* prevail in action, presumably in part through the force of the same minor premise. In short, the determination relation is stressed as part of the causal account of incontinent action; it does not preclude, and is not in tension with, the view that (normally, at least) practical reasoning has *both* an obviously implied judgmental conclusion as its terminal element and, typically, an action as its issue.

V The explanation of action

Clearly, practical reasoning as I have suggested Aristotle conceived it provides a way to understand and explain actions. It makes actions that are based on practical reasoning intelligible as conduct in accordance with one's practical judgment; these actions, in turn, are based on at least one proposition (the major premise) which is held as a guiding principle and is, in a reasonable person, at least prima facie correct. Aristotle's conception of practical reasoning also yields a causal account of actions based on such reasoning. There are at least two important points here. First, the agent is reasoning in the context of a desired end, at least typically in a way that includes a commitment to some principle; this provides *motivation* for the action issuing from the reasoning. Second, the minor premise expresses a perceptual grasp here and now of what the agent takes to be a means[16] to the end (or to acting in accord with the principle); this provides *guidance* for the action. The guidance is twofold: it is exercised in part by a belief to the effect that the end can be achieved by a certain kind of action, say reaching for a sweet; and it derives partly from a perceptual *event* with a kind of causal power that enables the belief to initiate action. The perception starts one's acting in an appropriate way, for instance reaching into the cabinet; the belief helps to sustain and guide the action, say to keep one searching the shelves until one finds the right container.

If Aristotle takes all our intentional actions, as opposed to merely voluntary ones, to arise from practical reasoning, as he sometimes appears to,[17] then his view of practical reasoning provides a good account of how intentional action in general is to be understood and explained. Suppose, however, that he should be read as placing practical reasoning only within the context of deliberation and he *also* allows for the possibility of intentional action that occurs outside this context, as where, after hearing *Finlandia* at a concert, one simply starts humming its melody because one likes it. Whether or not he is to be so read, there surely seem to be intentional actions that do not arise from practical reasoning,[18] and if so it is important to consider how Aristotle might account for them.

The first point to note here is that at least the paradigms of intentional actions are all of a kind that *can* arise from practical reasoning. If this is so, then it may be open to Aristotle to hold what we might call *the correspondence thesis*: the view that to every intentional action there corresponds at least one practical argument whose premises (in some way) express motivation and belief jointly sufficient to explain the action.[19] For instance, even if I spontaneously eat an apple because I am hungry, and without doing practical reasoning, I may eat it *in order to* reduce my hunger, which Aristotle might have taken to imply that, with no change in my motivation or beliefs, I *could* have reasoned from practical premises to a conclusion favoring eating one, say from the premises that eating apples relieves hunger and that eating this apple before me will relieve my hunger.

There is, however, some difficulty with this approach to defending the correspondence thesis. Consider actions performed for their own sake, such as playing tennis for pleasure. Let us start by setting aside an argument which, though unsound, can cause confusion: actions performed (entirely) for their own sake are ends in themselves, and if so they are not such that we can deliberate about them; hence, practical reasoning cannot be directed toward them either. Now even if it should be true that for Aristotle practical reasoning is deliberation, or is possible only for actions subject to deliberation, this argument is defective. For Aristotle's view that we do not deliberate about ends plainly permits deliberation about what *means* to take to an intrinsically motivated action, and in that way we can deliberate about the action. Indeed, Aristotle's view also allows that an end final in one context, say healing a patient, may be a means in another, say a means to making a living. His position is that every deliberation is relative to some end that governs the context and is not therein a subject of deliberation; but it is only the final end, happiness, that cannot (or at least cannot rationally) be pursued as a means to something further.

So far so good. But some apparent difficulties remain. Consider action both performed for its own sake and basic. Not only is it not *aimed*, in any obvious sense, at anything further; as basic, it is not performed *by* doing anything else. Hence, there appears to be no room to reason about what *means* will achieve it; and there is also no question of how to make *it* a successful means to anything else. We have already seen one Aristotelian response to the latter point; there is simply no need for deliberation to apply to every action *qua* means to something further, since not all actions are performed for a further end. This truth may be misleading, however, unless more is said. There is, for all intentional action, a final end – namely, happiness – and even actions performed for their own sake may be argued to be performed directly, even if not self-consciously, in order to realize part of that final end conceived as *activity* (as, for example, *NE*: 1098a–1099a); hence, the action may be conceived as a constitutive means to happiness. Happiness is not a *further end* of the action, but its intrinsic end. While the action itself, *qua* activity partly constitutive of happiness, might be the only relevant end, it is performed *for* the happiness it yields (or is expected to yield). This is not to say that it must be pursued under a conception that explicitly links it to happiness, for instance *being conducive to my happiness*. I think Aristotle is best read as allowing that it be simply the kind of thing that *is* partly constitutive of happiness and, on the basis of reflection, may be so viewed, and accordingly sought. This allows, however, that it be pursued in some way as a constitutive means.

These points about the sense in which intrinsically motivated actions can be constitutive means to happiness do not indicate how anything can be conceived as a means *to them* when they are basic. But this is not a problem for the correspondence thesis. A proponent of that thesis needs a way to exhibit basic action performed for its own sake as in some way reasoned, but not as done *by* performing some more basic action. If, for all intentional action, there is a corresponding practical argument, then all such action must be in some sense *aimed*; but this does not imply the possibility of being *aimed at* by some other action, and for basic action there is no distinct action capable of being so aimed. Granted, one can do something – such as free one's schedule – to *cause* oneself to swim for pleasure, but this is not trying to swim for pleasure *by* doing something else as a means, as one locks a door by turning a key. It is not entirely clear, however, how intrinsically motivated actions can even be aimed; they are certainly not aimed at any further action or at causal consequences. Let us explore in more detail how such actions might be conceived in an Aristotelian framework.

Consider humming for pleasure, which is a special case of doing something for its own sake and would not normally seem to correspond to practical reasoning. Although one is not humming for a further end, one is humming because of something about doing so, say the distinctively pleasing sounds. If humming may be viewed as a (constitutive) *means* of experiencing these sounds, then there might after all be a corresponding practical argument. Its premises might be that these pleasing sounds are to be enjoyed in one's humming (roughly, enjoyably realized in humming), and that humming here and now (perhaps in a certain manner) constitutes the *way* to enjoy them. This may seem artificial, but it is intelligible. Indeed, acceptance of the minor premise may readily be seen to yield an Aristotelian decision, manifested in (or indeed identical with) the agent's acting straightaway. The idea is twofold. First, even when one is doing something for its own sake (and basically), there is something *about* it, such as its pleasing sound, which one wants. Second, one can believe, *without triviality*, that doing it (in a certain way) constitutes getting that, if only because it is possible, and perhaps all too easy, to do the thing in question without what one wants, say the pleasing sound. One's pleasure (or other end sought for its own sake) is constituted by doing the thing in a certain way, not just by doing it. Hence, it is intelligible for the minor premise to connect the action with the intrinsic character that action has when performed in a relevant way. The intrinsic end supervenes on the humming, which is a constitutive means to it; but it does not supervene on just any humming: this is why, even in humming for its own sake, one can be doing so as a 'means' to the supervenient pleasure. The suggested account is consistent with Aristotle's view of pleasure,[20] so if it is successful then the correspondence thesis can be extended to all intentional action, including intrinsically motivated basic action.

VI   The structure of action

The correspondence thesis rests on the idea that intentional action has a certain structure, whether it actually issues from practical reasoning or not. Even if the correspondence thesis as developed in section V does not provide an account of how Aristotle could use his conception of practical reasoning to understand intentional action in general, other views he held about action might accomplish this, and they can also clarify his account of practical reasoning.

Central to the structure of action as Aristotle understands it is the good. He first considers what we might call subsidiary goods, the kinds that govern deliberation in a given sphere, yet are not final in the sense that they could never be sought as a means to something further. He says that in each art the good is

> that for the sake of which other things are done . . . in medicine this is health, in generalship victory . . . in every action and decision it is the end.
>
> (*NE*: 1097a18–21)

> But the best good . . . must be something complete . . .
> Now happiness more tha. anything else seems unconditionally complete, since we always [choose it, and also] choose it because of itself, never because of something else.

> Honor, pleasure, understanding and every virtue we
> certainly choose because of themselves, since we would
> choose each of them even if it had no further result, but also
> choose them for the sake of happiness, supposing that
> through them we shall be happy.[21]
>
> (*NE*: 1097a28–1097b5)

It appears, then, that happiness, in the sense of flourishing, stands
as our final unifying end: we may seek other things for their own
sake, but only when we believe that 'through them' – as constitutive and not merely instrumental means, I take it – they will make
us happy.

More specifically, in a given context, say medicine, we may not
have happiness *in mind* in acting, for example in prescribing a
remedy. For here our deliberation and practical reasoning are
governed by the end of health. But that end in turn is *sustained*
by the final end, presumably in the sense that our desire for
happiness, together with our belief that achieving the relevant
virtue, say the medical virtue that commits us to healing, conduces
to happiness, is what explains why we seek to fulfill this subsidiary
(if intrinsic) end. There need not be in our minds any *inferential
chain* from our final end to our action, nor even from our main
subsidiary end, say to practice healing, to the action. That is, we
need not actually infer, in each case of action, from the ultimate
premise that happiness is to be achieved, to the intermediate
conclusion that (say) health is to be promoted, to the practical
judgment that (for instance) I should prescribe this medicine.
Given the large number of both our subsidiary ends and our
instrumental beliefs, this would create a false, and un-Aristotelian,
picture of rational action. But there is always a psychologically
less intrusive causal chain – what we might call a *purposive chain*
– which unifies all our actions in relation to our final end, which,
at least in a mature, reflective agent, is their ultimate ground. The
existence of such a purposive chain underlying an action implies
at least this: if challenged as to why we are doing the thing in
question, the chain is always *accessible* to us as an explanatory
device (provided we are rational and not, for instance, acting in
ignorance). For ordinary purposes, citing a single practical argument may serve to explain an action. But to an agent with sufficient knowledge, a full explanatory story is always available.

A natural interpretation of purposive chains is to take each link to be constituted by a *practical basis relation* analogous to the *theoretical basis relation* by which one belief is grounded in, and in that way based on, a second when the latter expresses an evidential reason for which the former is held. Thus, if I prescribe medicine *in order to* heal, the former action is based on my wanting (or being in some way motivated) to heal. If I want to heal in order to fulfill my medical obligation, the chain has another link, and my healing is based on my wanting to fulfill my obligation. On Aristotle's view, there will be further links until we come to one anchored in the intrinsic desire for happiness, or at least to an intrinsic desire for something that, like virtuous activity, is part of happiness and can be so conceived on reflection. But notice that the practical basis relation is *non-transitive*: I can, for instance, heal in order to fulfill my medical obligation and do that in order to contribute to my happiness, even if I am not healing in order to contribute to my happiness. For I need have no belief (or minor premise) to the effect that by healing I will contribute to my happiness. No such connection need be made in every case of intentional action; and if I make none, my action is only *indirectly* grounded in my desire for happiness, a point that has by no means always been appreciated.[22]

The importance of this *indirect eudaemonistic grounding* of actions, as we might call it, should not be underestimated. Even when an action is so grounded, it still has both a causal link to the desire for happiness and, since that desire sustains it (for instance, via sustaining my wanting to fulfill my obligation) a potential explanatory link to that desire. In short, purposive chains ground all intentional actions in the desire for happiness (or for its constituents), directly or – far more often, it would seem – indirectly. (There are counterpart relations between the corresponding abstract entities, for example between the content of my desire to heal and the action-type, prescribing tablets, a type whose concrete realization is warranted by its capacity to realize that content; but my concern here is mainly with the concrete entities related by singular causal connections.)

For Aristotle, explanation is linked not only to causation, but also to reasonableness. This is in part why he wants to ground our characteristic actions in syllogisms and thereby in 'right reason.' From this point of view, it is not our desire for happiness, but the identity of happiness with the good, that is crucial. Happiness is not only our motivationally final end; it is also *the good*, and thereby *rationally* pursued for its own sake. Aristotle's reasons for identifying it with the good are rooted in his teleological conception of nature as a realm in which the good of things is constituted by their proper functions; and I am not concerned to evaluate his resources for defending this conception. My point is simply that, by virtue of purposive chains, the good unifies his *normative* theory of what constitutes reasonable (including moral) action, as well as his theory of motivation.

Moreover, if it is by a use of reason that we come to know that happiness is the good, then reason is *normatively practical*, in the sense that it suffices to generate beliefs expressing at least one ultimate standard of conduct. (Such beliefs may represent knowledge; I am simply not building truth or knowledge into the basic characterization of reason as normatively practical.) If, in addition, reason's leading us to form such a normative belief must generate in us some motivation to pursue as an end (for its own sake) the goal it expresses, say happiness, then reason is also *motivationally practical*. Given the grounds Aristotle offers for taking happiness to be our appropriately fundamental end – including the point that as rational beings we by nature seek it for its own sake – there is some reason to say that he took reason to be motivationally as well as normatively practical. His apparent unwillingness to allow that we ever act against our better judgment without a defect in our knowledge also suggests that he took reason to be motivationally practical. If these points are correct, then *both* our desire for happiness *and* our knowledge about what contributes to it are sources of practical reasons. Our knowledge, moreover, would be doubly practical: it provides motivation for action we see to be conducive to happiness, and it yields a normative ground for such action. It would thereby give us both motivating and normative reason to act. Yielding reasons that are practical in both ways, such knowledge is itself practical.

If this section is correct, Aristotle holds three mutually supporting doctrines crucial for understanding practical reasoning. Each concerns the centrality of the good, conceived as happiness, in human life. The first two are explanatory, the third normative.

The first is *motivational foundationalism:* on the assumption that there is a use of 'want' sufficiently broad to cover motivation in general,[23] the thesis may be briefly expressed as the view that there is at least one thing we want for its own sake, and everything else we want is wanted by us, directly or indirectly, for its contribution to something we want for its own sake. (If 'want' is too narrow, we may substitute 'are motivated to realize'.) The second doctrine simply roots action in the motivational framework just described; it says that all intentional action is linked by a purposive chain to at least one thing the agent wants for its own sake. Call this *behavioral foundationalism*. Both are suggested by Aristotle's remark that 'Hence it is always the object of desire that produces movement, but this is either the good or the apparent good' (*De Anima* III.10.433a27–9). Aristotle's version of both doctrines makes happiness central and is thus *eudaemonistic*: we all desire (our own) happiness for its own sake, and everything else we desire is desired, directly or indirectly, at least partly for its contribution to our happiness, where this may, but I believe need not, include explicitly taking it to be partly constitutive of our happiness. Assuming that actions are rooted, by the practical basis relation, in some kind of desire, all of our actions are explicable in this unifying framework.

The normative counterpart of this motivational view is a third major doctrine in Aristotle's theory of action, concerning what is good: *axiological foundationalism*. It says, in outline, that the intrinsically good is fundamental in the theory of value and hence basic to all other goods. Aristotle's eudaemonistic version is the thesis that whatever is good is either good in itself, and hence identical with either happiness or some constitutive means to it, or instrumentally good by virtue of making a suitable contribution to happiness, as practicing medicine may do by restoring health and thereby contributing to happiness as an exercise of the appropriate virtue(s). On the assumption that it is reasonable to act in pursuit of the good, Aristotle thus provides a eudaemonistic framework both for judging the reasonableness of actions, and for explaining them.

VII   Conclusion

We can now summarize where Aristotle, as interpreted here, stands on the six questions that largely guide our inquiry into practical reasoning. I shall be very brief.

1   A rational person characteristically answers a practical question by deliberation and, given sufficient knowledge, by producing a practical syllogism which yields a conclusion in favor of an action that is judged, in the light of the end governing the deliberation, to be suitable. The action may be represented by the premises as necessary for achieving the end, but Aristotle also allowed for other cases, such as those in which the agent simply takes the action to be the best means, or simply a good way, to achieve the end. There may also be more than one syllogism favoring the same action, and there may be conflicting syllogisms, one of which prevails in action.

2   To act for a reason is to act in order to achieve (briefly, to act *for*) an end, whether ultimate or, more often, subsidiary, as when we prescribe medicine in order to cure. Actions performed for a reason very commonly issue from practical reasoning; and if Aristotle does not think they always do, he at least holds that they are motivationally anchored by a purposive chain which terminates in a desire for happiness and can be associated, link by link, with practical arguments that concern the relevant want, belief, and action. This conception of the motivational unity of action, or at least of all action performed for a reason, is behavioral foundationalism.

3   The existence of purposive chains connecting actions with their ultimate sustaining basis constitutes the structure in which intentional actions can be explained. Even when intentional actions exhibit weakness of will, they are motivationally in the structure, by virtue of a desire, say for pleasure, ultimately traceable (even if through mistaken beliefs) to a desire for happiness. This is one reason why such actions, like other intentional actions, can express, or at least provide a basis for appraising, the agent's character. But such actions are normatively in conflict with the structure, since they oppose one's better judgment and arise because of an inadequacy in one's knowledge of (at least) one's premises. They are thus causally intelligible but, if rationally intelligible at all, not rational.

4   What mediates between reasons and actions based on them is apparently a perception of (what one takes to be) an appropriate means to the end governing the action, say the end of healing a patient. This perception yields an actual conceiving of the end at which the action aims and, at least in practical reasoning, also produces a judgment. But if (as I have left open) Aristotle's view allows that an action for a reason need not be performed on the basis of practical reasoning, he would have a good case for some sort of perception operating in the former case too, in a similarly causative way.

5   Acting for a given reason can be seen to be at least prima facie rational in the light of that reason because the relevant minor premise

connects the action with achieving the end that is associated with the reason. If, for instance, the reason is to give the patient penicillin, then reaching for the penicillin tablets is connected with that end by one's belief that it will lead to realizing it. Moreover, every action performed for a reason is ultimately rooted in the final, and presumably rational, desire for happiness.

6   Practical reasoning is like theoretical reasoning in exhibiting an inferential pattern of drawing a conclusion from premises. But it differs both in being undertaken in the service of an end to be realized in conduct and in concluding with a practical judgment. Its origin is a different kind of problem, and its concluding element is correspondingly different as well. Its upshot, moreover, is, when the reasoning succeeds, action that realizes the end in whose service it is done; the upshot of successful theoretical reasoning, by contrast, is knowledge (or at least belief that meets an appropriate standard). In the context of the premises, a practical judgment normally plays a causal role in producing, and may help to guide, the action it favors; it also normally plays a justificatory role in warranting that action. If parallel points hold for theoretical reasoning, then knowledge or belief, and not action, constitutes the object of the causal and justificatory influence exercised by the premises of that reasoning.

As I understand these Aristotelian views, they are all quite plausible. But they suggest a variety of problems which an account of practical reasoning should address. Is all intentional action grounded in practical reasoning, as Aristotle may have thought, and, if so, how? Is motivation intrinsic to a practical judgment, say that one must avoid eating sweets, and, if so, what is the implied *degree* of motivation relative to the agent's other desires? Connected with this is the problem of just how clear an incontinent agent's practical knowledge can be and whether, as Aristotle apparently thought, incontinent action is always irrational.

All of these and related questions will be addressed in part 2. This is not to suggest that one could not find answers to them in Aristotle's work. Perhaps it contains excellent answers. There is certainly a great deal more to say about his account of practical thinking in general and of practical reasoning in particular. An entire book could easily be devoted to these matters, but I cannot pursue them further here. If, however, what has been said about Aristotle in this chapter is sound, it shows him as developing a generally consistent, highly plausible, and powerful account, and it gives us a basis for understanding later treatments of the subject.

CHAPTER 2

Hume and the Instrumentalist Conception of Practical Reasoning

David Hume said much about the nature and scope of reason, but spoke little of what I have called practical reasoning, and the term seldom if ever occurs in his major works. He did say much about kindred topics, however, and implicit in his writings there is a conception of practical reasoning. In formulating it I shall concentrate on *A Treatise of Human Nature*, but in places it will help to compare its doctrines with passages in *An Enquiry Concerning the Principles of Morals*. I shall also connect Hume's view on some points with Aristotle's and, later, Kant's, but my purpose in discussing Hume is not mainly comparative. His views on practical thinking are among the most important in the field and are intrinsically plausible. As in the case of Aristotle, I make no claim to give a detailed overall interpretation; I seek only to offer a plausible reading of a number of his central points.

1 The instrumental role of reason

The paradigms of practical reasoning are cases of means-end reasoning, provided we include constitutive means, as where one is reasoning about how best to enjoy a free evening. There is no question that Hume took what he called reason to have a role in means-ends reasoning. The following is a good expression of the core of his account of that role:

> It has been observ'd, that reason, in a strict and philosophical

sense, can have an influence on our conduct only after two ways: either when it excites a passion by informing us of the existence of something which is a proper object of it; or when it discovers the connexion of causes and effects, so as to afford us means of exerting any passion. These are the only kinds of judgments which can accompany our actions, or can be said to produce them in any manner; and it must be allow'd, that these judgments may often be false and erroneous. . . . They extend not beyond a mistake of *fact*, which moralists have not generally supposed criminal, as being perfectly involuntary. . . . No one can ever regard such errors as a defect in my moral character. A fruit, for instance, that is really disagreeable, appears to me at a distance, and thro' mistake I fancy it to be pleasant and delicious. Here is one error. I choose certain means of reaching this object, which are not proper for my end. Here is a second error; nor is there any third one, which can ever enter into our reasonings concerning actions.[1]

The main point here is that reason, conceived in part as a source of beliefs about instrumental relations, influences our conduct only in two ways: (a) through arousing a passion by informing us (perhaps mistakenly) of the existence or properties of something it is a passion *for*, say tropical fruit, and (b) through giving us (again perhaps mistakenly) causal information about how we can attain the object.

This point is confirmed and developed elsewhere. A few paragraphs later, for instance, Hume says that while 'reason *alone* is incapable' of 'an influence upon our actions,' still 'Reason and judgment may, indeed, be the *mediate* cause of an action, *by* prompting, or by directing a passion' (462, emphases added). Clearly passion is the motivating force behind action; reason simply arouses or directs passion. This point, and Hume's conception of what unifies the passions, are evident in a passage about the relation between will and, on the other hand, desire and aversion. As the passage suggests, he apparently takes them to be equivalent to, or at least the central motivational elements in, the direct passions:

Desire arises from good consider'd simply, and aversion is deriv'd from evil. The will exerts itself, when [the agent considers that] either the good or the absence of the evil may be attain'd by any action of the mind or body.

Beside good and evil, or in other words, pain and pleasure, the direct passions frequently arise from a natural impulse or instinct, which is perfectly unaccountable. Of this kind is the desire of punishment to our enemies, and of happiness to our friends; hunger, lust, and a few other bodily appetites. These passions, properly speaking, produce good and evil, and proceed not from them, like the other affections.

(439)

On the plausible assumption that (intentional) action is (or in some way represents) an exertion of the will, the first paragraph suggests that (i) desire for some good and aversion to some evil (which may be roughly considered desire to *avoid* it) are the fundamental motivators (passions) and (ii) our desires to act, or at least our desires that lead us to act, arise when we take some action to be a means to achieving something we want. Roughly, desire, guided by belief, is what produces action. When Hume adds that good is equivalent to pleasure and evil to pain, it looks as if he is committed not only to the *valuational hedonism* with which that claim is normally identified, but also to *psychological hedonism*, the view that all our actions are motivated, directly or indirectly, by desires for pleasure, or to avoid pain. This impression is reinforced by his saying such things as that 'the passions, both direct and indirect, are founded on pain and pleasure' (438).

Later in the same paragraph, however (and elsewhere), Hume qualifies his apparent psychological hedonism. Not only does he acknowledge non-hedonistic direct passions, such as the desires for punishment of one's enemies and for the happiness of one's friends, that arise from a 'natural impulse'; he also says that these passions *produce* good and evil, rather than proceeding from them, as do the other direct passions. The point is apparently that satisfying the desire for one's friends' happiness can produce one's own happiness, whereas 'the other affections' arise through getting pleasure or pain from experiencing their objects, for example from eating delicious foods. If this is part of his point, then he is not only rejecting psychological hedonism as an account of *what* we intrinsically want, but also *genetic hedonism* – the view that what we intrinsically want arises from our experiences of pleasure and pain – as an account of *why* we intrinsically want what we do. He suggests that the satisfaction of a natural impulse may also produce such wants. This is consistent with that satisfaction's being generally pleasant, but Hume seems to be denying that the satisfaction produces them only *by* producing pleasure. Roughly, he holds *both* that we have intrinsic desires directed toward what we naturally find pleasurable and that we take pleasure in doing or experiencing certain things because, antecedently, we have an intrinsic desire to do or experience them.

It appears, then, that Hume's theory of motivation is *pluralistic*, in the sense that there is no one thing which he takes to be the sole kind of entity we desire for its own sake. To be sure, if pleasure is essentially tied to, and determined in its specified nature by, the experience or activity that yields it, then, like Aristotelian eudaemonism, even hedonism is perhaps only superficially monistic. There would be as many kinds of pleasure as there are enjoyable experiences and activities. But unlike Aristotle, Hume does not conceive pleasure in that way. Nonetheless, desire remains his fundamental motivational notion, as seems implicit in what I have quoted.

If passions are roughly desires (including aversions), how does Hume conceive the *in*direct passions? He says of 'the *in*direct passions' that they

> arise from a double relation of impressions and ideas. . . .
> Thus a suit of fine clothes produces pleasure from their
> beauty; and this pleasure produces the direct passions, or the
> impressions of volition and desire.

> (439)

The idea, I think, is that the desire for the fine clothes is indirect in the sense of being *based on* the desire for their sartorial beauty, which in turn is based on the direct passion for the pleasure of contemplating that beauty. This passion is direct because it is not based on any further one; one desires such sartorial pleasure for its own sake. In *An Enquiry Concerning the Principles of Morals*, Hume describes the motivational structure in question quite clearly:

> Ask a man *why he uses exercise*; he will answer *because he
> desires to keep his health*. If you then enquire, *why he desires*

health, he will readily reply, *because sickness is painful*. If you push your enquiries further, and desire a reason *why he hates pain*, it is impossible he can ever give any. This is an ultimate end, and is never referred to any other object.[2]

The overall view seems like Aristotle's in being a motivational foundationalism: some of our passions, the direct ones, are fundamental and not based (in the instrumental way just illustrated by Hume) on others; and all our other, indirect passions are instrumentally based on one or more of the former by virtue of our believing, of each indirect passion, something to the effect that satisfying it will (or that it might) satisfy one of our direct passions. Most of the time Hume talks hedonistically; but his considered view allows for foundational desires whose objects, though wanted for their own sake, are not wanted for pleasure. Indeed, he even allows for what seems a distinctively moral kind of motivation, though he insists that 'Since morals . . . have an influence on the actions and affections, they cannot be deriv'd from reason. . . . Morals excite passions, and produce or prevent actions. Reason is utterly impotent in this particular' (457). Passions are still the fundamental motivators, but some are aroused by moral judgments, such as that an action is a duty, as others are by factual judgments, such as that a fruit is delicious.

II Reasoning as an element in the genesis of action

Hume's conception of practical reasoning, so far as we can formulate it, can be located within the pattern I have described, namely, the foundationalist account of motivation in which reason plays the instrumental role indicated, by virtue of arousing and directing our desires. To see how he conceived practical reasoning, we might first of all note some of his points about probable, as opposed to demonstrative, reasoning. He maintains that

all probable reasoning is nothing but a species of sensation. 'Tis not solely in poetry and music, we must follow our taste and sentiment, but likewise in philosophy. When I am convinc'd of any principle, 'tis only an idea which strikes more strongly upon me. . . . Objects have no discoverable connexion together; nor is it from any principle but custom

operating upon the imagination, that we can draw any
inference from the appearance of one to the existence of any
other. . . . A person, who stops short in his journey upon
meeting a river in his way, foresees the consequences of his
proceeding forward; and his knowledge of these consequences
is convey'd to him by past experience. . . . But can we think,
that on this occasion he reflects on any past experience . . . ?
No, surely; this is not the method in which he proceeds in
his reasoning. The idea of sinking is so closely connected with
that of water . . . that the mind makes the transition without
the assistance of memory. The custom operates before we
have time for reflexion.

(103–4)

A major point Hume is making here is that the reasoning which
leads the agent to stop short of entering the river is neither reflective nor based on a 'discoverable connexion' between jumping
into a river and sinking. I do not know, and cannot discover, a
priori, that whoever jumps into a river sinks. Moreover, at least
normally I do not apply such a generalization to my circumstances
and infer that if I jump in I will sink. Instead, the agent is assumed
to associate the jumping and the sinking so closely that the idea
of the former elicits, by a customary, and presumably in some
sense inferential, transition, the idea of the latter. The latter idea,
on the basis of past experience, gives rise to knowledge[3] of the
consequences of proceeding forward, and that knowledge prevents
his doing so.

There apparently is, then, a kind of reasoning – or at least of
inference – here; and, even if it results in action only through a
transition of thought rooted in custom, the reasoning is surely
practical. Plainly the minor premise would be something like this:
if I go forward, I'll sink. What would be the major? Given Hume's
view that reason, which is the 'discovery of truth or falsehood'
(458) and is in itself 'perfectly inert' (458), affects action only
through arousing or directing desire, we would expect the major
premise to concern some object of desire (or aversion). This is
what we apparently do find; for in the same passage Hume
describes the idea of sinking as closely connected with that of
suffocating (104), and we may certainly take him to be assuming

44

that the agent is averse to suffocating. Thus, the major might be something like: suffocating is to be avoided.

There are at least two kinds of conclusions that would fit the context. The first would be in some sense normative and might thus be readily seen, from Hume's perspective, to have motivating power, since if he took moral judgments to have such power it is to be expected that he might regard other normative judgments as similarly motivating. Taken together with the minor premise that (say) not going forward would prevent sinking and suffocating, the major premise that suffocating is to be avoided would probabilistically imply the (judgmental) conclusion that one should not go forward. *Given* the motivation underlying the major, that concluding judgment in turn would normally lead to acting accordingly. The reasoning would then be practical in much the way Aristotelian practical reasoning is. On the other hand, if we think of reason as inert, we may want to construe the conclusion of Humean practical reasoning more narrowly, say as a judgment to the effect that one must either stop or else one will sink and suffocate. Making this judgment, *together* with the agent's desire to avoid suffocating, can be seen to motivate stopping. The judgment thus plays a practical role without itself having normative – and in that sense practical – content. Similarly, on this narrow interpretation, even the major premise should not be taken to be in any way normative. That suffocating is to be avoided, for instance, should be taken to express something like this: I want to avoid suffocating.[4]

We must be cautious here. While Hume himself uses the terms 'reasoning' and 'inference', he does not tell us what the major premise would be, nor specify the conclusion. On the other hand, in this passage he is at pains to show how we automatically act on information suitably connected with our desires. We might thus suppose that he takes as obvious what sort of content the major and the conclusion would have. This idea receives some support from a quite general point he makes about reasoning:

> All kinds of reasoning consist in nothing but a *comparison*, and a discovery of those relations, either constant or inconstant, which two or more objects bear to each other. This comparison we may make, either when both the objects

are present, or when neither of them is present, or when only
one.

(73)

In Hume's example, there is an implied background comparison
– which one makes rapidly and unreflectively – of one's entering
the river and one's sinking. This may be based on a more general
comparison, itself grounded in past experience, of people's entering such a body of water and their sinking in it. The comparison
of one's own entering with its associated effect leads to formation
of the general belief that the former would produce the latter.
Moreover, we cannot understand, in terms of Hume's theory of
motivation, why the agent stops at the river bank unless we suppose that there *is* a comparison of going into the river with sinking
(or perhaps suffocating). If there is no major premise concerning
sinking, then with what is going forward into the water compared?
And if there is no conclusion, what represents the result of the
comparison?

It is natural to suppose that there is something like enthymematic reasoning here: the major premise – say, that suffocating is
to be avoided – is only tacitly accepted by the agent on the basis
of his desires, and so is not expressed or even entertained in
the reasoning process; and the conclusion – say, that to avoid
suffocating I must stop going forward – is not explicitly drawn, if
only because, first, it is both too obviously implicit to need affirmation and, second, one is in a position to act on it at once,
without 'reflexion.' On this view, while we cannot be sure just
what forms Hume would take the major and the conclusion to
have – and several are open to him – he is taking practical reasoning to occur in at least some cases of action based on a desire and
on a belief to the effect that a certain action will realize the desire.

This interpretation accords well with another passage in which
Hume appears to be thinking of practical reasoning. He says:

'Tis obvious, that when we have the prospect of pain or
pleasure from any object, we feel a consequent emotion of
aversion or propensity, and are carry'd to avoid or embrace
what will give this uneasiness or satisfaction. 'Tis also
obvious, that this emotion rests not here, but making us cast
our view on every side, comprehends whatever objects are
connected with this original one by the relation of cause and

effect. Here then reasoning takes place to discover this
relation; and according as our reasoning varies, our actions
receive a subsequent variation.

(414)

The case imagined (which Hume does not illustrate in the immediate context) appears to be one in which the satisfaction of desire
is only in 'prospect' and *deliberation* may be appropriate. Deliberation is certainly one way to 'cast our view on every side' in order
to determine an appropriate means. Here we reason in order 'to
discover this [causal] relation.' Hume may well take it that in this
kind of case we *conclude* our reasoning with a judgment (or
belief or other cognitive element) indicating a means to avoid the
'uneasiness' or to realize the 'satisfaction.' It is still unclear what
the major premise would be; but if what we desire is in prospect,
it might well be something like 'That is to be obtained' or, more
personally, 'I've got to get that'.

There is, however, a weaker interpretation of Hume. He might
have held simply that when one *has* a suitably strong desire, such
as to avoid suffocation, then one's simply forming an appropriate
instrumental belief, say that one must stop in order to avoid
suffocation, normally leads to the action. One may be said to
reason because one sees, on the basis of experience, that if one
proceeds one will suffocate, associates proceeding with suffocating, and is thereby motivated to cease proceeding. This would give
Hume an instrumental account of intentional action and would be
consistent with his overall views on reason and motivation.

It is quite possible, of course, that Hume would apply the
weaker account, which I shall call the *simple instrumentalist
account*, to automatic or at least non-deliberate actions and use the
stronger account, which I shall call the *inferential instrumentalist
account*, for deliberate actions and, certainly, for those that arise
from *reflection*. That is, non-deliberate intentional action is simply
based on appropriate desire(s) and belief(s), and thus arises from
practical reasoning only in a weak, *associational* sense, whereas
deliberate and reasoned actions are based on practical reasoning
in the full-blooded, *inferential* sense. It is certainly open to him
to hold this, as indeed Aristotle might have. Both points are
harmonious with behavioral foundationalism, which Hume, like
Aristotle, seems to have held. As it stands, however, it may not

47

be possible to say decisively whether in accounting for at least some intentional actions Hume invoked practical reasoning in the inferential sense apparently illustrated by Aristotle's typical examples. We may, however, conclude that *if* Hume does imply that there is such practical reasoning, then while it is not clear just what forms he would attribute to the major premises and conclusions, the former would in some way concern the object of the motivating desire(s) and the latter would in some way favor the action which, according to the minor, would (or might) realize the desire(s).

III   Reason, rational action, and moral judgment

Hume is famous for his striking remarks about the limited power of reason. To understand his views of rational action and his resources for dealing with weakness of will, we must consider some of these views against the background of the positive account so far given of how Hume conceives reason as a force in human action.

Two of Hume's famous pronouncements about reason are that 'Reason is, and ought only to be, the slave of the passions' (415), and that ''Tis not contrary to reason to prefer the destruction of the whole world to the scratching of my finger' (416). These statements are closely connected with his views concerning the relation between reason and morality. On this he says, in another famous passage, that

> men are often govern'd by their duties, and are deter'd from some actions by the opinion of injustice, and impell'd to others by that of obligation.
>
> Since morals, therefore, have an influence on the actions and affections, it follows, that they cannot be deriv'd from reason; and that because reason alone . . . can never have any such influence.
>
> (457)

As to how morals influence action, Hume's view of their influence on action is quite understandable in the light of one of his important statements about the meaning of moral judgments. He says that when you pronounce any action or character to be vicious, you mean nothing, but that from the constitution of your nature you have a feeling or sentiment of blame from the contemplation of it. Vice and virtue, therefore, may be compar'd to sounds, colours, heat and cold, which, according to modern philosophy, are not qualities in objects, but perceptions in the mind.[5]

(469)

Calling an action vicious does not identify a quality *in* it, but expresses a connection between the object and one's own sentiments. These sentiments, however, have a 'passional' (certainly motivational) component. Hence, it is to be expected that they, unlike judgments of reason proper, can lead one to act. Moreover, insofar as the making of the judgment produces or arouses such sentiments, say a feeling of blame with a constituent desire to censure, the judging may indirectly generate action. But the direct motivator of action in the moral case is not judging (or at least not judging as reflecting reason); it is something passional.

How are the other two pronouncements to be explained? In the light of what I quoted from Hume in sections I and II, it is clear that in calling reason the slave of the passions he does not mean that it cannot influence them. As he repeatedly says, it is only 'reason *alone*' that 'can never have any such influence' (457), though even this may be too strong to accord with all of his considered views on the matter. His most important view here, I think, is this. Reason can *arouse* a passion by discovering an appropriate object, such as a kind of fruit for which one has a desire; and *given* a passion (or desire), it can *direct* action toward the satisfaction of that passion. It can, for instance, lead us along a chain of means to what we want until we get it.

There are, moreover, at least two ways in which reason may arouse passion. One is *identificational generation*: reason informs us (perhaps falsely) of the existence of something which we intrinsically want. Here it identifies an appropriate thing, usually but not necessarily an object of a standing desire, such as a glass of water when we are thirsty, or it identifies a *kind* of thing we antecedently want, or simply *like*, for its own sake, say a chance to see a beautiful painting: in this case we may *come* to want the identified thing, even if at the time we had no standing want for a thing of that sort, say to see a beautiful painting. The other kind of arousal is *instrumental generation*: reason informs us of the existence of an object, or indicates a possible action, that is (in some sense) a means to something we want, whether we want that for its own sake or not. In producing both kinds of arousal – and perhaps yet other kinds – reason serves passion by aiding its satisfaction. But it is a servant without which the passions would be satisfied only at the whim of fortune. The master is blind, and depends on this slave to see.[6]

The second pronouncement must be understood in the light of the first. *If* I have no desire which reason shows me will be thwarted by the destruction of the world, then given my natural desire to avoid pain it is not contrary to reason to prefer the destruction of the world to the pain of a mere scratch. Hume of course did not suppose that we have no desires that would be thwarted by the destruction of the world. His point, or at least the point implicit in his theory of motivation, is that *reason* does not give us any such desires *non-instrumentally*: it yields them only if we have some foundational desire whose satisfaction reason shows us would be thwarted by destruction of the world.[7]

There are two important Humean doctrines here. One is that reason is not *motivationally* practical, in the sense that by itself it cannot originate, as opposed to arousing or directing, desire. The second – which Hume takes to be implied by the first – is that reason is not *normatively* practical, in the sense that by itself it cannot tell us what is (non-instrumentally) good or bad, or what (non-instrumentally) ought to be. If it did, it would have to have at least some motivational force, and passages like those just cited argue that it does not. In these two respects, reason is not practical; and on both points we have a substantial departure from Aristotle. In contrast to Aristotle, Hume holds in effect that reason provides no ultimate premises for practical reasoning.

One could put the point more strikingly and say that for Hume there *is* no practical reason.[8] This formulation goes well with the slave metaphor and other vivid statements Hume makes in assessing the power of reason. But those statements are easily misinterpreted, and it may be preferable to say simply that Hume's account of practical reason is wholly instrumentalist, in the ways I have illustrated. This view still allows reason a powerful influence on action. The motivational influence, through arousing and directing desire, is clear. However, since Hume acknowledges that we may be mistaken about the nature or the existence of an object desired, as well as about how we may attain it, his account also makes room for reason to have a normative role, even if the normative force of its directives is *conditional* on one's basic desires: an action may be said to be instrumentally unreasonable if it is based on a mistake of any of the three kinds just mentioned (and possibly in other ways, though Hume does not seem to deal with others).

To be sure, Hume says at one point that 'Actions can be laudable or blameable; but they cannot be reasonable or unreasonable' (458); but in the context he is denying the non-instrumental *causal* power of reason, not the point that actions can exhibit mistakes due to the inadequate use or the insufficient influence of reason. Indeed, earlier he acknowledges two senses in which

> any affection can be called unreasonable. First, when a passion, such as hope or fear . . . is founded on the supposition of objects, which really do not exist. Secondly, when in exerting any passion in action we choose means insufficient for the design'd end, and deceive ourselves in our judgment of causes and effects.

> (416)

The same points apply to action; indeed, the second seems an even better indication of when an action is instrumentally unreasonable than of when a passion motivating action is. Whatever his terminology, then, Hume's overall view provides the materials for an instrumentalist conception of rational action.

IV Weakness of will, practical judgment, and Humean internalism

Suppose that weakness of will is construed as acting incontinently: roughly, as acting freely and intentionally (or at least knowingly) against one's better judgment, for instance in doing something which one takes to be contrary to what one ought to do. How might Hume account for it, or indeed for incontinence conceived in any similar way? He apparently did not talk of weakness of will using that phrase itself. He certainly discussed the general issue, however, and there is much we can see from considering some of his main points.

In one passage, Hume seems unhesitatingly to affirm the possibility of a kind of weakness of will:

> Men often act knowingly against their interest: For which reason the view of the greatest possible good does not always influence them. Men often counter-act a violent passion in prosecution of their interests and designs: 'Tis not therefore the present uneasiness alone, which determines them. In general we may observe, that both these principles operate on the will; and where they are contrary, that either of them prevails, according to the *general* character or *present* disposition of the person. What we call strength of mind, implies the prevalence of the calm passions above the violent. (418)

Unlike Aristotle, Hume does not elaborate on the kind of knowledge involved when one acts against one's interest, but he seems to be thinking of some of the same kinds of cases Aristotle presented, in which violent passion prevails over one's better judgment. Moreover, Hume's position at least leaves room for incontinence in such conflict situations. Consider competing practical reasonings, say one yielding the conclusion that I should not indulge, the other the conclusion that this indulgence would be delightful. Hume's view leaves room for the possibility that I act, intentionally and freely, against the former, cool judgment, which, we may suppose, represents both my calm passions and my interest. In addition, where Hume speaks of 'strength of mind' he is clearly not talking about intellectual strength, and we may reasonably suppose he means something like strength of will.

At least two problems remain, however, before we can formulate a Humean account of weakness of will. First, suppose that, as one might assume from Hume's point of view, knowingly acting against one's interest implies conduct about which one believes something to the general effect that it will yield less overall desire satisfaction than abstaining from the action in question. How *can* one so act? How could the strongest set of desires not prevail? Second, in the moral case (as the passage quoted from p. 457 indicates), Hume held a form of *internalism*: a sincerely held moral judgment, say that one ought to vote against a friend, implies (has 'internal' to it) motivation to act accordingly. How, then, can we act against our moral judgments, as people surely do in certain cases of weakness of will?

The first difficulty is serious, but Hume has various resources for dealing with it. He may have in mind a notion of what is in one's interest which gives that notion some degree of independence of the concept of what one actually desires. In *An Enquiry*, for instance, he speaks of virtue as 'desirable on its own account . . . merely for the immediate satisfaction which it conveys . . .'[9] This seems to imply that something can be desirable because of satisfaction it *would* bring, even if it is not at the time *desired* by anyone for whom it is desirable (such statements also suggest that Hume is not unqualifiedly a valuational hedonist, since the relevant satisfactions need not be unqualifiedly construed as matters of pleasure; but I leave that issue aside). The notion of desirability here is still instrumentalist; we simply go beyond *narrow (or categorical) instrumentalism*, which makes desirability entirely a matter of satisfaction of *actual* desires, to *broad (or mixed hypothetical) instrumentalism*, which makes desirability a matter of both actual desires and suitable hypothetical ones. Hume can employ the broader instrumentalism, or at least appeal to the relevant hypothetical desires, in explaining weakness of will. For he might point out that reason need not *always* arouse desire for a thing the agent regards as (say) enjoyable or essential to avoiding pain – or at least a *strong* desire for it – when it tells us that certain conduct, such as abstaining from indulgence, *would* obtain the thing and hence is instrumentally desirable in the broad sense. Incontinent action may then occur because the stronger passion, though for the less desirable end, prevails in action.

On this view of incontinent action, reason fails to prevent it because there is no existing passion – or no sufficiently strong one – that it can direct against the incontinent action, which itself is motivated by some overriding actual passion. Actual desires *direct* action; but it may be *assessed* in part by appeal to hypothetical desires suitably related to actual ones, for instance likely to be formed by reflection on how to maximize satisfaction of one's present desires. Hume might, then, hold a narrow instrumental view of the explanation of action and a broad instrumentalist account of its assessment.

There is an analogy to Aristotle here. On the suggested account of Hume, incontinence is possible because reason, like Aristotelian practical knowledge, is inadequately *integrated* into the agent's motivational system. One may, for example, realize that exercise would save one suffering in later years, yet simply fail to want to avoid that suffering enough to overcome one's resistance to undertaking the required regimen. If one's expectation of future suffering fails to arouse motivation strong enough to produce abstinence, even though, if that suffering were an immediate prospect, one would have a desire strong enough to produce resistance, then reason, as yielding the well-grounded expectation of future suffering, is insufficiently integrated into one's motivational system. A narrow instrumentalism would, however, be unwarranted in criticizing the indulgent act, since it would maximize satisfaction of *present* desires. A broad instrumentalism, as I suggest Hume may perhaps be taken to hold, could justifiably criticize it.

Hume's resources for understanding weakness of will include his plausible point – which supports the broad instrumentalist reading – that 'The same good, when near, will cause a violent passion, which, when remote, produces only a calm one' (419). At least in the common cases of weakness of will in which one acts incontinently for immediate pleasure (or immediate avoidance of pain), there often is what Hume would call a violent passion. This could well prevent one's reason, manifested in instrumental beliefs, from having its usual effect of evoking desire, or at least sufficiently strong desire, to experience the less immediate satisfactions that are to be ultimately obtained through abstention. Note that there is a further parallel with Aristotle, for here, too, it seems that reason may be *obscured* by passion, particularly violent passion. That it is the master who interferes with the servant does not make the resulting action acceptable as a way of furthering the master's ends; nor are violent masters, or masters in a violent state, any more worthy of service than calm ones.

Given these two resources for dealing with the first difficulty, our finding a Humean solution to the second one – how an internalist view of moral judgment would allow one to act against such a judgment – should not be as hard, provided Hume is not taken to hold *strong internalism*, that is, the view that (sincerely) judging that one (morally) ought to do something implies that one desires, *on balance*, to do it, i.e., desires it more than one desires any set of things that one believes to be (individually or collectively) incompatible with doing it. (A similar internalism can be formulated for moral beliefs, but we need not consider other formulations here.) If one judges that one ought not to insult someone, Hume's position implies that one has some motivation to abstain, but not that this motivation is stronger than one's desire to retaliate (by the insult). This vengeful motivation may represent one's desire on balance. Moreover, especially if this desire is violent, it may prevail over one's recognized best interest, in the sense of what one sees *would* be one's greater satisfaction if one should abstain.

There is, however, at least one textual obstacle to my account of Hume's resources for dealing with weakness of will. In the quoted passage concerning the influence of reason on action, Hume says, of judgments that excite a passion by 'informing us of the existence of something which is a proper object of it,' and of judgments that afford us 'means of exerting any passion,' that 'These are the *only* kinds of judgment, which can accompany our actions, or can be said to produce them in any manner' (459, emphasis added). These points raise a problem. They make it appear that 'Hume failed to notice [a third instance] in which reason shows us that the achievement of a desired end will probably result in the occurrence of something which we have a greater desire to avoid.'[10] On my interpretation, it appears that this third sort of judgment, a kind that is at least implicitly comparative, *can* in some sense accompany action. Indeed, acting against such a judgment can be a paradigm of incontinence.

This difficulty can be resolved in the light of the following points. First, in the passage in question Hume is talking about judgments that excite a passion or instrumentally direct action, as though he had in mind only passions which actually *yield* action. In the case of weakness of will, however, whatever passion there is on the side of one's 'interest' does *not* yield action; hence, judgments representing one's interest would not be included under his description of those that 'produce' action. This brings me to my second point. On my interpretation, Hume does not deny that a passion can be aroused by a judgment or belief to the effect that a satisfaction would be lost if one did a certain deed; all he need deny in order to solve the problem is that the judgment must arouse a passion *as* strong as the one on which the agent acts.

Third, we might stress Hume's notion of judgment that 'can accompany' action. Acting knowingly against one's interest does not require – and is harder to understand if we assume – one's rehearsing the very judgment against which one is acting, such as that indulging now should be avoided on pain of a hangover later. Knowingly acting against one's interest simply requires holding the betrayed judgment and having it sufficiently in mind to act *against* it rather than merely *inconsistently* with it, as one might do by unknowingly imbibing vodka thinking the drink to contain only spicy tomato juice.[11] This is acting in a way against the *content* of one's judgment, since one does the proscribed thing; but it represents cognitive error, not incontinence. Finally, if we are to make good sense of either Hume's notion of *knowingly* acting against one's better judgment or his apparent references to deliberation in the genesis of action, it is difficult to see how we can avoid taking him to make room, if only implicitly and in assessing the rationality of actions, for judgments concerning the effects of one or another action on the satisfaction of desires besides the one(s) that actually produce action.

V Conclusion

Enough has now been said in interpreting Hume to suggest where he stands on the important questions guiding this book. But, more than with Aristotle, I must be conjectural regarding his overall conception of practical reasoning.

1 For Hume, a rational person answers a practical question within the constraints of a foundationalist psychology of motivation and an instrumentalist conception of rational action. Thus, above all, agents in some way consider what they want (though not necessarily under a description mentioning wanting) and seek appropriate means to getting it. If the question is, say, how to reconcile quarreling friends (which we may suppose one wants for its own sake), one considers the situation, draws on one's experience to arrive at various means of reconciliation, and selects a promising one. Whether the action must emerge from reasoning, as opposed to arising in a simple non-inferential way from the desire and the belief, Hume does not make plain. But particularly if one's standing habits or relevant experiences do not make the choice automatic, Hume could allow that such an

action might emerge from practical reasoning and even from a stretch of deliberation.

2   To act for a reason, on Hume's view, is to act instrumentally in the service of a desire. This includes the special case in which one acts for pleasure, though Hume does not address specifically how the relevant means here – simply doing the thing in question – is constitutive.[12] The desire may, but need not, be for pleasure. But it is either a desire for something wanted for its own sake or traceable to such a desire through a chain of instrumental beliefs. Here Hume is, I think, Aristotelian. On Hume's overall position, practical reasoning may or may not be necessary to acting for a reason, but the most important textual evidence, including his emphasis on the pervasive influence of habit in action, suggests that, in his considered view, it is not necessary.

3   Intentional actions are explainable in the motivational structure just described: all are performed in the service of one or more desires. Hume seems to be both a behavioral and a motivational foundationalist. Weakness of will is possible in this structure, with or without practical reasoning in the genesis of the incontinent action or of the practical judgment it contravenes. Its occurrence is explicable because the desire(s) for something against one's better judgment can outweigh whatever desires support that judgment. This seems possible in at least two cases. First, calm passions that motivationally support practical judgment may be overridden by violent ones. Second, such judgment may be based on an assessment of one's best interest, say of what *would* be desirable in the future, and a judgment of this kind may lack support from any actual desires.

4   In describing what mediates between reasons and actions based on them, Hume mentions perception, say of the waters one judges will engulf one if one proceeds. But his framework for understanding action allows that drawing a conclusion of practical reasoning, such as the conclusion that one must not enter the water, may also mediate. His overall view seems to be that the central mediating factor is some event, typically perceptual or volitional, that brings into clear view, or moves one towards, something one takes to be a means to realizing the desire(s) preponderant in the situation of action. Where the agent acts upon the external world, this event is presumably perceptual. The event might be simply seeing fruit; and given an appetite for fruit, taking some might follow straightaway. For simple bodily action, such as moving a limb, the mediating event might be volitional. It may be, moreover, that Hume took volitions invariably to mediate between motivation and intentional action, as suggested by his

statement that 'The motion of our body follows upon the command of our will.'[13]

5   If acting for a reason fits into the Humean framework as suggested, it is clear how such actions can be seen to be at least prima facie rational in the light of the motivating reason(s). A motivating reason is conceived as a desire, and an action for that reason is, in the agent's view, a way (or possible way) to satisfy that desire. From the point of view of instrumental rationality, this will make the action prima facie rational; for the only constraints on rational action concern its suitability for overall desire satisfaction. There is, then, a sense in which Hume's conception of rationality is *functionalist*: the function of reason, and, I have suggested, implicitly of action, is to serve intrinsic desire. The rationality of our intrinsic desires is not in question, and indeed he leaves little if any room for their assessment in this dimension, though he might well have considered them unreasonable if it is impossible to realize them, or at least if the agent should see that this is impossible. Indeed, I have argued that he might have been a narrow instrumentalist in his psychology of action, taking all action to be explainable in terms of means-end relations to actual desires, and a broad instrumentalist in his normative theory of action, taking the rationality of action to be determined *both* by actual desires and by hypothetical ones suitably related to the former. Whatever the kind of instrumentalism best attributed to Hume, he does not give us a calculus, say a maximization of expected desire satisfaction (utility) view on which a rational action is one that scores at least as high in expected utility as any alternative the agent has. That is, if one (a) notes the (subjectively) possible (relevant) outcomes of each alternative action – say, for the action of drinking whiskey, the pleasure of the drink and the pain of the hangover – (b) multiplies the positive or negative satisfaction value of each outcome by the probability one takes that outcome to have, and (c) adds these products, then the rational thing to do is an alternative with the highest total score. But this view of rational action, though it is not quite implicit in Hume, seems consistent with at least most of his main points.[14]

6   On the degree of unity between reasoning directed to practical questions and reasoning directed to theoretical ones, it is difficult to see where Hume stands. He stresses that reason is concerned with the true and the false, but he also goes to great lengths to show how, through its relation to desire, reason influences action. When it does, and when reasoning occurs as an element in reason's influencing action, Hume gives us no good grounds for thinking that the reasoning must differ in kind from reasoning on theoretical matters. It might, after all, simply identify, in the major premise, something as desired,

and, in the minor, assert that some action is a means to it. He does seem to regard the practical case as at least typically involving probable reasoning, in part because it is concerned with causal relations and, more important, because the practical arguments he apparently had in mind (and it is difficult to formulate Humean practical arguments) do not in general seem deductive. But without a definite range in which to locate the major premise, it is hard to see how, in detail, he would draw the contrast.

There is, then, much that the text enables us to say about Hume's conception of practical reasoning and, especially, about the operation of reason in practical contexts. But on some points we are forced to offer several possibilities and speculate on which best represents his overall views. Moreover, we are left with a number of pressing questions about practical reasoning. Is Hume correct in denying that reason has normative force? On the other hand, does moral judgment have the kind of motivational force which his internalism posits, and, if it does, would this prevent it from being in some sense based on reason? And if he differs from Aristotle, who offers a more detailed dynamic account of the genesis of action – through, for instance, his discussion of the chain of causation terminating in choice and effective through perception – how might the apparently volitionalist dynamic view that seems to fit Hume's overall position be developed, and how plausible is such an account? These issues will be treated in part 2, which defends a conception of practical reasoning and rationality quite different from Hume's and more like Aristotle's. Hume is, to be sure, like Aristotle in many important respects, particularly in his conception of the structure as opposed to the content of motivation. But Hume's views about the scope and power of practical reason are very different. Its normative as well as its motivational power is wholly instrumental. Ultimate ends cannot be evaluated as reasonable or unreasonable, except, possibly, insofar as achieving them can be made a means to realizing other such ends, in which case they are not purely ultimate; and for the many actions to which Hume would apply psychological hedonism, their believed contribution to the agent's pleasure or pain is the only Humean basis of their rational appraisal.

CHAPTER 3

Kant and the Autonomy of Practical Reason

Immanuel Kant wrote voluminously about practical reason, but his view of practical reasoning, like Hume's conception of it, is largely implicit. It must be formulated through a study of his examples in the light of his doctrines about reason in relation to motivation and action. For this purpose, the most important text is his *Foundations of the Metaphysics of Morals* (the *Grundlegung*), and this will be my primary, though not my exclusive, source. In addition to representing his overall position on the relevant problems, it is an important and very influential text in its own right, and probably Kant's work that has been most closely associated with the Kantian account of practical thinking in general. It is that account which, in part, this chapter attempts to formulate.

I Practical reason in the moral sphere

Kant's most developed examples of practical thinking are in the moral domain. A central element in that domain is good will. He opens the first section of the *Grundlegung* with the thesis that 'Nothing in the world – indeed, nothing even beyond the world – can possibly be conceived which could be called good without qualification except a *good will*.'[1] A good will, moreover, is intrinsically good: 'not because of what effects it accomplishes or because of its adequacy to achieve some proposed end; it is good only because of its willing, i.e., it is good of itself' (394). Now reason is what determines the goodness of the will; for

> reason is given to us as a practical faculty, i.e., one which is meant to have an influence on the will. As nature has elsewhere distributed capacities suitable to the functions they are to perform, reason's proper function must be to produce a will good in itself and not one good merely as a means, for to the former reason is absolutely essential. This will must indeed not be the sole and complete good but the highest good and the condition of all others, even of the desire for happiness.
>
> (396)

Reason, then, through its influence on the will, is the central underpinning of goodness, although there are apparently other (intrinsic) goods besides good will, which is not 'the sole and complete good.'

If good will is not the only thing that is intrinsically good, it is the only thing unconditionally good. Kant does not explicate this unconditionality. But from the contrasts he draws we might suppose that *one* basis of the unconditional goodness of good will lies in this: that, unlike pleasure or even happiness, it cannot be undeservedly possessed. It is itself the condition for the worthiness to possess it.[2] As one would expect from the centrality of good will among the things that are good, moral goodness is in some way traceable to the will and hence to practical reason; a thing's goodness does not consist, for example, simply in its contribution to happiness. If we can understand how moral goodness is traceable to the will, we shall be in a position to locate practical reasoning in Kant's philosophy of action.

In order to connect morally good actions – those having 'moral worth' – to the will, we should note what Kant introduces, in the first section, as the three propositions of morality. The first, which he often reiterates, is that 'to have moral worth an action must be done from duty' (400). This is an explainability requirement: the action must be explainable as performed in order to fulfill a duty.[3] The second is that

> An action performed from duty does not have its moral worth in the purpose which is to be achieved through it but in the

maxim by which it is determined . . . the principle of volition
by which the action is done. . . . The third principle, as a
consequence of the two preceding, I would express as follows:
Duty is the necessity of an action executed from respect for
law.

(400)

Roughly, one's duty is what one must, from respect for (moral)
law, do; doing one's duty has moral worth only if the action in
question is done *from* duty; and the reason for this condition of
moral worth is that only such actions arise from the volitions
('willings' or perhaps intendings) which constitute a good will
and thereby enable its unconditional goodness, as expressed in a
morally sound maxim, to endow those actions with moral worth.
Actions done from duty stem from good will and thereby inherit
their moral worth from the goodness of the volitional elements
underlying them.

What, then, is it to act from duty? Kant's answer is evident in
his contrast between acting in accordance with duty and acting
from it. Most people, he says,

> preserve their lives according to duty, but not from duty. But
> if adversities and hopeless sorrow completely take away the
> relish for life, if an unfortunate man, strong in soul, is
> indignant rather than despondent or dejected over his fate
> and wishes for death, and yet preserves life without loving it
> and from neither inclination nor fear but from duty – then
> his maxim [that even in such circumstances it is his duty to
> preserve his life] has a moral import.

(398)

As I understand Kant, the action in question is preserving one's
life, *not* preserving it from duty. To see this, note that 'preserving
it from duty' reports both the action and its explaining motive.
Granted, Kant sometimes speaks as if specifications of operative
motives belonged in the crucial act description, as they may seem
to in certain Kantian principles and maxims, for instance the 'law'
that an agent 'ought to promote his happiness, not from inclination
but from duty' (400). But I do not think the view that specifications
of motives belong in the crucial act descriptions is supported by
Kant's four famous examples in 422–4. Moreover, if he is so read,

62

then on the plausible assumption that our (direct) duties are to do things which are under direct voluntary control (roughly, performable at will), we should take him to hold an implausible view: that agents have such control over the motive from which they act, in the sense that they can bring about at will their acting on a particular motive, or at least on one motive from a perhaps limited range, such as those of their present motives satisfiable by the action they are considering. It is far from clear that he held this, and his overall view does not require it. His view may require, and is more plausible if taken to presuppose, that by and large we have only indirect voluntary control over such motives, for instance the capacity to cultivate both certain motives and a tendency to act on them.[4]

We might say, then, that what is essential for the moral worth of an act is not that the agent determine its having the right motive, but that the right motive determine *it*. The crucial point is apparently that (considerations of) duty be both what provide a motive *to* perform the act and constitute the agent's actual reason *for* performing it. This is why Kant stresses the contrast with actions motivated by inclination or fear. It is not enough that the agent *have* a motive of duty, say an awareness of a duty or even a respect for duty; the action must be based on duty in the sense that it is performed for the relevant reason of duty.[5] Kant's example is particularly apt for illustrating the idea because the agent seems both to be using reason to arrive at what his duty is and to be consciously pursuing that duty against his wish for death. This attempt is an expression of the autonomy of the rational will against the heteronymy of ignoble inclination. Even if there is no such conflict, however, acting on a maxim seems a clear case in which it would be natural to engage in practical reasoning. Let us consider how, in another Kantian example, practical reasoning might occur.

In illustrating his fundamental principle of morality, the categorical imperative, Kant gives four famous examples. In one formulation the principle is this: 'Act only according to that maxim by which you can at the same time will that it should be a universal law' (422), hence a principle that is followed by everyone. One example concerns a man who needs to borrow money and knows he will not be able to repay it:

he also sees that nothing will be loaned him if he does not firmly promise to repay. . . . He desires to make such a promise, but he has enough conscience to ask himself whether it is not improper and opposed to duty to relieve his distress in such a way. Now, assuming he does decide to do so, the maxim of his action would be. . . . When I believe myself to be in need of money, I will borrow money and promise to repay it, although I know I shall never do so. . . . He changes the pretension of self-love into a law and then puts the question: How would it be if my maxim became a universal law? He immediately sees that it could never hold as a universal law. . . . For the universality of a law which says that anyone who believes himself to be in need could promise what he pleased with the intention of not fulfilling it would make the promise itself and the end to be accomplished by it impossible.

(422)

This example suggests what sorts of premises Kantian practical reasoning has. Clearly the agent is reasoning; and if he decides to make the false promise, then his major premise, on Kant's view, would be the maxim Kant states, and the minor premise would be the instrumental proposition that making an insincere promise to repay the money to be borrowed will get one that money. Moreover, Kant suggests that both the agent's decision to act, and, later, his action itself, would be *based on* this maxim. It would be so based because *the intention with which he acts* is to deceive by making an insincere promise, and what motivates both that intention and the promise which is its object is the desire to borrow money and the belief that such a promise is the only way to do so.

The role of the agent's intention (or at least primary intention) is especially important here. That intention reveals *what* description of the action is crucial in determining *on* what maxim(s) the agent acts. We might call this Kantian view *the descriptive primacy of intention*. If, for instance, one hands a creditor money with the intention of fulfilling a moral duty to repay it, one is – given a suitable commitment to a maxim that one should repay money one owes – acting *on* that maxim; whereas if one repays it simply with the intention of avoiding punishment, no moral maxim underlies one's action. One's maxim might instead be that one must repay borrowed money if this is required to avoid punishment. Kant does not make clear how a moral maxim itself must figure in the genesis of a moral action, but much of what he says suggests that acceptance of it partly underlies both the crucial intention and the resulting action. The idea is roughly that the action is intended under a description, such as 'fulfilling a moral duty to repay', or at least under a concept expressible by such a description, and thereby intended in a way that brings the action under the maxim. In our example, commitment to the maxim is at least part of what produces the intention to fulfill the duty to repay; and because the action is performed with that intention *as* grounded in the maxim, the action has moral worth.

The example is typical of intentional action as Kant conceived it. He apparently took intentional action in general to be governed by maxims, at least in a tacit way that does not require reciting them. He says, for instance, that 'The will is thought of as a faculty of determining itself to action in accordance with the conception of certain laws' (427) and that maxims – which he takes to be subjective expressions of laws (or at least of certain kinds of them) – 'arise from desires and inclination under the cooperation of reason' (427). He even goes so far as to speak of intentions as 'maxims of the will' (435), and he holds that 'in the use of means to every end I should restrict my maxim to the condition of its universal validity' (438). His view seems to be that the will moves us to action only if some principle informs it: the principle figures, at least tacitly, in the content of the intention to do the thing in question; and if we do it with that intention, we tend to take our doing it to realize the principle. If Kant did not regard all intentional action as rule-governed in this way, he at least so regarded a huge range of cases, including both moral and prudential action and apparently the entire category of rational action.

There may, of course, be more than one maxim applied by an agent to the same situation, say a maxim of morality and one of prudence. If so, both may be reflected in the content of the crucial intention or – though this seems less likely – Kant might suppose that such an action is performed with two or more intentions, each reflecting a different maxim. But if the agent acts on two maxims, then Kant's position would seem to imply that the action is moral only if the role of the non-moral intention is such that the action is still *from* duty, whatever else may jointly influence it. This point is speculative, however, since Kant did not treat such cases in detail and usually assumed that for each intentional action that is to be morally assessed there is just one intention with which it is performed, and its content is either moral or not, as opposed to moral and prudential. As he says in speaking of actions grounded on a sound moral principle, 'What is essentially good in it [the action] is the intention, the result being what it may' (416).

It is less clear what the conclusion of Kantian practical reasoning is supposed to be, but Kant is certainly talking as if it is a judgment appropriate to underlie both deciding to do the deed and the doing of it. In his fourth example Kant actually embeds the maxim in what appears to be a judgment of what one will do. He represents an agent who intends to practice indifference rather than do benevolent deeds as concluding (or at least closing) his deliberation with the thought, 'I will not take anything from him or envy him; but to his welfare . . . I have no desire to contribute' (423). Having this thought is not merely predicting what one will in fact do, while disavowing desire. It is the expression of (i) an intention, or even a resolution, regarding what, as a matter of policy, one should do, and (ii) aversion to contributing to the needy ('have no desire to' in such contexts normally means 'desire not to'). In Kant's first example, moreover, the agent's question to himself is 'whether it would not be contrary to his duty to himself to take his own life' (422). Given his 'despair' that motivates his asking the question and inclines him to act on his answer to it, we can suppose that even if the answer his reasoning yields is that it would not be contrary to duty, that answer will obliquely express an intention to act accordingly (to dispatch himself). If the answer is positive, it will of course be a statement of duty (which is to abstain).

To put the point broadly, Kant apparently takes the conclusion of practical reasoning to be a judgment *favoring* the action which the minor premise represents as fulfilling the maxim contained in the major. The major premise might even contain the categorical imperative itself, or at least an approving reference to it, since an agent might take a specific action to be required by it (through a specific imperative that passes its universalizability test) and might thereby conclude in favor of so acting. To be sure, in a situation of difficult moral decision, one would normally settle on a specific action only by first applying the categorical imperative to arrive at a subsidiary principle. One might, having done this, subsume the projected obligatory action under the master principle itself. Thus, in deciding which of two students to aid when there is time to help only one, I might describe their degree of need and my relation to them, formulate a universalizable principle expressing a priority of one kind of case over the other, and judge that in such cases I should aid the less advanced one. I might then act accordingly, and might or might not think of my action as according (indirectly) with the categorical imperative itself. But I would at least be acting from the subsidiary moral principle. If practical reasoning is genuinely moral (and not just couched in moral terms), the conclusion will be a judgment of obligation, based on premises the agent takes to show that there is an obligation. If the reasoning is not moral, the conclusion is an expression of intention, resolution, or perhaps just strong motivation, as in the indirect expression of aversion, 'I have no desire to expend my energies doing deeds of charity.' In any of these cases, one's drawing the conclusion can, given one's acceptance of the premises, explain both why one decides to do the thing in question and, normally, why one does it.

Practical reasoning so conceived may be viewed as having a means-end structure, provided we include constitutive means. For instance, preserving one's life out of the duty to do so is not an ordinary causal means to fulfilling that duty, but *constitutes* fulfilling it. But Kant also seems to envisage practical reasoning that is both outside the moral sphere and concerns ordinary causal means. Speaking of happiness, he says that

> To secure one's own happiness is at least indirectly a
> duty. . . . But the precept of happiness is often so formulated
> that it definitely thwarts some inclinations, and men can make
> no definite and certain concept of the sum of satisfactions of
> all inclinations which goes under the name of happiness. It is
> not to be wondered at, therefore, that a single inclination,
> definite as to what it promises, can outweigh a fluctuating idea,
> and that, for example, a man with the gout can choose to
> enjoy what he likes and to suffer what he may, because
> according to his calculations at least on this occasion he has

not sacrificed the enjoyment of the present moment to a perhaps groundless expectation of a happiness supposed to lie in health.

(399)

The man described here calculates the pleasure of indulgence and the possible bad effects of it and concludes that he should (or will) 'enjoy what he likes.' Kant speaks of this as a case in which 'the universal inclination to happiness' determines the man's will. Thus, despite the presence of a duty to secure his happiness, the action is not performed *from* that duty, and hence is not of moral worth even if it conforms to the agent's duty. In addition to calculation, the case also exhibits deliberation; for the agent both calculates and assesses the effects of his various options. Presumably he acts from a maxim, accompanied by an underlying desire, that he should enhance his pleasure. His minor premise, in the reasoning that leads to his action, might be something like: I can enjoy this rich meal without seriously impairing my health. His conclusion might be to the effect that he should (or will) take the food. The case might also exhibit weakness of will, but I leave that topic for section III.

II The motivational and normative power of reason

Following Kant, I have stressed the importance of acting from duty. An action's being performed from duty is a condition of its having moral worth. But acting from duty as opposed to other motives, such as a desire for pleasure, is possible only if duty – or the judgment or sense of it – has motivational power. Kant's considered view seems to be that judgments of duty – roughly, judgments that an act is one's duty – do have such power (presumably by necessity). He is indeed an internalist regarding judgments of duty (and obligation), a *deontic internalist*. He is more than a (deontic) *minimal internalist*, one who holds that judgments of duty have some motivational power inclining the agent to act accordingly, but less than a *strong internalist*, one who holds that judgments of duty yield overriding motivation to act accordingly. What he seems to hold is *moderate internalism*: the view that judgments of duty (or obligation) are sufficient (in the context) both to produce and to explain the action in question.

On the assumption that making a judgment of duty provides a motive of duty, we could also express Kant's internalism as a thesis about *motives* of duty, to the effect that judgments of duty entail motives of duty. Moreover, regardless of how we express the motivational component in his internalism, it is apparently an *unmediated internalism*, one that views the appropriate motivation as embodied *in* accepting the judgment, as opposed to a (less plausible) *mediated internalism*, an impure internalism that takes the motivation to be internal to accepting the judgment only in the weaker sense that it is in some (perhaps indirect) way entailed or otherwise implied by accepting it. Such mediation might occur where, say, a desire to keep one's promise is implied in judging it to be a duty, not because the desire is a constituent in accepting the judgment, but because one has a general tendency (possibly grounded in benevolence or even prudence) to want to do one's duty.[6]

Since the maxims of duty are derived from reason, Kant's internalism commits him to the view that reason itself is *motivationally practical*, a position he in fact states. He says, for instance, that will *is*

> nothing else than practical reason. If reason infallibly
> determines the will, the actions which such a being [a rational
> being] recognizes as objectively necessary are also subjectively
> necessary. That is, the will is a faculty of choosing only that
> which reason, *independently of inclination*, recognizes as
> practically necessary, i.e., as good.

> (413, emphasis added)

Clearly, then, as rational beings we can act on the basis of the dictates of reason. When we so act, the will is autonomous; when we act from inclination, it is heteronomous.

There is another respect in which reason is practical. It is *normatively practical*. Speaking of philosophical principles in general, Kant says that 'reason alone dictates' them:

> These fundamental principles must originate entirely a priori
> and thereby obtain their commanding authority; they can
> expect nothing from the inclination of men but everything
> from the supremacy of the law and due respect for it. . . .
> Thus everything empirical is not only wholly unworthy to be

an ingredient in the principle of morality but is even highly prejudicial to the purity of moral practices themselves.

(425–6)

As for the fundamental principle of morality, the categorical imperative, Kant says of it not only that 'it must arise from pure reason,' but also that

By this principle all maxims are rejected which are not consistent with the universal lawgiving of will. The will is thus not only subject to law but subject in such a way that it must be regarded as self-legislative and only for this reason being subject to the law of which it can regard itself as the author.

(431)

As practical reason, will is the author of the categorical imperative and thereby of the subsidiary principles of duty; but since, in addition, 'will is a kind of causality of living beings so far as they are rational' (446), it is self-legislative, and in that sense autonomous. It is also a powerful creative force. In one capacity, it provides the principles expressing its own rationality and moral commitments; in another, it provides its own executive powers. By virtue of these two capacities, rational beings are doubly autonomous.

I propose to call the twofold doctrine that reason is both motivationally and normatively practical the thesis of *the autonomy of practical reason*. First, reason need not derive motivation from any other source, such as inclinations to seek pleasure or avoid pain; second, it lays down, independently of empirical considerations, such as facts about human psychology, the moral principles which it motivates rational beings to obey. Here Kant contrasts with Hume, who explicitly rejected the first view and implicitly denied the second. In one important way, however, Kant is like Aristotle, who apparently accepted the second view, though without specifying that reason lays down moral principles a priori (he may indeed not have employed the relevant notion of the a priori). But Kant differs from Aristotle on the status of practical reason in at least two ways, which I take up in turn.

First, Kant maintains a stronger internalism. Aristotle held at most a weaker form, requiring only that practical judgment, including moral judgment, implies some degree of motivation to act accordingly. Indeed, in some passages Aristotle seems to endorse externalism: the view that practical judgments motivate one only if they are appropriately connected with one's (independent) desires.[7] It is difficult to tell whether Aristotle is a kind of externalist, in part because the desire for happiness is both motivationally omnipresent and appropriate to explain, by virtue of one or another purposive chain, any intentional action. Hence, this desire will in some sense accompany – and will be difficult to sort out from – a practical judgment even if the judgment is in no way grounded in the desire. By contrast Kantian moral motivation is grounded in the agent's judgment, say that something is a duty here and now, whether or not the agent may be said to have an independent desire to act dutifully.

Second, there are various ways in which reason may be normatively practical, and Kant differs from Aristotle here too. Reason may be *epistemically practical*, in the sense that it provides knowledge (or at least justified beliefs) of normative truths. It may be *legislatively practical*, in the sense that it lays down such truths as standards of conduct. And it may be *constitutively practical*, in the sense that its deliverances create normative standards. Both Aristotle and Kant take reason to be practical in the first sense; but, unlike Kant, Aristotle apparently does not conceive it as practical in the second. In part, this is because Aristotle is not a rule theorist: right action, for him, flows from character suffused by reason, not from application of principles or maxims; and while this allows virtuous agents to use rules, rule following is not the basic notion underlying his conception of rational conduct. If reason can be, for Aristotle, legislatively practical, it is *retrospectively* so, in that it enables us to draw normative generalizations from previous experience. But in Kant reason is *prospectively* legislative: there is no moral action apart from following rules expressing our duties, hence no field of moral action not already done in obedience to rules and thereby appropriate for retrospective generalization. Regarding constitutive practicality, it is not clear that even Kant attributed this power to reason, but there are places where it might seem so, for instance in the third section of the *Grundlegung*.[8] To be sure, even if dictates of reason somehow constitute normative standards, these dictates may still be based on premises, or at least supportable by propositions we can know. The constitution need not be written without cognitive raw materials. Nonetheless, while it is not clear to what extent Kant saw reason as normatively constitutive, he contrasts significantly with Aristotle, and sharply with Hume, by taking it to be both epistemically and legislatively practical.[9]

The practical reasoning that occurs in the background of moral action, then, is both subject to a priori standards of adequacy and capable of motivating action independently of inclination. Inclination may of course also yield practical reasoning; and when it does, ordinary desires apparently carry the motivating force, though it is perhaps not inconsistent with what Kant says to read him as also holding *prudential internalism*, the view that judgments that one ought, prudentially, to do something have independent motivating force. Kant may not be committed, however, to the claim that every intentional action emerges from practical reasoning. In places he talks as if he holds this, however, and he apparently does hold it for rational actions, at least if an action's being rule-governed in the way he imagines rational actions are, implies practical reasoning in its genesis. In any case, he is committed to the structural thesis that a practical argument corresponds to every rule-governed intentional action. There need be no *actual* deliberation or calculation: the agent may act from duty, and certainly from inclination, even if the relevant maxim is simply presupposed and the action is in some sense automatic. But there is still a practical argument corresponding to the structure.

III Weakness of will and the conflict between reason and inclination

If Kant affirms the autonomy of practical reason as full-bloodedly as I have suggested, then at least in moral cases there is some question whether his view can accommodate weakness of will. If my judgment that it is my duty to keep a promise has motivating power sufficient to explain my doing so if I in fact keep the promise, how can it lack motivating power sufficient to produce the action, even when I have strong contrary inclinations?

One might think that Kant could simply say that despite the power of reason, inclinations opposing it can motivate an agent more strongly. But in places he sounds like a strong internalist and seems to rule out this solution. In discussing the imperative to develop one's talents, for instance, he says of the agent in question that 'as a rational being, he necessarily wills that all his faculties should be developed, inasmuch as they are given him for all sorts of possible ends' (423). If developing my faculties is my *will* and is thus backed by volition and presumably also by intention to act accordingly, how can I want more to do something contrary to that?

The answer might seem to lie in the difference between willing (or intending) that, in general, my faculties be developed and willing that some particular faculty, such as my piano technique, be developed. Here we would have a failure of *volitional integration*: owing perhaps to a failure of one's motivation to extend from an end to a means, one's overall will is not sufficiently integrated into one system of volitions regarding particular actions. But Kant cannot unqualifiedly appeal to this view because of his doctrine that 'Whoever wills the end, so far as reason has decisive influence on his action, wills also the indispensably necessary means to it that lie in his power' (417–18). If I know I need practice for my technique, and will to develop that technique, I must surely will to practice, even if I intensely dislike the exercises. Thus, the problem of accounting for incontinence persists.

There are at least two solutions open to Kant. One is to say that even what one quite specifically wills need not be motivationally overriding; hence, contrary motivation can prevent one's doing what one wills. This would locate weakness of the will in its executive power and not in its conformity to reason. However, in Kant, as well as in most other philosophers, before and after him, who use the notion of volition in dealing with weakness of will, volition is normally the immediate determinant of action, or at least taken to prevail in action unless the agent is prevented from acting. This move, then, is unlikely to be Kant's response. In addition, it seems to assimilate *weakness of the will* as normally understood, to *weakness in the will*. The first is a volitional failure to conform to reason and is consistent with ability to do otherwise; it is a deficiency of volitional content, not volitional power, a failure to will the right action rather than a lack of sufficient energy to bring about that action. A good Kantian example might be judging that one should punish one's child, yet failing to do so because one 'cannot' overcome one's compassionate inclinations to let the matter pass with a scolding. The second phenomenon, weakness *in* the will, is a matter of inadequate volitional power, a failure to produce the right action once it *is* willed. A paradigm case would be that of a decision to do something difficult but within one's capacity – say, to move a boulder – followed by setting oneself to do it, yet failing to muster the effort to mobilize one's full power. I think, then, that Kant would instead propose a second solution, noting that it is only when *reason* has 'decisive influence' on one's action that one must will what one takes to be an available necessary means to one's end. Thus, weakness of will is, if not a species of irrationality, at least a failure of reasonable self-control. It is possible because of limits on the extent to which reason influences action.

I take this interpretation to be broadly Aristotelian, at least insofar as failure of integration is central to understanding Aristotle's views on weakness of will. In any case, the interpretation is supported by other passages. Commenting on what it is like to 'observe ourselves in any transgression of a duty' – which Kant seems to conceive as at least sometimes a case of observing our own weakness of will – he says that

> since we regard our action at one time from the point of view of a will wholly conformable to reason and then from that of a will affected by inclinations, there is actually no contradiction, but rather an opposition of inclination to the precept of reason. . . . Although this cannot be justified in our own impartial judgment, it does show that we actually acknowledge the validity of the categorical imperative and allow ourselves (with respect to it) only a few exceptions which seem to us to be unimportant and forced upon us.
>
> (425)

This passage occurs in the context of the four examples and might apply, for instance, to neglecting a talent. Here, too, Kant's emphasis is on inclinations as affecting the will in competition with reason, presumably in a way that leads (with or without competing practical reasoning) to a volition, and thus action, that is contrary to a judgment one makes (or belief one forms) in accordance with the categorical imperative. On the other hand, we 'allow ourselves' the transgression; this suggests that Kant is not speaking of compulsion, but of something more a matter of insufficient exercise of will.

The text does not tell us whether the imagined case occurs following practical reasoning, or simply against the background of a judgment which may have been made either without practical reasoning or through practical reasoning much earlier and no longer actively in the agent's memory. It appears that Kant is thinking of a situation in which the agent, who is after all considering a moral question, does do practical reasoning. In any event, Kant can certainly countenance weakness of will even where one has just inferred, from premises that clearly support it, a practical judgment against which one then acts. Granted, if we were perfectly rational, weakness of will would not occur, nor would we ever act immorally, in the sense of performing acts with no moral worth; for our actions would be not only in conformity with reason but also based on it, and such actions cannot be immoral. But Kant is certainly not imagining the offending agent as perfectly rational.

While Kant's main interest in action is rooted in his concern to develop an adequate moral theory, he apparently allows for weakness of will in non-moral cases. The structure of his account would be as just indicated: the agent would act against a judgment (or belief) that accords with the relevant imperative, and the explanation would be one or another kind of influence by contrary inclination. If the imperative is one of prudence, for instance, the agent might fail to heed its warning because of desire for immediate pleasure. Kant's gout example (cited above) might serve here. It is true that we cannot tell from Kant's description whether it is a case of weakness of will or simply *self-indulgence*, in the sense, roughly, of pursuit of pleasure in accordance with corrupt judgment, or without the agent's making any serious judgment, pro or con, regarding it (Kant's case sounds more like self-indulgence). But suppose that the man simply wants to nourish himself and draws the prudent conclusion that he should decline sweets in favor of fruit. Imagine that he then yields to his inclination and, trying to keep his prudential judgment out of mind by talking intently as he reaches for the pastry, takes several pieces. This is incontinent action which Kant could describe as such. It is not that moral principles, such as those concerning self-preservation, are irrelevant to the action; the point is simply that Kant's overall view allows for weakness of will where the agent does not consider a moral principle and acts against only a non-moral imperative.

If these points of interpretation are approximately correct, then Kant can explain some incontinent actions as due to a failure of volitional integration, others as attributable to obscured knowledge, still others as due to inadequately integrated knowledge, and some as combining all three defects. Weakness of will, moreover, may be moral or prudential or indeed a breach of any kind of normative standard. What marks it as weakness of will is above all the agent's failure to conform the incontinent action to reason.

IV   The unity of practical and theoretical reason

I have already stressed that Kant conceives reason as practical. Is reason as it manifests itself in theoretical matters fundamentally the same faculty, and how is theoretical reasoning (which is paradigmatically what Kant calls speculative) different from practical reasoning?

In the Preface to the *Grundlegung* Kant says:

> I require of a critical examination of a pure practical reason, if it is to be complete, that its unity with the speculative be subject to presentation under a common principle, because in the final analysis there can be but one and the same reason which must be differentiated only in application.
>
> (392)

The crucial difference in application Kant took to concern what he called the objects of the two uses of reason. As he said in the *Lectures on Ethics*:

> Philosophy is either theoretical or practical. The one concerns itself with knowledge, the other with the conduct of beings possessed of a free will. The one has Theory, the other Practice for its object – and it is the object which differentiates them. . . . Practical philosophy is such not by its form, but by reference to its object, namely, the voluntary conduct of a free being. The object of practical philosophy is conduct.[10]

It is important to see that in these passages (among others) Kant may be implying – and is certainly providing for – a twofold distinction: between the practical and theoretical aspects of reason as each appropriate to different subject matters, and between theoretical reasoning as undertaken *in order to* acquire knowledge and practical reasoning as undertaken in order to ascertain what to do, or at least as part of one's overall effort to determine what to do. Each distinction corresponds to a different kind of 'application' of reason.

Take the first distinction. If one reflects on what moral imperatives are true, one is doing practical philosophy because one is concerned in some way with the voluntary conduct of free beings, whereas if one reflects on whether there is a necessary connection between cause and effect one is doing theoretical philosophy. We have, then, a distinction of *content*. What I take to be Kant's second distinction between the practical and the theoretical cuts across this one. The latter is a distinction of *purpose*: when he says that the 'object' of practical philosophy is conduct, he has in mind, I think, more than its object conceived as its subject matter; he also has in mind philosophy done with the underlying purpose of guiding conduct. Now one might reflect on what moral imperatives are true simply out of intellectual interest in ethics; in that case one's thinking might be described as *practical in content* and *theoretical in purpose*. It is, to be sure, not of *narrow practical content*, in that it concerns action in general and not the options any specific agent faces or has chosen; yet even narrowly practical reflection need not be aimed at guiding action. We should also grant that there is a sense in which theoretical reasoning may be thought to guide belief formation. But while belief formation is an event, it is at least not normally an action.

How should practical reasoning be located in relation to these two distinctions? If my sketch of Kant's conception of practical reasoning is correct, such reasoning is *both* contentually and purposively practical. It concerns voluntary conduct, but it is also undertaken to determine, or at least as an element in one's effort to determine, what to do. In part because it is undertaken in this way, and in part because it is subordinate either to an imperative one accepts or to an inclination one has, its conclusion is motivating and thus tends to produce conduct. In this sense, Kantian practical reasoning is also *genetically* practical. It is like theoretical reasoning in being *inferential*;[11] but it differs from some theoretical

<del>77</del>

reasoning in content and from all such reasoning in its purposive and genetic character. It is in virtue of this second, sharper difference that it represents a substantially distinct 'application' of reason, one in which reason is, in the widest sense, instrumental and, if not prevented, expresses itself in conduct as well as in belief.[12]

V Conclusion

Enough has now been said about Kant to show where his views, at least in the *Grundlegung*, stand with respect to the guiding questions I have stressed in discussing Aristotle and Hume. In answering these questions in relation to Kant, I shall consider mainly the moral sphere, but it should be clear how to extend my points about his thinking to non-moral cases.

1 Kant is very explicit about how a rational person answers a practical question. It is by appeal, possibly tacit in an experienced person, to an appropriate imperative. Answering a practical question may even demand, especially in a situation of conflicting moral considerations, that one formulate a new principle, where this requires bringing to bear many relevant facts about the situation. If the practical problem is moral, the overarching principle is the categorical imperative. But commonly a moral question, say whether to make an insincere promise, can be settled by reflecting on a subsidiary, but also unconditional, imperative concerning the kind of conduct at issue.

2 To act for a reason is to act *from* that reason. This implies that the reason actually motivates the action and is sufficient to explain it. In the moral case, the reason must be one of duty. This is consistent with acting from a *desire* to do one's duty for its own sake. But if such a desire figures in acting from duty, it must be grounded in – and presumably must also be a constituent of – the agent's acceptance of the imperative. The desire cannot be grounded in inclination.[13] Moreover, if, when one acts in accordance with duty, one has an inclination to perform the action in question, either the inclination must play a limited role if any, or the action is not done *from* duty. Kant seems to rule out the inclination's being motivationally necessary or sufficient, but leaves open whether it can play some lesser motivational role. If it is present side by side with a motive of duty, we may be unable, at least by simply willing this, to prevent its influencing the action. It may be *unharnessable*, at least by anything short of

special efforts of self-intervention. Whatever Kant's view on this matter, he maintains that we cannot in general know that an inclination *has* been unharnessed.[14] His paradigms of acting for a moral reason, then, are actions *against* inclination.

3 The Kantian structure for explaining actions is a means-end framework in which constitutive means are a central element. It is to that extent like Aristotle's. But some of the ends are dictated by reason a priori; no such view seems to be expressed in Aristotle. Hume explicitly rejects this view; and the Kantian framework for conceiving action, in emphasizing motives grounded in the a priori application of reason, is radically different from Hume's thoroughgoing instrumentalism. Like both Aristotle and Hume, however, Kant leaves room for weakness of will; and for him, as for Aristotle and probably Hume, it exhibits a kind of irrationality. But whereas in Hume weakness of will simply represents the victory of one set of desires over another set, or over a judgment not backed by actual desires, for Kant it represents, at least in the moral case, the contravention of an *end* laid down by reason as normatively correct. There are normative as well as motivational practical reasons. They are grounded in truth and discoverable by reason; they provide a normative basis of action; and they endow with moral worth actions that are performed from duty and thereby express commitment to an appropriate imperative.[15]

4 On the question of what mediates between reasons and actions, Kant says little in the *Grundlegung*. He is not much concerned there with the dynamics of action. But he certainly speaks of willing as if its occurrence can trigger action; and he leaves open a place for perception – say of opportunities to get what one seeks – to play a major role. Since practical reasoning as he conceives it concludes in judgment (or at least in belief formation), we may suppose that where actions arise from practical reasoning, a mental event of judgment or of belief formation will be available in the Kantian picture as a potential proximate cause of action, or at least of a decision or a volition which, in turn, leads directly to action.

5 In exhibiting actions for a reason, and particularly moral actions, as rational in the light of the agent's reasons for them, Kant presents a powerful account. The actions can of course be *instrumentally rational*, in the sense that they appropriately contribute to satisfying the agent's basic desires. Beyond that, however, an agent's basic desire – or motive if 'desire' is too narrow a term – underlying the action may be laid down by an a priori and necessary principle, such as one licensed by the categorical imperative. The desire itself is thus rational; and in virtue of being based on that desire, in the sense of being performed from the motive constituted by the desire, moral

actions and other actions for reasons may be said to be, as they are for Aristotle, *telically rational*: appropriately grounded in the pursuit of a normatively proper end. Third, since reason itself has motivating power sufficient to yield actions independently of inclination, those it does produce may be *motivationally rational*: appropriately grounded in a rational judgment.[16]

6   These points bring us to Kant's account of practical reason in relation to theoretical reason. For they emphasize his unification of the two: the a priori truths that determine our duties are accessible to theoretical reason, yet their apprehension, at least when we apply them to our own potential conduct, motivates and is thereby practical. Reason operates as an a priori force, then, in both the domain of speculation aimed at simply ascertaining truth and the sphere of human conduct. This applies despite differences between the two uses of reason; and it holds even where reason is both motivationally practical – being purposively subordinate to the aim of acting in response to concrete problems – and contentually practical – being concerned with what conduct is appropriate to free beings. In both the practical and theoretical spheres, moreover, reason, conceived as a capacity with causal power, may issue in an actual process of reasoning; and when the reasoning is practical, its motivational power need not derive from inclination.

However Kant might have filled out the details of his account of practical reasoning, he conceived it as a process in which reason applies maxims to specific actions and thereby guides conduct in the light of normative standards. For him, reason is both motivationally and normatively autonomous. Rejecting the externalist view that reason can motivate only with the aid of independent desire, and the instrumentalist view that allows rational appraisal only of means to ultimate ends which are beyond the reach of rational assessment, Kant gives us a ringing affirmation of the scope and power of practical reason.

There remain many problems to be explored in appraising Kant's conception of practical reasoning. One of his most important and most controversial theses is the view that reason can determine, a priori, a set of correct normative principles. One may grant this, however, and still question Kant's internalism. And one may question whether, in order to be truly moral, an action must be done from the appropriate motive, as opposed to being, say, performed with a suitable awareness that it is obligatory for the reason expressed by that motive. Supposing that it must be done from the motive, there remains the question whether it must arise from practical reasoning in the application of a moral rule; and similar questions arise about the way, if any, in which non-moral intentional action must be rule-governed. These and related issues concerning the foundations of practical reasoning and the grounds of rational action will be explored at several points in this book. My concern will be more with Kant's position on practical reasoning than with his views on the status of practical reason, but that issue, too, will be considered. The problems I address will not in general be discussed in relation to his work – nor indeed to that of Aristotle or Hume. But it will be clear that the account of practical reasoning I develop is an attempt to respond both to many of the problems they raise and to a number that they leave unsolved.

PART 2
Practical Reasoning, Intentional Action, and Rationality

CHAPTER 4

The Varieties and Basic Elements of Practical Reasoning

Historically, practical reasoning has been conceived as a kind of means-end reasoning. This conception is prominent in Aristotle, and we saw it, though less explicitly, in Hume and Kant. But even in Aristotle the conception is not developed sharply, and we certainly have not noted any specific means-end pattern that all three take every instance of practical reasoning to have. Moreover, the unifying notions I have used in framing examples of practical reasoning also leave open just what pattern, if any, is unique to such reasoning. Those notions are chiefly these: first, practical reasoning is undertaken in order to determine, or at least plays a purposive role in determining (or in trying to determine), what to do; second, it expresses at least one reason for action; third, it is, in some way, suitable for producing action that is in line with its content; and fourth, on all three counts it contrasts with theoretical reasoning, conceived as undertaken in order to ascertain, or at least as playing a purposive role in ascertaining (or in trying to ascertain), what is true.

If these notions are, as they seem, among the main elements influencing one's conception of what practical reasoning is, it should be no surprise if there are many views of what constitutes such reasoning. There are indeed so many that it is difficult even to sharpen the fourfold characterization just given without eliminating some cases plausibly taken to represent practical reasoning. This chapter will first explore the variety of cases and, in that light, formulate an account of what practical reasoning is. My aim is to be as inclusive as possible, yet also to bring out the features that seem, on historical and other grounds, to be the central characteristics of practical reasoning. Fidelity to examples, however, will not be my only concern. An adequate account of practical reasoning should also represent it in a way that enables us to give at least partial answers to the six theoretical questions I have stressed as central in locating practical reasoning in the philosophy of human action.

I   The diversity of practical reasoning

A philosophical account of practical reasoning should exhibit the role that reason plays in human conduct. This demand is reflected in the question (which I have raised for Aristotle, Hume, and Kant) of how practical reasoning might exhibit the structure of acting for a reason so that actions for a reason can be seen as prima facie rational in the light of the agent's reason(s) for them. If this question guides our understanding of practical reasoning, it should be useful to group conceptions of it according to the kind of relation they take the agent to envisage between the action in question and the goal expressed in the content of the reasoning.

Using the variables '*S*' to range over agents, '*A*' to represent actions, and the Greek letter φ to stand for the agent's goal as expressed in the reasoning, we can schematically describe conceptions of practical reasoning. Perhaps the most widely illustrated are *necessary condition schemata*, which represent *S* as taking *A* to be necessary for realizing φ; *sufficient condition schemata*, which represent *S* as taking *A* to be sufficient for this; *sufficient reason schemata*, which represent *S* as taking *A* to be a (sufficiently) reasonable way – for instance a probable way, even if not necessary or sufficient – to realize φ; and *rule schemata*, which represent *S* as taking *A* to be required by a particular rule.[1] Let me illustrate these schemata with examples, most of them from the literature.

A necessary condition schema might be as follows:

(a) From now on *S* considers that, unless he does *A* no later than time *t'*, he cannot bring about φ at time *t*.
Therefore, no later than when he thinks time *t'* has arrived, *S* sets himself to do *A*, unless he forgets about the time or is prevented.[2]

Varieties and Basic Elements

A necessary condition schema might also specify, in its premises, a duty, as in many Kantian cases, or a need, purpose, plan, or various other things. What is crucial is that the action be conceived by *S* as necessary for realizing whatever goal governs the reasoning. Thus, if *S* is rational, no other action will be seen as an *alternative* way to realize the goal.

A similar diversity of goals may be exhibited by sufficient condition schemata. Let us consider some. Here is a sufficient condition schema with an optative goal representation:

(b) Let it be the case that I convince my examiner that I am a competent driver. If I signal for a turn, I will convince my examiner that I am a competent driver. [Hence] Let it be the case that I signal for a turn.[3]

S might also do practical reasoning in the service of a felt need:

(c) I really need a peaceful visit in the country. Accepting their invitation for a weekend in the Catskills would be a good way to have such a visit, so I'll accept it.[4]

A sufficient condition schema may be developed beyond this, with the idea of representing the reasoning as valid, in the sense that the truth of the premises entails *S*'s *A*-ing (and presumably also entails that in some sense *S* should *A*):

(d) I want ϕ.
A-ing is a way for me to bring about ϕ under these circumstances. There is no other way to bring about ϕ now which is as preferable to me as, or more preferable to me than, *A*-ing.
There is no sufficient reason for me not to bring about ϕ under these circumstances.
Therefore, let me do *A*.[5]

The validity of practical reasoning is not always of much concern to philosophers in their discussions of practical reasoning. This is one reason why sufficient reason schemata have been taken to represent at least some practical reasoning. It has been suggested, for example, that the simplest schema is:

(e) Doing *A* would be desirable (or, would bring about a desirable situation); I can do *A*, so I ought to do it.[6]

In other sufficient condition schemata, prima facie (pf) qualifications may be explicit in the premises, though the conclusion is unconditionally accepted because S presupposes that the reason expressed in the major is not overridden:

(f) $pf(x$ is better than y, [given that] x is a refraining from fornication and y is a fornication); A is a refraining from fornication and B is an act of fornication; so A is better than B.[7]

Where agents reasoning in this way take the prima facie superiority of refraining not to be overridden, it is natural for them to conclude unqualifiedly in favor of it and to act accordingly.

A common source both of perceived necessary conditions for a goal and of sufficient reasons for actions is rules. Here is a good representation of a rule schema:

(g) I'm in circumstances C.
If I'm in C, then I ought to do A.
So, I ought to do A.
Therefore, I shall A.[8]

The description of circumstances may be complicated and may exhibit conflicting reasons. Take the case of Antigone. She believes that she is in circumstances in which, legally, she ought not to bury her brother Polyneices and, religiously, she ought to do so. Her comparative rule is that in such circumstances the decrees of the gods override the laws of kings. She concludes that she ought, all things considered, to do what the gods decree, and resolves, 'I *shall* bury Polyneices.'[9]

There is at least one other notion of practical reasoning that should be mentioned. It may lie in the background in some passages in Aristotle and in other historically important figures, but it has been explicitly articulated only in recent years. This is a *functionalist view of practical reasoning*. Here is one formulation: 'Practical reasoning . . . is, basically, the process by which intentions are formed from beliefs and desires,' where 'A subject's desire matrix includes his preferences about Aing, as well as his preferences about alternatives to Aing. Similarly a subject's belief matrix includes his beliefs about his opportunity and his ability to A . . .'[10] Thus, given Antigone's desires to obey the gods and to avoid breaking the law, together with her beliefs about her

options, she forms the intention to bury Polyneices, and her forming it on this basis may be an instance of practical reasoning
whether or not she consciously reasons in the usual sense implying
the drawing of a conclusion on the basis of one or more premises.
On the functionalist view, since any of the kinds of schemata
just cited can play the appropriate role in representing the relevant
beliefs and desires, no one kind is favored as uniquely fitting the
functionalist notion of practical reasoning. It will indeed be an
empirical question what kinds of schemata are typically instantiated when intentions are formed from beliefs and desires in the
way supposed to constitute practical reasoning. Moreover, since
intentions can be formed in this way without *S*'s considering premises or a conclusion, the functionalist view does not require their
being recited or even entertained, and it leaves open what sorts
of processes are required, if indeed any conscious mental processes are required, for practical reasoning to occur.

In the light of the examples just given and those taken, or
reconstructed, from Aristotle, Hume, and Kant, how can we gen-
eralize about practical reasoning? Let us start by trying to ascertain what are its basic elements. They are of three kinds, one
corresponding to the major premise, one to the minor, and one
to the conclusion. The major premise can surely be taken to
represent a goal, even if the goal is not indicated by an expression
of, say, a desire or intention, but only implicit in *S*'s commitment
to a rule, for instance that one must place religious obligation
above legal obligation if they conflict. The minor premise clearly
represents a belief that indicates how *S* sees the action in relation
to the goal, say as necessary or as sufficient. The conclusion is the
most difficult to characterize. I have cited diverse examples of
conclusions, ranging from judgments of what one ought to do, to
the optative (and artificial) 'Let me *A*'. One trouble is that we
tend to think of the conclusion in a double role: as a proposition
concluded on the basis of the premises (drawn from and supported
by them), and as motivationally and normatively practical: it is
motivationally practical in tending to produce, or to play a major
role in producing, the action and thereby in solving the associated
practical problem, say what to do given Creon's forbidding one
to bury one's brother; and it is normatively practical by virtue of
having content that in some way supports the action it tends to
motivate.

To get a more detailed account of what practical reasoning is, we must observe some important distinctions and bring them to bear in understanding examples. One is the distinction, not always noticed, between practical *reasoning* and practical *argument* (in one use of 'argument'). A related distinction is between the *conclusion* of *S*'s argument, say the *judgment* that *S* should *A*, and *S*'s *concluding* that argument, say by *judging*, on the basis of the premises, that he should *A*. These and other distinctions must be developed and connected with the notion of practical judgment. This is the main task of the next section.

II Practical reasoning, practical argument, and means-end inference

Like the term 'argument', 'practical reasoning' may designate either a process or the corresponding abstract structure to which we directly refer when we logically appraise someone's practical argument (or reasoning) as valid or invalid. It is essential that we distinguish between a practical argument as a structure of propositions (or other bearers of truth value, such as perhaps equivalence classes of sentences) and the process of passing, in the way we do in reasoning, from the premises of such a structure to its conclusion. The same dual usage is exhibited by 'practical reasoning'. To avoid confusion, I generally use 'practical argument' for certain structures of propositions, 'piece of practical reasoning' for an instance of the corresponding process, and 'practical reasoning' for processes of that kind. Similarly, we must distinguish between the conclusion of a practical argument, which I take to be a proposition, and what corresponds to it in *S*'s reasoning: his *concluding* that reasoning, by inferring the conclusion from the premises. Typically, the conclusion will be the kind of proposition we think of as a practical *judgment*, and the concluding of the reasoning with that judgment will be an instance of *judging* that the action in question is, say, necessary for realizing the end in view.

If, as I have suggested, we may think of practical reasoning in general as a way of responding to a practical question, a parallel distinction suggests itself. We might call the *conclusion* of *S*'s practical argument *S*'s (actual or possible) *answer* to the relevant practical question, and his *drawing* that conclusion his (specific) *response* to that question. His *general* response is the entire piece of reasoning, of which his drawing the conclusion is the terminating element. If his drawing the conclusion is the making of a practical judgment, such as Antigone's judgment that she ought to bury Polyneices, the response is cognitive; if drawing the conclusion is forming an intention, the response is intentional; if drawing the conclusion is making a decision (which apparently implies but is not implied by forming an intention), the response is decisional; and if drawing the conclusion is the action itself, the response is behavioral.

In making these distinctions, I have spoken of the process *corresponding* to the practical argument. It turns out to be both difficult and important to say what the corresponding process is. Clearly it involves some kind of representation of the argument. We might call it a *tokening* of that argument, though no particular *sentence*-tokens, such as specific sentences of English, need be used: indefinitely many different sentences could express the relevant propositions. Moreover, surely one could express a practical argument, whether to oneself or aloud, *enthymematically*: one need not state or even entertain, for each of its propositions, a token of some sentence (or other representation) expressing it. If *S* says, 'That river is swift enough here to carry one away, so I've got to find another crossing,' *S* has expressed practical reasoning even though *S* leaves tacit an instrumental premise to the effect that finding another crossing is necessary to avoid getting carried away. The example also illustrates the indirect way in which the goal – here, getting safely across – can be expressed in actual tokening of a practical argument. I leave open the difficult question whether mental events other than sentence tokenings can play the necessary representational role. The typical representations, at least, and those of most interest here, are linguistic.

In the light of these distinctions, we can consider the schemata set out above as candidates for representation of either the forms of practical arguments or, on the other hand, of the actual tokening process that partly constitutes a piece of practical reasoning. The former aim – exhibiting the abstract structures of practical argument – seems closer to what the proponents of the schemata had in mind in proposing them, and I want to consider the schemata primarily in that light.

If our interest is in framing a comprehensive schema that indicates a kind of argument appropriately thought to underlie all the plausible examples of practical reasoning, then none of the schemata will seem wholly satisfactory. Necessary condition schemata fail to do justice to cases in which S regards A-ing as sufficient (in the circumstances), but not as necessary, for realizing φ. Sufficient condition schemata have the converse defect. Schema (e) is broad in leaving open the point of view from which S regards A-ing as desirable. But certain cases of weakness of will show that practical reasoning in the service of inclination need not contain a major premise to the effect that the thing wanted is desirable, unless seeing something as desirable is taken with such great breadth that it is implied by simply *wanting* it. Schema (f) is restrictive in a different way, and some of our examples suggest that it is also too narrow. It requires, for instance, that S make a comparative judgment, if only between A-ing and not A-ing, and draw a comparative conclusion. But surely one can simply judge that an action will realize a goal which one non-comparatively seeks, and on that basis conclude that one should perform it.

The rule-following schema is narrow in still another way. It requires one to conceptualize one's circumstances in relation to a normative rule. The minor premise is then taken to describe the action as a (constitutive) means to obeying the rule. Kant may well have so regarded practical reasoning; and apparently rational action, as he conceived it, is grounded in adherence to an appropriate rule. Granting that *some* kind of rule can be formulated to correspond with any kind of goal – say, the rule that good fruit is to be tasted by a hungry person who has it available – it does not appear that we are always acting *on* such a rule when, in envisaging a goal, we do practical reasoning, arrive at a way to achieve our goal, and act accordingly. We are perhaps *disposed* to justify (or even explain) such action by a relevant rule if the appropriateness of the action is questioned. But that would only show that such practical arguments are available in retrospective reconstruction, not that they represent the structure of our actual practical reasoning. The rule to which we appeal may be one we are formulating, or perhaps even accepting, for the first time as we think about the matter. Reflection on why we did something, or on why it was appropriate to do it, does not merely elicit beliefs we had at the time; it creates new beliefs and even new knowledge.

Suppose we now ask how well schemata (a) to (g) represent, first, the process of *S*'s tokening the premises and, second, whatever it is that constitutes *S*'s drawing the conclusion. From what has already been said, it is plain that none of them is fully adequate to capture the diversity of processes we surely want to call practical reasoning. Since not all such reasoning embodies (or even enthymematically presupposes) beliefs of the sort indicated by the premises of any one of the schemata, for example beliefs to the effect that *A*-ing is necessary for φ, no tokening of these premises need occur in every case of practical reasoning. Concerning the conclusions of the schemata, there is the deeper issue of what constitutes the concluding element. As mentioned in discussing Aristotle, some commentators take him to conceive the concluding element as action. In schema (a) it is setting oneself to act; and on the functionalist view cited, it is forming an intention. Let us first consider the view that the conclusion is an action, beginning with its resources for explaining what it is to conclude practical reasoning.

Recall Kant's gout example. Suppose it occurs to the agent that he would love some sweetbreads, and he realizes that to get some he must go out before six. He might conclude that he should go out before six. Surely this is one way a piece of practical reasoning can be concluded: with a judgment in favor of a future action. Making this judgment, however, if it is an action as opposed to a mental doing not properly considered action, is not the action in favor of which the reasoning concludes: going out before six. Moreover, *that* action need never occur; he might later change his mind and not go. Thus, the action-as-conclusion view does not provide a necessary condition for concluding practical reasoning. The view also seems not to give us a sufficient condition for concluding it. Suppose that *S* does not infer from the propositions in question that he should go to the store, but instead resists their influence and resolutely adopts the belief that he should not go. (He might form this belief as a result of competing practical reasoning.) If, being weak-willed, he later goes in spite of himself – and without judging that he should – must we say that *by* going he did complete the original practical reasoning? He has indeed acted in accordance with practical premises he accepts; but it appears that he stopped short of drawing the conclusion they supported, and drew a different, incompatible one. The incontinent action he performs, then, arises (as Kant might say) from his inclination, not his reasoning.

One might reply that where *S* completes practical reasoning that favors *A*-ing, yet does not *A*, he at least *decides* to *A*, and decision is then the practical response that constitutes his concluding the reasoning.[11] But surely the same range of examples already given argues that *S* can complete practical reasoning without even deciding to *A*. Susan might conclude that she should do some heroic deed, yet fail to decide to because, as she thinks about the high risk, she changes her mind.

Granted, the action-as-conclusion view has the virtue of closing the gap between practical reasoning and the action it indicates – by making the action itself the concluding element. This implication may indeed be the chief attraction of the view. But the view has serious defects. It makes practical reasoning a hybrid process composed of what is, intuitively, reasoning and, on the other hand, action based on it. It leaves us with no adequate account of the concluding of that reasoning. And it fails to accommodate cases in which the action that should be the concluding element does not occur. There is of course more to be said on this issue. But rather than present further direct arguments against the action-as-conclusion view, I propose simply to try to develop an alternative account of practical reasoning that deals better with the relevant problems. Let us start by asking what, besides the action, might be the concluding element.

I have already proposed one important guiding idea: drawing the conclusion should be a good candidate for *S*'s response to a practical question, both by having a content appropriate to answer it and in being such that accepting this content on the basis of the premises is a prima facie response to the question. The most general notion that seems to fill these requirements is that of judging. In particular, it is making a practical judgment, generically, a judgment that one should *A*. I say 'generically' because *S*'s point of view may be moral or prudential or something else again. Moreover, we should include relativized judgments, such as, 'Given what I know, *A*-ing is best'. For we want to include all the judgments favoring *A* such that normally *S*'s accepting them on the basis of the premises can constitute responding to the practical question and having a reason for action.

To account more fully for the sense in which reasoning may be

94

practical, we want something whose occurrence can also help both in explaining *S*'s *A*-ing simpliciter and in explaining why he *A*'s straightaway. Practical judgment – strictly, judging – is appropriate here, since it often provides both kinds of explanation. Moreover, the view that such judging is the concluding element captures part of the Aristotelian idea that (successful) practical reasoning *concludes in* action, just as theoretical reasoning (typically) concludes in belief. For judging that, say, I must repay a loan, is doing something, though it is probably not action under direct voluntary control, i.e., performable at will. In so far as one can judge at will – and we may leave open to what extent, if any, one can – judging does not imply *believing* the proposition judged. It may, for instance, be self-deceptive (in ways I shall later discuss). One may also judge that something is so on the basis of premises one does not believe, but has only supposed in order to see what they imply; here one may judge only suppositionally that the inferred conclusion is true. But typically one believes the conclusion of one's practical reasoning, just as typically one has the motivation and cognition expressed in its premises, and one's judging the conclusion to be true thus tends to motivate and guide one's action.

III   A cognitive-motivational conception of practical reasoning

I now want to characterize practical reasoning in more detail. In addition to keeping in mind the six theoretical questions that largely give the topic of practical reasoning its special interest, I shall proceed in the light of the threefold distinction made in section II. There are practical arguments as structures of propositions; pieces of practical reasoning as appropriate tokenings of such structures; and actions, decisions, intentions, and other motivational states or events based on practical reasoning. The conclusion of a practical argument is an answer to a practical question; *S*'s drawing that conclusion constitutes (in part) his responding to it; and *S*'s doing the thing favored by the conclusion is, from his point of view, normally an appropriate solution to the practical problem motivating the question.

   Let us start by trying to formulate a very inclusive schema for practical arguments. There is wide (though not universal) agreement that the major premise expresses (possibly by explicitly reporting) some want of S's, in the broad sense of 'want' encompassing any kind of motivation, extrinsic or intrinsic.[12] The relevant notion of expression must allow for the premises to express a want one does not have. Just as, in presenting practical reasoning to others, S may lie, he may also mistakenly, for instance self-deceptively, express a want; he may thereby falsely attribute it to himself. What is essential to the adequacy of a tokening as a representation of the major premise is that it would normally be taken to express motivation. The same holds for the minor premise in relation to a means-end belief. Suppose Susan reasons: I must not make an insincere promise to do the job Ann wants done, and to avoid making such a promise must decline the payment she is offering me, so I had better decline. This may plausibly be considered practical reasoning even if Susan in no sense wants to avoid making an insincere promise to Ann and even if, because Susan is deceiving herself about the conditions of the promise, she does not really believe that taking the money without certainty of succeeding in the job would imply insincerity.

At least two important points about practical reasoning are implicit in our discussion of the examples so far considered. One concerns conditions for reasoning, the other conditions for the practicality of reasoning. First, as logical exercises and hypothetical cases illustrate, whether one is reasoning does not depend on whether one believes the premise(s) and conclusion of the inferential process that constitutes one's reasoning. Second, one's reasoning can be practical even if one does not have the motivation or cognition expressed in one's premises and conclusions. The latter case is of course atypical and bears comment.

Where S in no sense wants the goal expressed in the major premise, the practical reasoning would be *motivationally empty*: motivationally, S would be just mouthing the words, however sincere he is; and the reasoning could not normally be expected to have A-ing as an upshot. But it appears that S could still believe the premises and conclusion. Even if that is not so, however, we should allow motivationally empty reasoning as a limiting case. It is analogous to theoretical reasoning from a proposition one does not believe to another, which one may or may not believe, as in certain cases of drawing out the consequences of a proposed view, with an eye to seeing what it commits one to. There is also theoretical reasoning from suppositions to a further supposition, and we can find practical analogues of these and other kinds of theoretical reasoning. We might call practical reasoning *motivationally suppositional* provided S is aware of lacking accompanying motivation, *cognitively suppositional* provided S is aware of lacking the belief corresponding to the minor premise, and *wholly suppositional* provided both conditions hold. Such reasoning may play an important role in practical thinking, for instance in determining which of several proposed lines of action would best suit one.

Suppose that, as in the normal case, S's practical reasoning is not empty, either motivationally or cognitively. Must S have, corresponding to the major premise, a want *on balance*, i.e., one stronger than any incompatible want(s), where S's wants for ϕ and ψ are incompatible if and only if S believes that ϕ and ψ cannot be jointly realized? As our examples suggest, most writers on practical reasoning talk as if S must want ϕ on balance, or at least must think he does. After all, if the want is to count as expressing a practical reason, S's having it should provide a strong motive to act, and his believing he has it should yield a strong prima facie reason to act. But if we recall that practical reasoning often occurs in the course of deliberation, and that S may be affected by competing practical reasonings at the same (or about the same) time, this restriction seems unreasonable. Imagine that Samuel simply wants to savor the prospect of realizing ϕ. This might lead him to reason about how to get it, and thereby to conclude in favor of doing so, even if he wants more to realize something he believes incompatible with ϕ. It is true that in that case, he might draw only a *conditional conclusion*, say that *if* he wants ϕ he must A. We would then have practical *thinking* that perhaps falls short of practical reasoning. We might call this *conditional practical reasoning*, though it might be better to restrict that term to cases in which the condition in the conclusion is not a change in one's motivation, but an external event, such as someone's helping one buy a rug, which one intends to do *if* properly funded.

Deliberation about alternatives may also result in a related phenomenon, a kind of *overall conditionalization of the reasoning*, as opposed to the conclusion alone: roughly, one reasons in order to see where one is led. One might, for instance, just imaginatively try out a means-end sequence in weighing things up. Here the conclusion might be unconditional, though one is quite consciously uncommitted to acting on it: one will act on it only if the prospect seems reasonable enough when it is adequately before one (or meets further tests). The reasoning is conditional in the sense that one's commitment to its (unconditional) conclusion is itself conditional on (say) deciding that the action it favors is desirable from one's overall point of view.

A related case occurs where S does practical reasoning when, unable to choose between two incompatible things he wants equally, he constructs a practical argument for each, hoping thereby to establish a preference by putting each means-end sequence in prospect. In both these cases we might speak of *exploratory practical reasoning*. This serves one's effort to determine what to do; but unlike the typical cases it is not produced with a disposition to act on its conclusion without further thought. It is, as it were, conditional in purpose though not in content.

There is less controversy about the minor premise of practical reasoning. If we take 'means' to apply to constitutive as well as instrumental means, we may say that the minor premise is to the effect that A-ing is (or that it may be) a means to realizing ϕ. It is thus a *connecting premise*: it links the action to the relevant end. Similarly, S's belief of it is a *connecting belief*. Many kinds of content are appropriate to such beliefs. Commonly, S believes simply that his A-ing will realize (bring about, produce, etc.) the goal. But if the goal is very important to S, then even the proposition that A-ing has a slight chance of realizing it can serve as the minor premise, and S may act on this slim chance. One might try to climb a cliff on the slim chance of saving a child who will otherwise fall from it.

It is also possible for S to have a number of beliefs about the connecting relation, say that A is necessary for ϕ, and that it nonetheless has only a slight chance of realizing it. If S is determined to realize ϕ, reflecting on this slim hope may result in his forming either a conjunctive minor premise, say that A-ing and B-ing together will likely produce ϕ, or in framing two or more supplementary practical arguments, say one favoring A-ing and another B-ing, or in other complexities that promise to increase the chances of realizing ϕ. A parallel point holds, of course, for the case of two or more goals which S thinks can be realized by a single action. *S* may, for instance, frame a major premise expressing both goals.

Regarding the concluding element in practical reasoning, I have already suggested that it is the making of a practical judgment, say that one must find a safe river crossing. I have also indicated how, given the motivation and cognition expressed in the premises, *S*'s making such a judgment is a practical response to the question what to do, both by virtue of its content and in its power to produce, or at least to trigger, intention, decision, or action. We can clarify the view further by applying it to cases in which what seems to be the concluding element is an expression of intention, or even the performance of the relevant action.

Suppose that, wanting to pull a friend from under a tipped motorcycle, Samuel says, 'the only way to do it is to lift this straight up, so here goes!' and straightaway lifts it up. Clearly, the propositions that one must free the friend, and that one's lifting the vehicle straight up is the only way to achieve this, self-evidently entail that one must lift it straight up. This makes it natural not to state the conclusion if there is no need to. In addition, since the action is possible (and needed) immediately, Samuel has some reason *not* to bother with stating the conclusion. But this does not imply that he does not *draw* the conclusion that he must lift. Drawing it not only does not require utterance but, given the urgency of the context, can be expected to lead to action at once. The reasoning thus produces the action immediately. But the immediacy is only *temporal*: *S*'s drawing the conclusion favoring the action is part of what mediates between his motivation and the action itself. To say that the action *is* the concluding element is to conflate the *practical upshot* of the reasoning with its conclusion.

On the basis of the points made so far, I suggest that the simplest basic schema for practical reasoning – a schema of which there are numerous variants – consists of a motivational premise; a cognitive, means-end premise; and, as conclusion, a practical judgment. We might represent this schema as follows:

Major Premise – the motivational premise: I want ɸ;
Minor Premise – the cognitive premise: My *A*-ing would contribute to realizing ɸ;
Conclusion – the practical judgment: I should *A*.

Several comments are called for here. First, I call this schema basic because it has just the three kinds of elements that seem essential, and simplest because it reflects no qualifications, such as a specification of the strength of the want or of the epistemic or psychological status of the belief, which might, for instance, be represented as justified or as confident. (The notion of simplicity is admittedly vague, but nothing significant in what follows will turn on that.) Second, in reasoning that fits this schema, S does not merely entertain the proposition that he wants ϕ; rather this proposition figures as a premise in the reasoning process. (If the reasoning is enthymematic, one or perhaps two propositions need not be entertained, but all must still figure in the process in some appropriate way.) Third, if this schema is to be suitably broad, then even for the intuitively simplest cases, ϕ must be allowed to include S's acting, and A must be construed as an action-type which, normally, S believes (or presupposes) he can perform. Fourth, 'should' may have either a specific force, such as a moral, prudential, or legal one, or an overall sense grounded on whatever S thinks relevant. Fifth, the minor premise, as illustrated, can express any of an indefinite range of beliefs, including beliefs that link the action to a complex plan, say by representing it as the first step in a prescribed sequence. Hence, 'contribute to' must be taken to encompass many kinds of beliefs, including all the means-end beliefs which our examples in this and earlier chapters have exhibited.

It turns out, then, that what I am calling the simplest basic schema is doubly schematic. It can itself be instantiated by more specific schemata, depending on how the motivational, cognitive, and judgmental elements satisfy its three schematic representations. These other schemata may also be considered basic, whereas, if certain further details are included, such as S's adding, to wanting ϕ, that he is obligated to realize it, or adding a second goal in the same premise (say, a quite different end he takes A-ing to realize), we get a non-basic schema. Roughly, many schemata may be constructed by adding specificity to the simplest basic one; but when additional cognitive, motivational, or judgmental propositions are brought in, the result is normally a more complex and non-basic schema. Furthermore, practical reasoning can be embedded in a stretch of thinking which expresses many propositions not belonging to the reasoning, possibly including some that are irrelevant to it. Practical thinking is broader than practical reasoning, and the former can occur even in the midst of a daydream.

It appears that practical reasoning can always be seen to contain elements interpretable as fulfilling the basic schema just set out. This applies, I think, even to *social practical reasoning*, which occurs when two or more people reason together in the way a unanimous committee might as it decides in favor of collective action, such as voting for a policy.[13] For people can want the same ends, agree on a means to accomplish them, and participate jointly in realizing them by those means. Practical reasoning may, however, contain much more than the basic schema indicates. As sufficient condition schema (d) in section I illustrates, there may be more than two premises; and as other schemata we have considered show, the motivational premise may express S's wanting something through attributing to him a commitment to a rule. Take Aristotle's dry food example, whose major is 'Dry food suits any human.' In the context, we may probably take this to express S's wanting to eat food which is suitable for a human being.[14] If so, then the conclusion, 'This food suits me,' is plausibly thought to express something to the effect that I should eat the food. The 'should' is appropriate in the light of 'suits'; and without some such approbative term it is difficult to see why it is reasonable to expect S to act on the reasoning.

There is another difficulty we must face. If *any* mental process that instantiates the simple basic schema is practical reasoning, then we must countenance possible tokenings of such reasoning in deep sleep. It is doubtful that such a dreamlike tokening would be reasoning at all, and it would certainly not seem practical. We need some restriction to rule out parrotings and other incidental tokenings. The central idea is that the schema must be instantiated, in an appropriate way, in determining what to do. It is difficult to make this precise, but perhaps its vagueness appropriately matches that of 'practical reasoning' itself. A further point is that if the words, 'I want ϕ', said by S, express the same proposition as 'S wants ϕ', said by someone else on the same occasion,[15] then even with the restriction just made we might have to countenance second- and third-person tokenings of the basic schema as practical reasoning. For it would then be possible for someone else to token *my* practical argument. Susan might even do this in the course of trying, by analogy, to decide what she should do. Such arguments are of course practical in *content*, but reasoning that instantiates them in the second or third person is not what is commonly called practical reasoning. I shall adhere to that usage. In theory, however, there is no harm in countenancing second- and third-person practical reasoning, so long as we bear the differences as well as the similarities in mind; and some writers do seem to countenance them.[16]

IV Practical and theoretical reasoning

Practical reasoning understood as I have proposed is an inferential process that in some way instantiates (at least) the simple basic schema. On this view of it, its contrast with theoretical reasoning becomes of special interest. The contrast cannot be formal. Granted, if there are first-person propositions, roughly propositions whose content is intelligible only to the subject, who, in the first person, expresses them, then the form of practical reasoning is intrinsically tied to the agent. But this holds equally for theoretical reasoning that embodies first-person propositions. Moreover, we must also distinguish between a practical tokening and a mere parroting, and doing so would again take us beyond formal considerations. What distinction do the resources so far developed allow us to make?

First, let me indicate what elements in the action-as-conclusion view I do accept. I agree that the kind of concluding element appropriate to practical reasoning is a main point of contrast with theoretical reasoning. The making of a practical judgment (in the widest sense) is essential to practical reasoning, and such a judgment expresses at least a normative practical reason. While the proposition in question may also be the conclusion of theoretical reasoning, it is not typical of such reasoning to conclude in practical judgment, nor to have the kinds of premises represented in the simple basic schema. Granted, logically both kinds of reasoning may be taken to express arguments, conceived as certain kinds of propositional structures whose premises are viewed as (at least presumptive) grounds for their conclusions. Indeed, in one way, the term 'practical argument', applied to the structures tokened in practical reasoning, is misleading. The typical *uses* of such structures are practical, in that these arguments serve to guide conduct, and reasoning in accordance with them commonly yields the action judged appropriate; but the arguments, *as* abstract structures, are not intrinsically practical: they can be used for theoretical purposes. To be sure, this is a functional (and in some sense pragmatic) contrast; but it commonly marks the difference we seek to characterize.

My account of practical reasoning allows, then, for a significant distinction between the two kinds of reasoning process. Practical reasoning is undertaken in order to determine or, in a certain purposive way, in the course of determining (or of trying to determine), what to do; and one's drawing the conclusion will normally count as responding, by making a practical judgment, to the question what to do. This does not apply to theoretical reasoning, even when its underlying argument is the same.

It might be objected that simply in order to find out the truth, one could ask, 'Is it true that I should *A*?' and respond with reasoning expressing a practical argument. Since the proposition that I should *A* is equivalent to the proposition that it is true that I should, we apparently have the same question in different words. Hence, one might argue, reasoning that embodies the same arguments and is aimed at answering this question has as good a claim to be considered theoretical as practical. This objection is mistaken. For one thing, equivalent propositions need not be *identical*; and that the two in question are apparently not identical is suggested by the clear difference between reasoning undertaken in order to determine *what to do* (or even what I should do) and reasoning undertaken in order to determine *what it is true that I should do*. The latter phrase suggests the detachment of people who want to determine what their duties are *and then* see if there is any reason why they should fulfill them, or indeed have just an intellectual interest in what they should do. The phrase is at best unnatural as a description of what we do when, in the course of trying to solve a practical problem, we engage in means-end reasoning of the sort that fits the simple basic schema I have proposed and is paradigmatically practical.

Broadly speaking, practical reasoning is guided by a search for appropriate action, say action that will end a quarrel; theoretical reasoning is guided by a search for appropriate knowledge, or at least belief, say as to who wrote an anonymous note. Both kinds of reasoning are done with a certain sensitivity to reasons. But in doing either kind, we need not, and usually do not, consciously aim at finding reasons for action or belief. While a presupposition of our reasoning may be that the appropriate action or belief will be supported by reasons, we need not conceptualize the reasoning *as* partly a search for reasons, nor is finding reasons usually the main aim even of theoretical reasoning. The different ways our reasoning is guided by practical versus theoretical purposes are manifested in our dispositions. Above all, one has dispositions to act in different ways in the two different cases and to guide one's inferences and actions by different standards. For instance, if I reason to determine what to do, I am, by virtue of my reasoning for this purpose, directly disposed to act accordingly; if I reason to determine what it is true that I should do, I am disposed to act on my answer only if I am motivated to act in accordance with the normative belief in question. If externalism is correct, I must be *independently* motivated so to act, since the belief by itself need not motivate me. Even if internalism is true, my disposition to act on my answer may arise only *as* I (believingly) give it: the disposition is not part of my overall motivation *in* asking the question in the first place, as it is when (in the normal way) I ask the practical question. Moreover, if one is reasoning in order to determine what to do, then the judgment with which one concludes tends to give one a practical reason in the motivational as well as normative sense, since one is reasoning against a motivational background that makes it likely that one will be at least disposed to act on this judgment. Finally, even if there is no difference of the kind I have suggested, the distinct linguistic forms, together with differences in the kinds of role practical arguments play in human conduct, yield a significant contrast between practical and theoretical reasoning.

In denying that there is an intrinsic logical difference between practical and theoretical arguments, I do not mean to deny that cognitive and motivational attitudes, such as desires and beliefs, may have different kinds of *objects*.[17] Indeed, I think that they do, and I have spoken of what *S* wants as a state of affairs. While states of affairs are sometimes identified with propositions, they need not be. They are not naturally called true or false, for instance. Whether the objects of motivational attitudes are states of affairs or something else, it is noteworthy that we do not use the indicative to express wants and other motivational attitudes: we want *to* clarify practical reasoning, or *that* it be distinguished from theoretical reasoning. States of affairs are brought about (realized) or not, just as the objects of desire (however we construe them) are. Granted, the obtaining of a state of affairs, such as one's keeping a certain promise, is equivalent to the truth of the corresponding proposition, that one keeps the promise (i.e., necessarily, this state of affairs obtains if and only if that proposition is true). But this equivalence does not entail that an existing state of affairs simply *is* a true proposition. Supposing it is, however, that would show only that there is something special about at least one premise of a piece of practical reasoning: it expresses, at least tacitly, a motivational attitude. But in that characteristic it need not differ from certain kinds of theoretical reasoning. For the motivational attitude is not the premise (a point easily missed if one embraces the functionalist view); the motivational premise is an expression of such an attitude, not the mere having of it.

If my view yields only a functional and broadly causal distinction between practical and theoretical reasoning, at least it has the advantage of giving us a ready account of what the two have in common: being appropriate tokenings of arguments, subject to rational assessment as such, and for both reasons having the potential to ground the justification of their conclusions and of actions based on the reasoning. This seems to me at least as important a merit as providing us a way to make the distinction.

There is a trade-off that we must recognize in distinguishing practical from theoretical reasoning. The more obviously *practical* our account of practical reasoning makes it appear – say by construing its conclusion as the action it favors – the greater our difficulty in construing it as *reasoning*; whereas the more obvious our account makes the process appear to be reasoning – say, by taking it to be an inferential passage from premises to the drawing of a propositional conclusion – the less clearly practical it appears. My account is proposed in the hope of yielding optimal results in this trade-off. Some of those results will emerge in the next section, others in the remaining chapters.

V   *Practical reasoning and actions for reasons*

Given the conception of practical reasoning developed in this chapter, three of the six theoretical questions I have been stressing can be partially answered. One, concerning the distinction between practical and theoretical reasoning has just been discussed. Let us briefly consider the two others on which this chapter has close bearing.

Regarding the question of how a rational person answers a practical question, I have suggested that practical reasoning plays a major role. It need not always occur in such a case. But answering a question like 'What should I do to free my friend from under the crushing motorcycle?' commonly evokes practical reasoning. In a sense, however, a practical question can *arise* for S without S's *asking* it or even confronting a situation evoking puzzlement. It may arise whenever one is aware of certain kinds of resistance to getting what one wants, or feels a need to figure out a means of obtaining it. To be sure, the less puzzlement there is about an appropriate means, the less practical thinking there is likely to be in the background of practical reasoning. One may quite quickly proceed to reasoning that yields a practical judgment on which one is ready to act. Practical questions can also arise after the fact. Suppose that, from good habits based on long experience, Samuel finds the appropriate means to his end in an automatic way not accompanied by reasoning, and acts to get what he wants. There is still a practical argument corresponding to his motivation and belief leading to his action, say to his simply lifting the motorcycle immediately on perceiving the trouble. Later, what we might call the *retrospective practical question* 'What should I have done?' may come up, say because the friend was injured. That argument is then available to Samuel (if he remembers his reason for acting) and may surface in reconstructive practical reasoning. It may or may not suffice to answer the question correctly.

From here it is a short step to bringing the proposed conception of practical reasoning to bear on the question of what constitutes acting for a reason. In the framework of this chapter, we might say that to act for a reason is to act *from* motivation and cognition *appropriate* to figure as the motivational and cognitive elements expressed in the premises of practical reasoning. (I assume these are some kind of want and belief elements.) Such an action need not actually arise from practical reasoning – as will be argued in the next chapter. But, as Aristotle thought – and apparently Hume and Kant also believed – for every intentional action (at least if intentional action is equivalent to action for a reason) there is a corresponding practical argument. When that argument is actually expressed in practical reasoning, and S then acts on the basis of that reasoning, we have a paradigm of action for a reason. It is not enough, as Kant clearly saw, that the action accord with antecedent or accompanying reasoning; in order to be based on the reasoning, it must be done *from* the motivation expressed therein.

Moreover, just as one can act for two or more reasons, one can act on two or more pieces of practical reasoning. The influence of a single piece of such reasoning can also extend far into the future. One may reason to a conclusion in favor of an activity, such as abstaining from sweetbreads henceforth, and the appropriate actions may all arise from the resolution with which one concluded one's reasoning. One's reasoning has thus led to longterm acceptance of a practical reason. If practical reasoning need not always underlie action for a reason, it often does, and it may influence one's entire pattern of future conduct. When it does not underlie an action for a reason, the structure of the motivation and cognition that do ground the action may still be expressed in a practical argument, and in principle the agent can appeal to that argument to articulate a reason that provides both an explanation and a prima facie justification of the action.

CHAPTER 5

Practical Reasoning
and Intentional Action

A paradigm case of intentional action is action based on practical reasoning. The agent considers a goal, realizes that A-ing is required to achieve it, concludes in favor of A-ing, and straightaway A's. If the *correspondence thesis* – the view that for every intentional action there is a corresponding practical argument – is correct, then there is some plausibility in the further claim that every intentional action is based on reasoning, even if tacit, which expresses that argument. Call this second thesis *inferentialism*, since it posits a piece of practical reasoning, thus an actual inference, as essential in the genesis of every intentional action. Inferentialism has been maintained,[1] and there is much to be learned from assessing it. To simplify matters, let us consider it where it is most plausible, namely, for intentional action that is performed for a further end rather than for its own sake, as where one swims simply for pleasure and not for one's health.

I The range of intentional action

If intentional action for a further end is too closely associated with *deliberate* action, the former may be unwarrantedly assumed to arise from practical reasoning, since that is often conceived as the final stage of deliberation, or at least of those deliberations that issue in action. Even if a deliberate action need not arise from a stretch of deliberation culminating in practical reasoning that yields the action, deliberate action is the kind of action that typically has this sort of genesis. If there are deliberate actions that do not arise from a process of deliberation, they are still likely to be based on practical reasoning. This is common, for instance, where the practical reasoning occurs in a situation that calls for calculation of means, but not for weighing of alternatives. Granted, calculation of means *may* be deliberative, but it need not be. In any event, there are surely intentional actions that are not deliberate. Walking in the woods, I may push aside a branch without even being distracted from my conversation. This is done in order to clear my way, but it is *automatic*, in a sense which precludes the action's being deliberate. Moreover, even if such automatic actions can arise from practical reasoning, it is not plausible to postulate any as essential to their genesis.

There are also things one regularly does out of habit, such as locking one's car door. These actions may, but need not, arise from practical reasoning; they are typically performed spontaneously as part of a standing practice. One might reply that an action can be based on practical reasoning even if the agent does not recite a practical argument before or after performing it.[2] True. But *S*'s doing practical reasoning surely entails the occurrence in *S*'s consciousness of some representation of the relevant argument, even if it is only an enthymematic tokening of it. What occurs in the case of automatic and certain habitual actions apparently falls short of this. When I lock my car, my consciousness may be virtually filled with other matters. All that is required for my intentionally locking it is the appropriate motivation, belief, and perception. I want to protect it and believe this requires locking it; my vision guides my hand to its accustomed turn of the key. The want and belief are standing dispositional states and need not surface in consciousness.[3]

This is not to deny that perception requires space in consciousness; but it does not require space in a way that implies reasoning. My perception shows me where to put the key; it need not be represented in my thinking about the key, and it need not produce in me a thought of an instrumental premise, say that my turning the key in the slot will lock the car. Even if I *do* lock the car on the basis of practical reasoning, some such perception is required in order for my instrumental belief – that to protect the car I must lock it – to yield action; and here, too, the perception can play the required guiding role without producing such thoughts. Once the role of perception in enabling practical reasoning to yield action is properly understood, there is less temptation to intellectualize that role and to think that since it is crucial for intentional action in general, such action requires practical reasoning.

My case against inferentialism depends, of course, on what events, if any, must occur in consciousness for practical reasoning to take place. This question is easily neglected if one is preoccupied with the structure or assessment of practical reasoning, or with its role in the explanation or rationality of action; and I think it has been neglected. If *S* can do practical reasoning in a wordless flash, there are fewer obstacles to establishing inferentialism. Is that possible? In answering, we would do well to keep in mind two questions: what do we experience when we clearly *are* doing practical reasoning, and what must one *say* to manifest practical reasoning orally? The second question might seem irrelevant, but I take it that inner and outer instantiations of practical reasoning are both tokenings of the same kind of process and so should have similar structures. Let us consider these questions in turn.

On the first point, practical reasoning, like any reasoning, requires an inferential passage from one or more premises to a conclusion. This does not imply reciting each premise; but it does require *attention* to at least one of them. If a proposition does not come to my attention in some way, then while my believing it can *cause* me to believe something else, I cannot *infer* something else from it. This is confirmed by the way we distinguish between *why we believe* a proposition and *reasoning on which our believing it is based*. Imagine that I say something you think groundless, such as that FitzJames is stuffy, and – expecting a supporting argument – you ask on what reasoning I base this. If I have not attended to one or more propositions in the light of which I drew this conclusion, I will candidly admit that what I expressed is, say, an impression. If I then pause and recall some points about FitzJames that seem to be the basis – and a reasonable basis – of my belief, I do not conclude that I must have reasoned after all. I back up my belief with an argument, but do not pretend that the argument had already issued in that belief through unnoticed reasoning. It *may* have; but it need not have. Retrospectively constructed reasoning need not be *recollected*; it may be *created* by the reflections that produce it.

A further point here is that there is a sense in which my reasoning is *guided* by my premises: it is in the light of one's premise(s) that one infers one's conclusion (even if the reasoning is invalid). It is at best difficult to account for this guidance without supposing that the premises are represented in some way in consciousness. This kind of representation is tied to the *thinking* of the premises or in some way entertaining them; it is not implicit in the relation of one belief's being based on another, even when the second expresses a potential premise for the first.[4] The difference is somewhat like that between a guidepost one reads in directing oneself and an unobstructed pathway one simply follows. We have to attend to the guidepost in order to read it; but we can follow a path even if its borders are only in our peripheral vision and we simply go forward with a perceptually grounded readiness to adjust our direction as necessary.

In pursuing the question of what one must say to express practical reasoning orally, we again find confirmation of the view that such reasoning requires both attending to at least one premise and making some passage from the premise(s) to the conclusion. This is obvious where, in explaining oneself to someone, or in thinking aloud, one fully articulates one's reasoning. The troublesome cases occur where we express just one proposition of the reasoning. If someone says to me, 'You've got to free him from under that motorcycle', I may accept this, respond with, 'The only way is to lift it straight up', and proceed to labor accordingly. Here, this one utterance might suffice to express my practical reasoning. But this is because, in the particular context, it is obvious that I attend to the major premise – that I must free him – and that, in the light of it and the minor – that the only way is (for me) to lift it straight up – I draw the self-evidently implied conclusion that I must lift it straight up. (Obligation on balance is not implied, but prima facie obligation is, and is sufficient for the practicality of the reasoning.) Thus, on the plausible assumption that mentally doing practical reasoning can be conceived as an internalization of, or at least an internal version of, what we do in orally expressing practical reasoning, there is good reason to conclude that intentional action can, and apparently often does, occur without underlying practical reasoning.

Some philosophers may find it natural to object that this interprets 'reasoning' too narrowly. It might instead be taken to be equivalent to 'inference', in the broad sense in which some

111

philosophers use that term, one for which it is sufficient for S's inferring a proposition, p, from another, q, that S's belief of p be produced by, in a sense implying that it is based on, his belief of q. Philosophers do commonly speak of *inferential* belief (and knowledge) in such cases. This is intelligible on the ground that even if S has not reasoned from q to p, he is *disposed* to do so if he considers their relation. But surely the suggested condition is not sufficient for reasoning from q to p. If it were, we must say that if, on the basis of a visual belief that the snowflakes are furiously swirling about, I believe the wind is blowing, I have reasoned from the first proposition to the second. This simply need not be so. I may not only 'just see' that the wind is blowing from my noting that the snowflakes are swirling about, I may also be quite occupied with speaking to someone about a quite different topic as I glance out the window, sufficiently occupied to preclude my doing anything properly called *reasoning* on some other matter. We can *use* 'reasoning' this broadly if we choose, and philosophers sometimes do so use 'inference'. But to do that is to assimilate reasoning, as an inferential process we engage in, to our automatic formations of beliefs on the basis of other beliefs which express evidence too plain to need focused attention.

It is at this point that the functionalist view of practical reasoning recommends itself. If practical reasoning simply *is* whatever process mediates between reasons and actions based on those reasons, say between a want and belief and, on the other hand, an action performed *in order to* satisfy the want, then *of course* inferentialism is true. For intentional action (for a further end, at least) obviously is action for a reason in this sense.[5] Now it is certainly true that *one* of the important questions motivating the study of practical reasoning is to account for what plays this mediating role. But this is not the only such question; and both the history of the subject and considerations of the sorts I have stressed argue against conceiving practical reasoning on functionalist lines. Indeed, unless the functionalist view is restricted (as it is not always clearly intended to be) to mediators in *consciousness*, it would allow that practical reasoning be simply a neurophysiological process with no conscious manifestations at all. That would certainly be an implausible conception; practical reasoning is never merely this. Suppose, on the other hand, that the mediating events must be conscious. I contend that if they have sufficient complexity and content to be plausible candidates for tokenings of practical arguments, they will be too complex to be required in the genesis of every intentional action.

The notion of practical reasoning, then, is not a functional concept, but a *process concept*; and when the right processes are identified, they can be seen to be paradigms, but not necessary conditions, of episodes generating intentional action. Indeed, I believe that the notion is, in addition, an action concept: we *do* practical reasoning, often intentionally, and still more often just knowingly as part of our thinking. If it can be done only intentionally, then the view that intentional action must be based on practical reasoning would generate a vicious regress of such reasonings. I do not claim that practical reasoning is always intentional, but there certainly seem to be cases of it that are intentional, yet do not appear to arise from further practical reasoning. We do practical reasoning naturally in certain situations; we do not by and large do it in response to reasoning to the conclusion that we should. To be sure, it may well be impossible to do it *un*intentionally, though one can certainly muse unintentionally over the relevant propositions, say where one may have tried unsuccessfully to put the matter out of mind, and one can engage in reasoning about solving a practical problem when one is trying to listen to a lecture. But if, as I doubt, there is a kind of intentional action, or even a kind of behavior, on which all other intentional action is directly based, it is not practical reasoning. The relation between practical reasoning and intentional action is more subtle than that, as the next section will show.

II   *The reconstructive role of practical arguments*

Inferentialism is not decisively refuted by what I have said, and I have intended only to show that it is far less plausible than the conception I have developed. But there is a weaker version of inferentialism that is not directly disconfirmed by my points. It is partly based on the plausible idea that practical reasoning can conclude in favor of a *kind* of action and can influence one's actions long after its completion.

To see how the view goes, recall one's locking one's car automatically, though intentionally. It is arguable that this action is *traceable to practical reasoning* even if not produced by it on this occasion. After all, one presumably has at least once considered whether to lock one's car, reasoned about the matter, and concluded in favor of locking it. One's now locking it may thus be regarded as ultimately based on that reasoning, in the sense that the reasoning generated the policy one is carrying out and remains, other things equal, a ground of one's locking one's car. We might call this qualified view *linear inferentialism*: it posits a causal line, possibly extending far into the agent's past, from every intentional action to at least one piece of practical reasoning favoring an action of that kind. In this sense, then, linear inferentialism implies that all our intentional actions have, at least indirectly, a foundation in practical reasoning.

Where the relevant reasoning is in the past, there are at least two kinds of linear grounding. If the original motivation and cognition that correspond to the generative reasoning have been preserved and indirectly support the action in question, then that reasoning is (to some degree) a *sustaining* basis of the action and presumably of actions in the same pattern, say lockings of one's car. Roughly, the action is performed for the same reason, and actions in the pattern have been performed for that reason all along, as opposed to one's having dropped the practice and resumed it for the same reason. If, on the other hand, that motivation and cognition cease to exist and, thereafter, some other ends or beliefs of the agent sustain the pattern, then the original reasoning is only the *genetic* basis of the pattern. Here the actions are not performed for the same reason. In either case, the relevant causal lines vary in historical length, in the number of practical reasonings favoring the action, in the number and variety of causal intermediaries between the reason(s) and the action(s) traceable to them, and in other ways. Both cases yield a linear inferentialist version of behavioral foundationalism.

Linear inferentialism is far more plausible than inferentialism simpliciter, which requires reasoning at or just before the time of action. But it still seems too strong. For one thing, it neglects important *social* cases, those in which we do things simply because we have been told to, say by a parent or trusted friend. Particularly with routine basic actions, such as handing someone a book one is holding, we may form intentions, and act intentionally, in response to such directives, without even considering the matter,

and certainly without reasoning. Furthermore, linear inferentialism gives too intellectualistic an account of actions that arise from
spontaneous *discovery*. Think of a complex activity like gardening.
One may simply observe that narrow nylon string has cut the
stems of one's laden tomato plants, and remove it. Granted one
does so because one wants to prevent the cutting of the stems,
but we have already seen that there is no good reason to postulate
practical reasoning in every such case. Suppose, moreover, that
as a practice, one now avoids narrow nylon string. Must one have
reasoned to the general conclusion that one should avoid it, or
can this practice be explained by appeal to a general belief, based
on the specific one originally formed, that narrow nylon string
tends to cut tomato stems? I doubt that reasoning *need* be involved
at any point here.

A different but related case concerns behavior in unpredictable
situations, such as explorations of unfamiliar territory. Here it is
not action based more or less directly on discovery, but *automatic-
ity* that inferentialism does not well account for. Exploring a field,
one might step over rocks and walk around, rather than through,
patches of unfamiliar tall grass. One does these things out of
caution, but not necessarily in carrying out a policy, to which one
has reasoned, of staying off rocks or unfamiliar grass. In one kind
of case, the behavior simply manifests a kind of Humean custom.
In some instances, moreover, perhaps because of a different
pacing or mood, one may do the opposite and step on many
stones and proceed straight through unfamiliar grasses. To be
sure, some unfamiliar grass also looks suspicious, and one may
have once concluded that one should avoid suspicious ground.
But if, for every intentional action, one must sometime have
drawn such a guiding conclusion, the necessity is, I think, psychological, not conceptual.

At this point it becomes evident that the plausibility of the linear
view depends largely on how we *describe* the action. Perhaps every
intentional action admits of *some* correct, broad description such
that the agent has, at some time, concluded practical reasoning
in favor of actions of the kind specified by the description. A case
can be made for this view, even with the proviso that there be an
appropriate causal connection between the action and the reasoning. Call this view *restricted linear inferentialism*. I shall not argue
that it is false; but it is far from plainly true, and I believe that if

it is true it is not a conceptual truth. Intentional action is *intelligible* even if it is in no way subsumable under actual practical reasoning. It may in any case be subsumable in the imagined way without being *traceable* to practical reasoning, in a sense implying that the reasoning is part of what explains the action. It appears that often we can arrive at a premise suitable for explaining or prompting an action, or at reasoning which becomes the basis of an action, only *after* we have had *experience* of acting for the relevant reason, or kind of reason. Imagine that James is surprised at his pronunciation of a certain word, and then realizes that he has heard it so pronounced in a recent lecture and must be trying to correct himself. It may well be that we must perform some actions for reasons before we can take anything to *be* a reason for acting, or at least before we take something to be a reason for action in the *way* we take as a reason for action the goal figuring in the major premise of our practical reasoning. If this is so, then we have even less reason to accept restricted linear inferentialism. For it would appear that acting for a reason, far from being a kind of action based on practical reasoning, is in some cases prior, at least genetically, to action so based.

III Inferentialism and the realization of practical arguments

There is a truth underlying inferentialism, beyond the point, already stressed, that intentional actions are *based on* reasons. This second truth is what I have called the correspondence thesis: that if S A's intentionally, say pushes aside a branch in order to pass through, there is a corresponding practical argument, one whose premises express motivation and belief jointly sufficient to explain the action (this is true, at least, if acting intentionally is equivalent to acting for a reason). In the case at hand, the argument might represent, in its major premise, S's motivating want (to pass through) and, in its minor, S's guiding belief (that to pass he must push aside the branch). But the correspondence thesis does not imply any kind of inferentialism. The relevant correspondence holds whether or not S actually reasoned from these premises to a conclusion. It is true that intentional action may be plausibly considered action for a reason; and the reason will be expressed in the premises of a corresponding practical argument.

Intentional Action

But the importance of the point that intentional actions are performed for a reason should not be exaggerated. Suppose *S* does act for the reason indicated by the premises. That reason need not be good; a reason for which one acts can be a bad one for so acting. It may well be, however, that wants in general (or at least intrinsic wants) provide prima facie good reasons to act.[6] But their doing so is not required for the *intelligibility* of an action to be implied by its being performed in order to realize a want, and my main points do not require the assumption that intrinsic wants automatically provide prima facie reasons to act.

A further truth underlying inferentialism is that acting for a reason may be construed as a concrete realization of a practical argument.[7] The point is not simply that *S instantiates* the argument, i.e., has the want and belief expressed in its premises and does the thing indicated by the conclusion. There are at least four other factors. First, the premises represent the *structure* of the causal and explanatory basis of the action, namely, the want and belief that explain why it is performed. Second, the explanatory relation which that want and belief bear to the action mirrors a kind of support (or prima facie justificatory) relation which the premises of the argument bear to its conclusion. Third, *S* is, at the time, disposed to appeal to the argument if asked to explain or justify his *A*-ing, rather in the way one may appeal, for explanatory or justificatory purposes, to a rule or practice one has been following. If, for instance, *S* is asked why he *A*-ed, he is disposed to say things like, 'Because I wanted φ and believed *A*-ing would enable me to get φ'. Fourth, if *S*'s *A*-ing is a realization of a practical argument, then even if the action is not based on practical reasoning, the explanatory relation between his reason and action is just what it would have been if (other things equal) he had *A*-ed on the basis of actual reasoning from its premises to its conclusion. He would, for instance, have *A*-ed for the *same* reason, though perhaps more deliberately for it, in part because, in the light of the reason, he would have judged that he should *A*. If all this is so, it supports an important thesis: even when *S* does not act on the basis of practical reasoning which expresses the underlying practical argument, such reasoning may be invoked reconstructively: recollectively if it is actually the basis of the action, hypothetically otherwise. I call this thesis *reconstructivism* regarding practical reasoning. Invoking such reasoning is appropriate to the action from the point of view of both explanation and justification. The reconstructive role of practical reasoning, however, does not require a genetic role.

There are different kinds of realization. When *S* simply infers the conclusion of a practical argument from its premises, I call the argument *inferentially realized*. One point here is that it need not be inferentially realized in order to be *behaviorally realized*, through a spontaneous action that expresses *S*'s motivating want and is guided by a belief which *S* need not entertain. In this case, intentional action occurs without being based (at least immediately) on practical reasoning. When a practical argument is both inferentially and behaviorally realized in the normal way that results in an action based on both its concluding judgment and the underlying motivation and cognition expressed in its premises, we have acting on the *basis* of practical reasoning. The action is performed both for the right reason – the one expressed in the premises – and in the right way: on the basis of the reasoning process.

Neither kind of realization implies the other. This is why practical reasoning, the inferential realization of a practical argument, can occur without *S*'s acting on that reasoning, as in some cases of weakness of will. There the practical argument is only partly realized, whereas its full realization implies *S*'s doing what its conclusion favors. On this score, we find another respect in which the inferential process view I have been developing is superior to the action-as-conclusion view. For on the latter view (interpreted without ad hoc qualifications), weakness of will implies that, far from being able to act incontinently against practical reasoning in favor of an action, if one acts incontinently one does not complete practical reasoning in favor of it.

Combined – as it may or may not be – with inferentialism, the action-as-conclusion view also requires that the incontinent action, being intentional, arise from competing practical reasoning. Yet there need not be any such reasoning; and if there always were, we would get a less plausible account of weakness of will, since the incontinent action, no matter how thoroughly one disapproves of it, would then accord with a practical judgment one makes – the one concluding the reasoning on the incontinent side – and in that (admittedly limited) way the action would be consonant with one's will. This judgment would not be one's 'best,' in the sense of the one expressing a judgment of what, on balance, one should do, but its presence would still reduce the degree to which the incontinent action contravenes one's judgment in general. In any case, we must surely countenance *purely passional incontinence*, in which desire simply overrides one's better judgment without the aid of another judgment favoring the object of desire, and so without reasoning that concludes with such a judgment. If one countenances passional incontinence, one has additional reason to resist inferentialism, which requires some underlying reasoning even for incontinent action.

IV Unconscious and self-deceptive elements in practical reasoning

The inferentialist view of intentional action would have us posit practical reasoning where we notice none, for instance when we act intentionally but automatically. The view thus invites us to suppose that practical reasoning may occur not only without recitation of the constituent propositions, but unconsciously. For if reasoning is unconscious, it is no surprise that it should go unnoticed, as inferentialists must grant it often does. This is particularly likely to be stressed by proponents of a functionalist inferentialism, since the mediating role in terms of which they characterize practical reasoning need not require consciousness of its elements. If practical reasoning is, as on my view, an inferential process, can it be unconscious?

There is an important ambiguity here. The question could be whether practical reasoning can occur without *manifestations in consciousness*, or whether it can occur without *S*'s *consciousness of it* as reasoning. In the second case, there are various possibilities: for instance, that *S* simply is not aware of it *as* reasoning; that – owing, say, to repression – *S* is incapable of becoming aware of it as such without special self-scrutiny; and that *S* is incapable of becoming aware of the underlying *motivation* of the reasoning. Unlike the functionalist view of practical reasoning, the inferential process conception of it rules out unconsciousness in the first, *awareness sense*. For *S* must in some way both attend to at least one premise and draw a conclusion from it; and one must surely be aware of these events, even if not under those descriptions. I have not, however, ruled out unconsciousness in the *recognitional sense*. Let us explore this.

A good place to observe how practical reasoning may involve unconscious elements is self-deception.[8] I take self-deception with respect to a proposition *p* – say, that one will survive one's brain cancer – to be a state in which *S* (a) unconsciously knows (or has reason to believe, and unconsciously and truly believes) that not-*p*, (b) sincerely avows, or is disposed to avow sincerely, that *p*, and (c) has at least one want that explains, in part, both why the belief that not-*p* is unconscious and why *S* is disposed to avow that *p*, even when presented with what *S* sees as evidence that not-*p*.[9] As I conceive it, self-deception centrally involves belief which is unconscious in the recognitional sense: it is not that *S* *cannot* come to know he has the belief, but the belief is sufficiently veiled from recognition to make doing so require self-scrutiny or outside help, such as the observations of one's behavior by another person.

It may appear that the inferential process conception of practical reasoning precludes its underlying motivation or belief from being unconscious in this sense. For if a want, say to do something one would be ashamed of, figures in one's reasoning leading to a judgment that one should *A*, it may seem that one must realize that one *does* want that to which one takes *A*-ing to contribute. But surely *S* might suppose he is only *imagining* what it would be like to realize that state of affairs, and could mistakenly take as revulsion the guilty anticipatory flush he feels on contemplating it. Moreover, since one can do practical reasoning enthymematically, without entertaining *all* its constituent propositions, even the conclusion need not be consciously confronted. One can acquire the belief expressing the minor premise *later* than the want figuring in the major, and then complete the reasoning when the want, though not manifested in consciousness, motivates the conclusion – judging that one should *A*. The most common case of this occurs when one notices a means to an already existing end one has.

If self-deception (or other sources of unconscious propositional attitudes) can occur in practical reasoning, there are many ways in which we might expect it (or another source of unconscious elements) to affect practical reasoning. Among the most interesting possibilities are these: self-deception might supply a cognitive premise; it might supply a motivational one; it might produce a self-deceptive practical judgment as conclusion; and it might lead to weakness of will. I want to consider each of these possibilities briefly.

Since self-deception embodies belief, it should be possible for a self-deceiver to engage in practical reasoning whose minor premise represents a belief produced by, or intimately connected with, self-deception. Imagine that as part of her self-deception with respect to her feelings about her cousin Ellen, Jane has an unconscious desire (hence unconsciously wants) to hurt Ellen. This may lead her to notice ways of doing so, even if she does not try to find them. Thus, if she discovers from her aunt (Ellen's mother) that Ellen would like to be invited to Jane's graduation, she may form the belief that if she does not invite Ellen, Ellen will be hurt. At some point when the question of whom to invite arises, Jane might judge that she should leave Ellen out. Making this judgment *could* be the concluding element in practical reasoning whose major premise, expressing the unconscious want, does not enter consciousness. That is quite possible even if the minor premise – that not inviting Ellen will hurt her – does enter consciousness; for Jane might have a rationalization, say that the guest list is already too long, which shields her from realizing why she excluded Ellen. The reasoning thus illustrates both how self-deception may help to produce a belief expressing the minor premise and how it may supply a motivating want which underlies the major.

Jane's reasoning here is a case of what we might call *self-deceptive practical reasoning*. For one premise, the motivational one, expresses an element in the associated self-deception, in this case the unconscious want to hurt Ellen. In addition, the belief corresponding to the minor premise arises in part because of the self-deception; and because it does arise in that way, the reasoning is even more closely connected with self-deception than it would be if only the unconscious want influenced the reasoning. There are, then, degrees to which practical reasoning may be self-deceptive. I offer no definition of just what constitutes self-deceptive practical reasoning, but we may say at least this: the greater the number of elements in the reasoning that are embodied in, or (non-accidentally) produced by, self-deception, the more self-deceptive it is, where the self-deceptive elements embodied in the reasoning count more than those produced by it.

The same example can be varied, however, so as to yield another case of self-deceptive practical reasoning. Suppose that, at the time of the reasoning, Jane *also* wants to do something nice for Ellen, believes that sending a present for Ellen's own graduation would achieve this, and concludes, on this basis, that she should send one. Imagine, however, that she believes sending a present is incompatible with hurting Ellen and wants to do that more than to do something nice for her. Then, although Jane might still engage in the reasoning just described, she might not be wholehearted in judging that she should send the present. Indeed, in making that judgment she may be deceiving herself, just as she is deceiving herself in saying that her exclusion of Ellen from the party is due to the size of the guest list. If Jane then does not give the gift, we could explain this as due in part to her not having *believingly* judged she should. Her practical reasoning is still genuine, however, in that she still *draws* a practical conclusion and *makes* the appropriate practical judgment. Nor is she lying if she says to a friend that she should give it; she is self-deceptively insincere, and so lying only to herself. We could rule that this is not really practical reasoning. But it seems artificial to do so; and if we countenance exploratory practical reasoning, whose conclusion need not be believingly drawn, then so ruling would narrow our conception of practical reasoning rather considerably.

Weakness of will has diverse connections to self-deception, and there are several ways in which self-deception can be linked with weakness of will in relation to practical reasoning. It might seem that one way has already been illustrated: if Jane does not act in accord with her (overall) judgment that she should give Ellen a present, she may appear to be acting incontinently and thereby not acting on her practical reasoning. But recall that she did not believingly make this judgment. For this reason, it is unclear that weakness of will occurs. To be sure, if the judgment is sound, then she does make an *error* by failing, in the way she does, to act on it. But at least if she holds a conflicting practical judgment which is aligned with her motivation – say, with her strong desire to avoid letting Ellen get into the limelight (by displaying and cooing over the gift) – the error should not be considered weakness of will. For in that case her action does accord with her actual, if misguided, practical judgment, say that she should not make positive gestures toward Ellen. If, on the other hand, Jane had believingly made the judgment that she should give Ellen the gift, but simply could not bring herself to give it, because of her entrenched unconscious desire to keep Ellen out of the limelight, then we would have incontinence that arises from self-deception by virtue of a strong want embodied in that deception. We might also have a case of incontinent action that is not irrational, provided Jane rationally wants to keep Ellen out of the limelight, is intelligently contributing to this end by withholding the gift, and has no overriding reason not to withhold it, which is possible if Jane is warranted in thinking that the slight to Ellen is minor.

These possible interactions between self-deception and practical reasoning illustrate the integration of such reasoning with actions that do not fit the everyday means-end patterns of inference that exhibit us as the manifestly rational creatures we like to suppose we are. If I have opposed the view that practical reasoning is an element in every intentional action, I have also tried not to restrict unduly the range of cases in which it can occur, or the requirements for its manifesting itself in consciousness. Even when it leads to action, there is a sense in which at least one major element in it can be recognitionally unconscious. On the other hand, even then its role in producing the action may endow that action with *some* degree of rationality after all. The agent may not be consciously in charge of the motivational process leading to action, but there may still be a good measure of instrumental rationality.

V Practical reasoning and reasoned action

In chapter 4, I argued for a cognitive-motivational view of practical reasoning; this chapter argues for an inferential process construal of that view. Using the resulting account, I have tried to show that not all intentional actions arise immediately from practical reasoning, that they need not all be traceable to such reasoning, and that they need not even constitute (non-trivially) a type of action in favor of which one has in *fact* concluded practical reasoning, whether or not it is part of the causal history of the action. But if practical reasoning is not *genetically pervasive* in intentional action, it is *reconstructively available*, at least for actions performed in order to achieve a further end. This can be so, even if the reasoning contains unconscious elements. For with appropriate efforts or suitable help from someone else, the agent could still formulate and appeal to the practical argument corresponding to the action. To be sure, there is no guarantee that an agent attempting to formulate, reconstructively, a practical argument underlying an intentional action will succeed, even with the help of a person who knows his psychology well. Confusion, loss of memory, rationalization, and other interferences may prevent it. But there *is* such an argument, as surely as there is a means-end structure underlying intentional action.

I have, then, tried to account for the main points that make inferentialism plausible and have left open the possibility that some restricted version of linear inferentialism may be true. But there is one more point to be made here. There is a common category of action which does at least roughly correspond to action based on practical reasoning. The category is not intentional action; for that can be automatic or spontaneous in ways that do not require reasoning. It is not deliberate action; for that arises from a kind of reflection which is at least implicitly comparative and not required for every case of action based on practical reasoning. It is not even action that is part of a plan. For one thing, there is *some* presumption that a plan must emerge from planning, or at least from a kind of prospective consideration of one or more options; if so, a plan is not automatically produced by every minimal episode of practical reasoning. In any case, unless 'plan' is stretched, perhaps beyond plausibility, there are actions based on spontaneous practical reasoning which do not fit into any pattern of aims and beliefs of the kind required by a plan.[10] But action based on practical reasoning does seem at least roughly equivalent to reasoned action. For if practical reasoning is understood as I have described it, it does fulfill the minimal conditions for reasoning; and I believe that when we speak of reasoned action we refer to action based on a process that includes or, minimally, is constituted by, practical reasoning.

Evidently, then, the account of practical reasoning so far developed in this book bears directly on the question of how practical reasoning is related to intentional action. To every intentional action (at least every one performed for a reason) there corresponds a practical argument – more than one if the action is performed for two or more independent reasons. The agent need not have reasoned accordingly; but the realization of the argument(s) in actual reasoning is appropriate to produce (or cooperate in producing) such an action whether the agent actually reasons accordingly or not. Practical reasoning, as a type of inference that an agent might instantiate, is thus reconstructively available for any such action, including actions exhibiting weakness of will. Indeed it helps to explain the possibility of incontinent actions, though without forcing us to construe them as rational – or necessarily irrational. Practical reasoning is also genetically fundamental in much intentional action, including all reasoned action. When it occurs, it may be conceived as an inferential realization of a practical argument. It is also something we do, or at any rate not merely something we undergo. It can produce, guide, and at least partly explain, actions even when some of its elements are unconscious. If it does not underlie all our actions, it remains a central element in human conduct.

CHAPTER 6

Practical Reasoning
in the Dynamics of Action

When actions arise in the normal way from practical reasoning, we can understand them in relation to at least three major characteristics. They are reasoned, end-directed, and in accord with a practical judgment. But this understanding is not the only kind one might seek from an account of practical reasoning. As a process constituted by a pattern of *events*, it is a candidate to account for the *dynamics* of actions based on it, above all for what causes them, and for how, in relation to causative events, they come about. The understanding so far stressed in this part of the book is roughly conceptual. One dimension of this understanding is, in linguistic terms, *redescriptive*: practical reasoning is conceived as providing a background against which we can see what the agent is 'really' doing, say rescuing a friend or slighting a rival. A related dimension of our subject concerns explanation: how practical reasoning can provide an understanding of why the agent performed the action in favor of which it concludes. The dynamic aspects of practical reasoning are quite different; and they are important for a causal theory of action, i.e., one which conceives action as behavior that is in some sense caused by motivational and cognitive elements in the agent. Some version of the causal theory has been dominant since Aristotle, and the theory appears likely to be correct.[1] I thus want in this chapter to consider how practical reasoning figures in the dynamics of action.

Dynamics of Action

I The need for a dynamic account

Historically, there has been deep disagreement among philosophers about whether actions are *deterministically* produced, but the picture of actions as simply caused by such states or events as the agent's desires, beliefs, decisions, and other intentional elements has dominated both philosophical and common-sense thinking about human action. Given the dominance of that picture, we can see one reason for inferentialism: it postulates a causal factor, namely, practical inference, which *genetically unifies* actions by constituting a kind of origin they all have in common. Connected with this is a second point. Practical reasoning provides a conception of how the actions we perform arise from the welter of psychological elements internal to the agent.

This second point is particularly important if one accepts the plausible view that, strictly speaking, (a) the causes of events are other events, and (b) events are (or at least entail) changes. For if this view is correct, then actions, which plainly are events, cannot be (directly) caused by dispositions, including desires and beliefs, since dispositions are not changes. Something can have a dispositional property, for instance solubility, from the time it comes into being until the time it ceases to exist, without changing in any way, or at least any way relevant to that property, such as dissolving. Roughly, a thing's dispositions are a matter of what, under certain conditions, it *would* do, not a matter of what it actually does. Hence, a causal theory of action, if it is to be adequately clear, must go beyond talking about the agent's beliefs, wants, and other dispositional properties; it should indicate certain kinds of events as causes of action.

Practical reasoning may help us understand the dynamics of action in another way. Consider intentions. They do not execute themselves. Indeed, as dispositional states, they presumably do not cause anything except by virtue of some event suitably connected with them, such as their becoming occurrent. For instance, one might have the thought, upon noticing a break in a discussion, that one will now raise one's hand; here the thought is what accounts for one's executing the intention at this point.[2]

Even if we do not conceive intentions and other propositional attitudes as causal factors, we need an account of the execution of intentions and of how other motivating attitudes generate action.

Practical reasoning can help to provide this even if it is not taken to be (as volition has been) that in virtue of which these dispositional states manifest themselves in such a way that they may (indirectly) cause actions. But for any causal theory of action which construes these states as causal explainers, it is desirable – and indeed crucial if only events are strictly speaking causes – to find one or more events that directly cause the action. Broadly, then, one might think of practical reasoning as a pattern of mental events that mediate between reasons and actions, or minimally, as containing at least some of these mediating mental events for certain sorts of actions based on reasons. This allows that something further, say volition,[3] can mediate between practical reasoning and action (or at least overt action), for example between a practical judgment that one should offer to help someone, and one's extending the offer. But one could bypass such executive events if, like some theorists, one regards the making of a practical judgment, in the context of a suitable belief or appropriate perception, as sufficient to trigger action.

If intentions do not simply execute themselves, they also do not provide in themselves much of a clue as to why they are carried out *when* they are; and the same applies to all the other action-explaining propositional attitudes. This is an important point. For at least with respect to causation of one event by another, there seems to be an important pattern which a dynamic account should capture. The pattern might be expressed in a *principle of the differential temporality of causation*. It says that there is an intimate explanatory relation between temporal properties of the cause and of the effect; and in a strong but not implausible form it asserts that the time at which the cause occurs explains why the effect occurs when it does, i.e., the fact that the former occurs at a given time explains why the latter happens when it does. Thus, if we want to know why a gangplank broke when it did, we might point out that it was at that time that it was overloaded by the added weight of the last person to mount it. Similarly, we might suppose that often we act when we do because we have just completed the appropriate practical reasoning. Having arrived at a practical judgment, and given the ability and the opportunity to act on it, we do so straightaway.

II Practical reasoning as a causative process

It has often been argued that reasons are not causes. Here the word 'reasons' does not designate what I shall call reasons proper, since they are abstract and thus not commonly taken to be even candidates for the terms of singular causal relations. Reasons proper are the *contents* of propositional attitudes, expressible by propositional and infinitive clauses, as where we say that her reason for not inviting her cousin was to slight her (or that it would slight her). What is usually meant by 'reasons' when reasons are said not to be causes is *reason states*, i.e., propositional attitudes themselves – which, as part of the reasons *why* people do things, are also properly called reasons. If reasons in the latter, explanatory sense are dispositions, and if causes, but not dispositions, are events, then it is true that (explanatory) reasons are not causes. But this does not imply that reasons have no causal power or play no causal role; and they certainly do play a causal role when, together with an appropriate event, they produce actions explainable by reference to them, paradigmatically, actions performed because the agent believes they will contribute to achieving something he wants.

It is in this context that practical reasoning plays a major role. For instance, if I want to free a friend from under a motorcycle, believe that to do so I must lift it straight up, and conclude with the judgment that I must now lift it, my *making* that judgment is well suited to trigger my action. The judgment is a kind of *directive*: its content directs that a particular thing be done. My making it is an impetus to my doing that. Given the want and belief expressed in my premises, my so judging is the sort of event we expect to lead to action straightaway, provided I have the ability and opportunity. Moreover, my so judging also serves to explain why I lift *when* I do. After all, I judged that I must *do it now*. Even if I had only judged that I should do it, with no specific time built into my judgment, my (partly perceptual) awareness of the circumstances, together with my *now judging*, might explain why I lift now. The time *of* a practical judgment, as well as the time indicated *in* such a judgment, can explain the time of action.

This is not to say that my practical reasoning is itself a cause of action. Even though, as a process, it is in the right category to be a cause, I prefer to call it a causal factor. One's drawing the conclusion, which at least in the normal case is equivalent to one's making a practical judgment, is more nearly what causes one's action. But even this is not quite right, for the judgment causes it only in the context of the relevant motivation and cognition. Its role is directive, not generative. In talking of the dynamics of action, we are often unable to cite some one event that is the crucial cause of an (intentional) action. It is usually preferable to speak of various causal factors, their interrelations, and their various (partial) contributions.

If inferentialism of any kind is true, then for every intentional action there is an event of judging, or at least of forming a belief of one's practical conclusion, which is a candidate for the triggering role just illustrated. This is another reason for the appeal of inferentialism. However, once we recall that practical reasoning is often concluded in favor of an action which S takes to be impossible at the time, it is plain that we shall still need an account of how intentional actions are produced by practical reasoning when they are temporally separated from it. Presumably, in these cases the judgment yields an intention to act, where this intention either clearly implies in its content, or is accompanied by beliefs which indicate, what would be an appropriate later occasion for action. What, then, later triggers the execution of such future-directed intention?

Here we do well to recall Aristotle's emphasis on perception. He said, of the genesis of one's taking a sweet, that 'a belief about something perceptible' 'controls action' (*NE*: 1147b9–10) (in the Ostwald translation, the point is that 'The final premise, consisting as it does in an opinion about an object perceived by the senses, determines our action'). There are at least two cases here which the text does not explicitly distinguish. First, S may be guided in carrying out his practical judgment, say that he should have *a* sweet, by a perception of a good opportunity, in this instance by perceiving an available sweet. Here, the major premise expresses a desire for sweet things and the minor is the unspecific, though perceptually applicable, proposition that I ought to taste one. Second, the minor itself may be directed toward a perceived object. It might be, say, that taking *this* sweet will give me the taste I want; and since I perceive it, I can and normally do act at once. There is no need, and scarcely psychological space, for my reciting the conclusion. That is in part why, in this second case, the action itself may appear to be the conclusion. However, the conclusion can be tacit, in ways pointed out earlier. What I would add now is that both drawing the conclusion and acting on it can be common effects of the same causal factors. These are above all the want and belief expressed in the premises, together with the perceptual events constituent in one's seeing the opportunity to act. Both cases illustrate how the generation of action is aided by perception and practical judgment.

The general picture that has so far emerged portrays both springs of action and its trigger. The springs of action based on practical reasoning are constituted by motivation and cognition; its trigger is the making of a practical judgment guided by perception, though sometimes perception by itself, whether visual, auditory, or of some other kind, may trigger action. The degree of motivation represents the strength of the spring; the stronger the spring, the stronger the agent's disposition to try to get the thing wanted. The cognition represents the psychological direction of the spring: what the agent believes he must do to get the thing wanted. Perception guides action physically, and the physical direction of bodily action – what one actually does – is determined by what one perceives, together with environmental factors, such as lighting conditions, obstacles to one's movements, and the like. Motivation without cognition and perception would be blind; cognition and perception without motivation would be impotent.

Mental action, to be sure, does not require a perceptual trigger, though there may be something analogous, such as a thought that now is the time for, say, reflecting on tomorrow's responsibilities. Even mental action, then, seems to depend on events, presumably on something like triggering by an event; but the events need not be physical.

The picture of action so far given is instructive, but also incomplete, at least in identifying triggers. There are still other events that can trigger action based on practical reasoning. Here are two cases in which the trigger is *motivational change*. First, suppose that Susan is already aware of an opportunity to *A*, say to help Bonnie find certain books, and believes that suggesting she get them for Bonnie would be the best kind of help to offer. It occurs to her that Bonnie is a person she would like to help, and she imagines, without feeling any aversion, the task of getting the books. She concludes that she really should offer, but does not, because her motivation is still insufficient to overcome her inertia. If her desire to help suddenly becomes strong enough, this motivational change can trigger her action, and she may offer help straightaway. Granted, her thinking, beforehand, that she really must help Bonnie may be what increases her motivation; but unless that motivation is strengthened beyond a certain threshold, we ought not to expect her having this thought to lead by itself to the action. A second case would be that of resolution of conflicting wants. Imagine that motivational change is needed, not to overcome inertia, but to outweigh opposing desire, say a desire to use the available time to go to a matinee rather than the library. If both prospects are before her as she looks at her friend in silence, it may be the altruistic desire's becoming stronger than its rival that triggers her action. If she has done practical reasoning favoring her attending the matinee, this case may also illustrate how one piece of practical reasoning can prevail over another. Any of these motivational cases may, of course, represent weakness of will if the dominant motivation leads to action against one's better judgment.

So far in this chapter, I have explored ways in which practical reasoning, together with judgmental, perceptual, or motivational events, figures in the dynamics of action. But examples similar to those used for this purpose also show that practical reasoning is not always *needed* to account for the dynamics of action. If it were, then contrary to what I have argued, a fairly strong form of inferentialism would be correct. Consider Susan again. If Bonnie is a close friend and sounds really distressed about how many books she needs over the weekend, Susan may offer help without having reasoned about whether to do so. Having a standing want to give Bonnie support, she may simply form the belief that she can give it by offering to go to the library, and straightaway make the offer to help. Here the formation of that belief may trigger her action, assuming there is a suitable opportunity for her to speak. If the distress is voiced in a conversation difficult to interrupt, the formation of the belief may initially lead only to Susan's intending to offer, and the actual offer may be triggered by her perceiving a break in the conversation. This perceptual event may not only help to explain why she offers, but may fully explain why, given her governing desires and beliefs, she does so at that time.

132

Clearly, then, practical reasoning can and often does play an important role in mediating between reasons and actions. Together with associated events, particularly perceptual events and motivational and cognitive changes, it may explain both how an action comes about and why it is performed when it is. But these same kinds of events can mediate between reasons and actions, and can account for the execution of intentions, even where no practical reasoning plays a part in the genesis of the action. Practical reasoning, then, is just one important element in accounting for the dynamics of action.

III   Causality, nomic connections, and intentional action

In chapters 4 and 5, practical reasoning is construed as a causal process. This chapter stresses its dynamic causal role. But this role is not causal in the sense that S's accepting the conclusion is *merely* caused by S's accepting the premises, nor is its dynamic role in action a matter of its merely causing the actions we think of as based on it. Drawing the conclusion is, in a complicated way, guided by one's acceptance (or at least entertaining) of the premises; and acting on the basis of practical reasoning similarly requires guidance by the agent's motivation and cognition. For the purposes of this chapter, then, acting on the basis of practical reasoning must be described further.

Imagine that Susan judges, on the basis of practical reasoning, that she should offer to go to the library for Bonnie. This judgment (given other factors normally present in such a context) may cause her to lean forward intently, awaiting a chance to break into the conversation and to raise her hand as if to say, 'Stop!' In raising it, she may knock over her glass. This action is caused by her practical reasoning, but is not *based on* it. It is not even intentional, much less performed *for* the reason expressed by her major premise, as is required by its being based on the reasoning in the full-blooded sense that interests us. The action is, we might say, an effect, but not the issue, of her reasoning. It is not the issue because, for one thing, it is not properly *guided* by the belief expressed in the minor premise – that offering to help is the way to give the friend support. Susan does not, for instance, take knocking over the glass to play a role in offering help. Second, it is not an action she adjusts, or is even disposed to adjust, in the light of beliefs about its contribution to either offering help or giving support. Moreover, she does not herself have the normal *sense* of agency in knocking over the glass, a sense which, when one does act for a reason, manifests itself in (among other things) a non-inferential disposition to attribute an action to the reason for which it is performed. For these reasons, the action is not *controlled* by her practical reasoning, in the sense of being both generated by it through an appropriate trigger and under the control of its constitutive motivation and cognition. The latter kind of control is very difficult to explicate,[4] but what has been said here should clarify, sufficiently for our purposes here, what sort of causal relation is in question.

If there is a causal connection between (explanatory) reasons, or reasoning processes, and actions, it is natural to ask whether it is *nomic*, i.e., instantiates a lawlike connection, even if the relevant law is framed in different sorts of concepts, say neurophysiological notions. On the covering-law theory of causation, which is perhaps the most widely held view of singular causal connections, whenever an event *e* causes an event *e'*, there is *some* law linking them, even if under descriptions alien to the vocabulary in which the causal relation between them is reported. A further question is whether the law must be universal in form, or may be a tendency or a statistical law. The question whether reasons are causes has often been discussed in relation to the covering-law view.[5] Some who apparently accept the view think that the nomically relevant descriptions are not psychological.[6] My position is that whether or not the covering-law view is correct, there *do* seem to be tendency laws (but apparently not universal ones) linking wants and beliefs to actions.[7]

It is arguable that unless there are laws of some sort linking psychological states to action, there cannot be a genuine science of psychology, at least not a scientific psychology of *action*. There is no need for this book to take a position on that issue. A philosophical account of practical reasoning may appropriately remain neutral on whether practical reasoning itself, or the motivation and cognition that figure in it, are nomically linked with the actions we use them to explain. My account is neutral on this score, though it can be coupled with a suitable covering-law account of causal connections. There is no need to develop that point here. But it is important that we consider how my causal dynamic conception of practical reasoning allows for weakness of will, and I now want to take up that topic.

IV   The dynamics of incontinence

Incontinent action of the kind that constitutes (behavioral) weakness of will is not merely action inconsistent with one's better judgment. That would allow it to be merely accidental, whereas what is wrong with incontinent action is precisely that it is at once intentional and in a certain way opposes one's better judgment. If practical reasoning has the causal power I have attributed to it, however, it raises puzzles about how weakness of will occurs. *That* it occurs I have been assuming, and how it *can* occur I have explained – as I think Aristotle, Hume, and Kant did in their different ways – in part by appeal to the influence of opposing motivation. The obvious principle here is that where two sets of wants conflict, the agent tends to act on the stronger one.

Another principle relevant to incontinence – a principle that also indicates why the former is only a tendency claim – is that one's believed chance of success also tends to figure in any such conflict, so that one may act to achieve what one desires less provided one believes that one's chance of getting it exceeds the likelihood of one's getting the thing desired more. Thus, I may want, on balance, to fulfill a duty to finish a report this afternoon more than to see this afternoon's matinee, but might also regard as less than even my chance of succeeding in finishing the report in the time I have. This pessimism about success may cooperate with my desire to see the matinee, with the result that I act against my judgment that I should do the report, and I take the afternoon off. We could bring this case under the principle that the stronger set of conflicting wants prevails, by supposing the result of my thinking about the matter is formation of a greater desire to perform the *action* seen as yielding the originally less desired end, here the action of taking the afternoon off. The idea is roughly that the strongest among conflicting *action* wants prevails, even if the strongest among conflicting wants simpliciter sometimes does not. I might still prefer actually finishing the report to the experience of seeing the matinee, but I prefer leaving my office, which

I do in order to get the experience, over staying at my desk, which I would do to finish the report, since I think the latter action likely to fail. Whether we *must* view the matter this way or not, it remains true that where the agent has probability beliefs about the options relevant in the context, those beliefs may contribute, at least in the suggested way, to incontinence. For in either case I act against my judgment of what I ought to do.

From a dynamic point of view, how does my account of practical reasoning help us understand the actual occurrence of incontinent action? There are three kinds of case I want to describe here.

First, practical reasoning often takes place in situations of either conflict or self-monitoring or both. Being conscientious, Samuel may wonder whether he should spend so much of the family's money on opera tickets. He considers other things he wants, realizes that he cannot have them if he buys the tickets, and concludes that he should not buy the tickets. But his powerful desire for them persists. His eye lights on the pre-season reduced prices, he says to himself that they *are* a bargain, and he writes the check. Here the opportunity for incontinence is at hand, and the desire underlying it simply overrides the motivation backing the practical judgment. There may, but need not, have also been practical reasoning favoring the purchase.

A second case occurs when practical judgment favors something specific, while the opposing motivation, unlike a single felt temptation, consists in a number of mutually supporting considerations. This time suppose that Samuel is considering an important charity and, aware of his resources and commitments, reasons to the conclusion that he should make a generous donation. On the other side, however, are several legitimate though self-regarding needs. He considers them one by one. Collectively they seem impressive. With discomfort, he decides to donate half of what he originally judged appropriate, and, with the other needs vividly in mind and still clouding his shame, rushes on to some other activity.

It is important to this case that his thoughts about other needs not alter his original *judgment*, say in favor of a lesser contribution. If they do, we would not have incontinence but, more likely, a kind of self-indulgence: a collapse of judgment in the face of desire. Rather, it is the consideration of those needs, together with the associated motivation, that enables him to go against the practical judgment he still holds. Reasons overcome reason; a crowd overthrows its would-be leader. This is not a case of reason overcome by passion. A string of prima facie good reasons for reducing the projected contribution pull together against his practical judgment, which expresses a reason, on balance, for making it. The pull may be dispassionate; but it may still obscure his knowledge of what he is doing in making the lesser donation. It need not do this, however, though certainly there is some defect in his rational self-control; and whether or not it is due to obscured knowledge, it constitutes one kind of deficiency in motivational integration.

From here it is a short step to a third kind of case, rather like one suggested by Aristotle, in which practical judgment is overridden precisely by virtue of what seems to be obscured knowledge. This is especially likely in conditions of either aroused desire, or mental unclarity, or both. There are many ways in which knowledge (or belief) can be obscured. A common one occurs with intoxication. Imagine that Tom, who is already partly drunk when a waiter offers another champagne, has a strong desire for more to drink but is too absorbed in conversation to reflect on the matter. Tom nonetheless knows, and has judged, that he should avoid drunkenness. But this judgment – based on that premise and arrived at shortly beforehand through practical reasoning – that he must decline drinks after having three, may not be entertained at all, and he may take the drink. The point here is that *attention* to a practical judgment one holds tends to increase its motivational power, just as attention to a perceived object of desire tends, when the object is recognized as the desired thing, to enhance that desire, or at least to lower the threshold for acting to satisfy it.

Hume may have been suggesting something similar when he spoke of the tendency of nearer objects of desire to raise the passions more than distant ones.[8] In Tom's case, however, there is no mental haziness or conscious interference with the understanding of the judgment. The clearly understood judgment simply does not enter consciousness to oppose the aroused desire for the champagne: like the knowledge of the principle the judgment is based on, the judgment is edged out of consciousness or remains on its periphery, where it is much less likely to influence action. Impetuosity, which Aristotle emphasized as a factor in incontinence, may also cloud judgment, though it also works through the goad-ing or even impelling effect of the perception or imagining of the object of desire.

It may happen, however, that the practical judgment is not straightforward in the first place and the agent's grasp of it weak-ened by other considerations. Here we find another variant of the third kind of incontinence, in which obscured knowledge is a major factor. Suppose one is asked to chair a committee. One's underlying view is that one should be a supportive member of one's team, and one thereby judges that one should promptly take the job. Still, the situation in which one so judges may present various legitimate obstacles, including one's own deficiencies. Reflection on those obstacles – say, on one's inad-equate information and poor report-writing skills – can cloud one's judgment so that one does not clearly see what is demanded, and indefinitely puts off taking over the committee. At some level one knows one has failed; but the description of the required act may be vague enough, and the sense of problems with performing it lively enough, to permit one's failing without a clear sense of going against one's better judgment. Alternatively, one may clearly see that one is not living up to one's better judgment, find oneself ashamed, and, as if to excuse one's failure instead of preventing it, resolve to do better in the future. This might occur where the problem is not the clarity of one's judgment or the knowledge (or belief) giving rise to it, but rather a failure to integrate that knowledge (or belief) adequately into one's motivational system.

Incontinence may occur, then, in many ways, even when the practical judgment outweighed is backed by practical reasoning from which it arises. The central factor may, for instance, be a single overriding desire, a set of collectively dominating desires no one of which could prevail in action, obscured knowledge of one's guiding principle or of one's practical judgment, a vague and poorly focused practical judgment, a failure to integrate one's guiding principle into one's motivational system, or an impetuous thrust toward the envisaged object of desire. There are other cases of weakness of will that occur despite practical reasoning in support of the judgment against which the agent acts. Moreover, disparities between action and judgment significantly like the kinds sketched can occur *without* the relevant judgment's arising from practical reasoning. But many of the disparities of both sorts can be understood on the basis of the points made in this chapter.

V *Causality and freedom*

If there is some kind of causal relation between, on the one hand, reasons and reasoning and, on the other hand, the actions they explain, one may wonder how the associated causal account of action bears on the possibility and extent of human freedom. This section briefly addresses that question.

To begin with, even if one goes so far as to hold that reasons are connected with actions by *universal* laws, one is not thereby committed to determinism, i.e., the view that *every* event is subsumable under some universal law and in that way deductively explainable by some antecedent (or simultaneous) set of events. But if one so much as leaves open the possibility that actions are subsumable under universal laws, those who take freedom and determinism to be incompatible will tend to think that one leaves open too much, since actions so explainable seem to them unfree. This is a large issue. I have elsewhere offered a detailed account of free actions which implies that freedom is consistent with determinism,[9] but here I simply assume that the kind of causation required by my account of practical reasoning does *not* entail the existence of universal laws governing intentional action.

If, as I believe, my account of practical reasoning leaves room for freedom and moral responsibility, it is appropriate to ask how it might help us understand just what they are. Plainly, among the clearest cases of free actions are those based on practical reasoning. It is true that unfree actions can also arise from it, as where the major premise is that one must at all costs save one's children and the minor is that giving up one's savings is necessary for their ransom. But even actions thus compelled are reasoned; and in the broad sense that is associated with being under the control of reason, they are voluntary. (This is the kind of voluntariness, incidentally, which Aristotle apparently had in mind in citing, as paradigms of the involuntary, actions that are neither done of one's own free will nor proceed *from* the will at all; see, for example, the *Ethics* 1109b30–1111b.)

The account of practical reasoning also bears on moral responsibility. Since strongly compelled actions can be based on practical reasoning, it would be wrong to say that the agent is morally responsible for every action so based. A kind of causal responsibility is implied by an action's being based on practical reasoning; but that does not entail moral responsibility. However, it does appear that if we act freely *and* on the basis of practical reasoning, then, other things equal, we bear greater moral responsibility than for intentional actions not so based. We thus tend to be more blameworthy or – where moral responsibility applies to laudable actions we have performed – more praiseworthy. The explanation of this difference is apparently that the action is both reasoned and undertaken in the light of a judgment which is itself based on reasoning. This indicates a kind of endorsement of the action by the agent. It also roots the action in reasoning; the action is not merely motivated, as where one spontaneously acts to realize a sudden desire one has never entertained. Other things equal, the action better represents the character of the agent, or at least represents both the intellect *and* the will.

There are other factors relevant to how practical reasoning bears on moral responsibility. If *S* has the concluding judgment in mind in acting, this tends to contribute to the degree of moral responsibility. For the action is thereby likely to be influenced, perhaps in some way encouraged, by the endorsement implicit in making the judgment. Related to this point, since the judgment is before the agent's mind, he has a chance to reconsider that judgment, and acting in line with it thus tends to confirm the endorsement it expresses. If the reasoning is careful, this, too, tends to contribute to the agent's moral responsibility for the action it favors, though if a mistaken judgment is sufficiently plausible the judgment may extenuate by providing a rationale for the action. If the reasoning is culpably sloppy, again the moral responsibility for the action may increase: the deed becomes, as it were, a manifestation of an avoidable vice. It is not easy to say just what has to be equal, of course. But my aim here is not to develop the connections in detail; I simply want to suggest some ways in which practical reasoning is important for moral responsibility.

It is, then, not only in producing actions, and in the execution of intentions, that practical reasoning plays a major role. It is also important in determining what sorts of actions the agent performs, for instance incontinent, rational, or responsible. Practical reasoning is a significant generative process; it is associated with motivation and cognition that can explain action; and both the formation of the belief expressing its minor premise and also its concluding judgment can trigger as well as guide actions. Its rationality as an inferential process, moreover, can reveal much about the agent and can significantly affect proper assessment of the action. Practical reasoning is also important in providing an understanding of rational action. It does so in complicated ways that remain to be explored. The rationality of practical reasoning and its bearing on rational action will be the central concerns of chapters 7 and 8.

CHAPTER 7

The Assessment
of Practical Reasoning

Chapters 4 through 6 construct a cognitive-motivational account of practical reasoning conceived as an inferential process. Their chief concerns are to explicate what practical reasoning is and how it figures in the explanation and dynamics of human action. This chapter considers the assessment of practical reasoning, particularly as bearing on the rational status, roughly, the degree of justification, of the judgment constituting its conclusion. Given this aim, it is quite important whether, as I do, we conceive practical reasoning within a logically univocal conception of reasoning, i.e., a conception for which the same logical criteria, such as those of standard deductive logic, apply to reasoning irrespective of its content. I do not deny that a single logic can be devised to cover both practical and theoretical reasoning when they *are* taken to differ logically and construed as having different sorts of conclusions.[1] But the task of assessing practical reasoning is simplified if standard deductive logic and (so far as there is one) standard inductive logic are taken to apply to it in basically the same way as they apply to theoretical reasoning.

A further simplification would be to regiment practical reasonings so that they can all be represented as (logically) valid. Aristotle may have wanted to represent them thus, at least in some contexts in which he discussed them, and that might partly account for the naturalness of his using the term commonly translated as 'syllogism'. An advantage of such regimentation is that it eliminates from actions based on practical reasoning whatever irrationality they might inherit from the invalidity of the practical argument

142

underlying them. But in the light of the examples cited in chapter 4 and the philosophical problems giving the subject of practical reasoning its special interest, I prefer to consider practical reasoning in a more psychologically realistic way. I therefore countenance all the variety found in its everyday occurrences, despite their not infrequent logical deficiencies.

It is true, however, that in many cases a small amount of rational reconstruction would exhibit as valid some of the practical reasonings which, as represented only by the propositions considered or entertained in the agent's thinking, fall short of validity. In any case, if we can formulate basic criteria for assessing practical reasoning in the diverse forms in which it actually occurs in the agent's thinking, this will give us a broad account of the quality of such reasoning and should enable us to see how to appraise it in forms that, though invalid, exhibit a relation of significant support between the premises and conclusions. The main purpose of this chapter is to work toward such a broad account.

In approaching the assessment of practical reasoning, it is natural to consider at least four sorts of criteria. Those governing the relation of the premises to the conclusion are logical criteria. Those that apply to the relation between the corresponding beliefs – of the premises and, on the other hand, of the conclusion – I shall call inferential criteria. Those concerning the justification of these beliefs (or of their propositional objects), I shall call epistemic criteria. And the criteria for the truth of the premises and conclusions I shall call material. I want to discuss the various criteria in that order, though for the most part the material criteria will be considered in relation to the others rather than separately.

I Logical and inferential criteria

I have stressed the distinction between inferential processes and inferential content, roughly, between reasoning as something we do and arguments as what reasoning instantiates. There is a related distinction between logical and inferential criteria. Logical criteria concern relations between propositions, particularly as they constitute premises and conclusions of arguments; inferential criteria apply to relations between the psychological elements – most notably beliefs – that have propositional objects and figure in reasoning processes. Logical criteria are crucial for appraising practical arguments, inferential criteria for assessing inferential processes. The former criteria concern relations of entailment, or – in the broadest sense – of inductive support, between *propositions*. The latter criteria concern chiefly the psychological and justificatory relations between, on the one hand, *beliefs* of (or other cognitive attitudes toward) the premises and, on the other hand, beliefs of the conclusion.

Inferential criteria depend in *part* on logical criteria. The dependence is obvious when we imagine someone's reasoning exhibiting a bad argument. Practical reasoning to a conclusion patently unwarranted by its premises is poor in a way that reflects on the agent's inferential capacities; it is vitiated by the defective argument it expresses. The reasoning, as an inferential process, is bad, though in this case its defect derives from the corresponding argument. But (I shall argue) inferential criteria do not depend entirely on logical ones: practical reasoning, *as* a rational process, may also be criticizable even when the corresponding argument is unobjectionable. This section will develop these points.

The simplest way to see that the adequacy of practical reasoning is not just a matter of the validity of the corresponding argument is to apply to practical judgment the Kantian distinction between acting from a principle and acting merely in accordance with it. Imagine that Samuel reasons from the premises that he ought, all things considered, to do something to relax, and that having another drink will relax him, to the conclusion that he ought (prima facie) to have another drink. Assume that he sees that the conclusion follows from his premises and infers it from them, where this implies that in some way he draws the conclusion in the light of them, in the sense, roughly speaking, that he draws it with an awareness of them and of its following from them. But imagine that he is *rationalizing* and really accepts the conclusion and the major premise *only because* he has a strong intrinsic desire for another drink. Such rationalization bespeaks a practical deficiency in his reasoning. The reasoning does not properly ground his practical judgment. For, other things equal, he would not hold this judgment if, despite accepting his 'premises' for it, he ceased to have his real reason for holding it, the one in whose clandestine service he is rationalizing. *What he judges* is justified by the premises, since his abstract argument is cogent. But *his judging* is not warranted by his believing them, since the explanatory basis of his judgment is not his believing the premises but the intrinsic desire for another drink. There is thus a defect in his practical reasoning: he concludes it on the wrong basis, even though he *has* (but does not 'use') a sound basis for concluding it.

One might object that if this is really reasoning, which is after all a causal process, then Samuel must believe the conclusion on the basis of the premises. But this need not be so. Granted, his accepting the premises – or at least supposing them to be true – must play some causal role in his *drawing* the conclusion. But his acceptance or supposition can play this minimal role even where the reasons for which he *holds* the conclusion are not the premises. It might be, for instance, that he would draw the conclusion only suppositionally if he did not want another drink. Samuel is thus like an agent who sees that her apologizing to a friend is required by duty, and, rather in the way one might in a logic book exercise, infers that she should apologize, but nonetheless *believes* that she should apologize, only on the basis of her desire to avoid annoying a second friend, and actually apologizes only *for* the second reason. Logically, Samuel's reasoning is unobjectionable (given a suitable interpretation of 'ought'); it corresponds to a valid argument. But inferentially it is not: his holding the conclusion is not based on, but only rationalized by, the premises.

We could put the point in part by distinguishing between the corresponding argument and *the underlying argument*: here the practical argument merely corresponds to, and does not underlie, his judgment in favor of the conclusion. He *has* beliefs that are of, and in that sense correspond to, the premises and conclusion; but his beliefs of the premises do not explain, and so do not provide a (causal) basis of, his believing the conclusion. The beliefs express a reason he *has* to believe his conclusion; but he is abnormal in that he does not believe it *for* that reason. In *that* sense the argument does not underlie his belief of the conclusion even if he comprehendingly goes through the motions of a kind of inference of the conclusion from the premises. In good practical reasoning, by contrast, a suitable practical argument underlies *S*'s reasoning; it provides a basis of it, not merely a corresponding structure available for use in reconstruction or rationalization.

A further deficiency in the kind of rationalizational practical reasoning just considered is that it lacks an appropriate practical upshot: neither Samuel's acceptance of the premises nor the reasoning as a whole yields a tendency to act accordingly. The premises and conclusion of his reasoning give him normative, but not motivational, practical reasons. This is not just a limitation on how practical the reasoning is. It indicates that the inferring of the conclusion is not backed by the normal motivating force of *reason* as represented by the agent's believing the premises and drawing the conclusion from them. The agent's tendency to act on the conclusion is grounded solely in a desire which is not expressed in his premises. We have, then, practical reasoning that is logically acceptable yet inferentially deficient. Its inferential deficiency is epistemic in nature but psychological in origin. The case shows, then, that the full assessment of practical reasoning is a manifold task that requires the use of standards from at least three different domains: the logical, the inferential, and the epistemic. The next section will focus mainly on the first of these.

II *Common patterns of practical reasoning*

So far, I have presupposed the notion of a logically acceptable practical argument. What range of such arguments *is* logically acceptable? Answering this fully would require a detailed logical theory, for the diversity of practical argument forms is very great. Here I simply want to get a few of the major logical criteria before us. My point of departure is the view that practical reasoning is very broadly a kind of means-end reasoning. I want to consider deductive and inductive standards separately. The relevant deductive standards are not in general derived from familiar argument forms, such as categorical syllogisms, and some do not seem formal at all; nor are the inductive standards of a familiar enumerative or analogical kind. The task of explication, then, goes well beyond the domain standardly covered in textbooks of deductive and inductive logic, and what follows is only a beginning.

We have already seen one kind of valid practical argument of the appropriate sort: one in which the major premise, say that on balance I must do something to relax, expresses an overriding need, i.e., one that the reasoning represents as taking priority over all competing ends relevant at the time, and the minor premise says that *A*-ing, for example having another drink, is necessary to satisfying the need.[2] We have here an instance of a necessary condition schema, and it is plausibly considered valid because its conclusion simply says that one should, on balance, do something necessary to realizing what one needs on balance – hence something one should on balance attempt to realize. Rule schemata may also be valid provided the rule figuring in the major premise expresses a similarly overriding demand (as Kant thought genuine moral rules do). Let us refer to valid practical arguments of this sort as having a *necessity pattern*.

It is more difficult to identify valid schemata where no such necessary condition pattern is exhibited. Consider a case in which the major premise sets out an overriding end and the minor says that *A*-ing is sufficient for it. It does not follow that *S* should *A*. Some kind of prima facie judgment does follow, since *S* has some reason to *A*. I have been calling such judgments practical, but it should be remembered that they may often fail to lead to action. Indeed, if there is an obvious alternative means that is far better than *A*-ing as a way to achieve the end, then *S* would normally be unreasonable to judge unconditionally that he should *A*. Suppose, on the other hand, that the minor premise says that *A*-ing is the best way to achieve the end. If 'best' is given a suitably broad sense, wider than, say, 'most efficient', then it apparently does follow that *S* should, all things considered, *A*. For that is the overall best *way* to realize the overall best *end*. The reasoning would exhibit an *optimality pattern*. Depending on whether the end is objectively or subjectively optimal, for instance is 'really' best or merely best in *S*'s opinion, the practical judgment will express objective or subjective reason for action. The terms 'objective' and 'subjective' conceal significant dimensions of contrast which I cannot pursue, but the point here is simply that the kind of reason implied by the premises will depend on the kind of end they posit.

In the more usual instances of practical reasoning, where the major premise does not state an end that is overriding in the strong sense sketched, even an optimality claim in the minor premise would not be sufficient for the argument's validity. For there might be some competing end in the situation in the light of which, all things considered, *S*'s doing something other than *A* is more reasonable. Granting that at a particular *moment* we often do posit ends *as* overriding, there are many cases in which we are too cautious to do this and hence can validly infer at best a strong prima facie judgment favoring the action which, in our minor premise, is represented as best for achieving our end.

If we drew only prima facie conclusions in practical reasoning, the assessment of that reasoning would be in one way simpler. For these conclusions are often sufficiently weak to follow from the sorts of premises we actually employ, such as that we want to free a friend from under a motorcycle and to do so must lift it straight up. However, in the actual context of practical problems, we are trying to determine what to do, and here it is often natural to draw unconditional conclusions yielding a kind of definite directive on which we find it natural to act straightaway. One *may* unhesitatingly act on a judgment that *A*-ing is prima facie best; but particularly if the matter is important, such a guarded judgment might cause one to hesitate or reconsider. We tend to respond much better to unqualified directives.

In many cases, then, it is natural to conclude practical reasoning with an unqualified judgment even if the judgment is not entailed by our premises. Thus, inductive – in the broad sense of 'non-deductive' – standards are more appropriate than deductive standards for appraising the reasoning. In these instances, the basic criterion is rather loose. It is the *reasonableness* of the conclusion relative to the premises, by which I mean that given the premises the conclusion is at least likely to be true, in a sense implying that it is a 'reasonable inference' from them. The intended notion is related to justification as an epistemic concept. Roughly, the idea is that if a rational, relevantly informed person had nothing to go on but the premises, it would be rational for him to draw the conclusion. This may be taken to imply that the conclusion is probable relative to the premises; but that is misleading in suggesting that we commonly have a way of assigning a probability here, or even a definite range of probabilities. At best we are likely to be warranted in saying that relative to the premises, the conclusion is more likely than not; but not even this specific warrant is clearly entailed by the notion of a reasonable inference.

It may be, however, that reasonableness implies that the premises make it at *least* as reasonable to believe the conclusion as to believe its negation. In any case, I propose to call any pattern that meets this standard a *minimal adequacy pattern*. This is a quite permissive standard. Practical reasoning whose underlying argument only meets, and does not exceed, this standard, is not unqualifiedly adequate. For one thing, such patterns allow that it might be *more* reasonable to suspend judgment on the conclusion. Where the premises support the conclusion to the extent that it would be unreasonable *not* to draw it, we might speak of a *standard adequacy pattern*. Here, relative to the premises, it would be a mistake to suspend judgment on the conclusion; and while one's premises might be far from entailing one's conclusion, they would surely provide adequate reason to draw it.

There is still another gradation to be noted. Suppose that an argument barely meets the demands of standard adequacy, in the sense that, given its premises, it is only just barely unreasonable not to draw the conclusion. One might say that such an argument is short of being *cogent*. When, on the other hand, the premises give more support than standard adequacy requires, we might speak of a (minimal) *cogency pattern*. For instance, *S* might reason: I want to get there safely, and the only good way is to wait out this storm, so I had better sit tight until it passes. Many cogency patterns will also be necessity patterns; but there will be disagreement, as there is with theoretical reasoning, over whether every cogency pattern must be valid. I am inclined to believe that the premises of a cogent argument need not entail, but only give strong support to, the conclusion; and I have thus characterized a cogency pattern in such a way that inductively strong arguments may instantiate it. For most non-skeptics, at least, there are certain good arguments whose premises do not entail their conclusions; some cogent arguments are of this kind.

Take some examples. Granting that one would not want to base any important judgment on premises that are only minimally supportive, suppose one is choosing between two almost equally attractive small gifts for a friend. Here, believing that one of them is fairly likely to please, and a bit more likely to do so than the other, minimally warrants the judgment that one should give it. It might be slightly more reasonable to suspend judgment, but one would be reasoning in a minimally adequate way if one judged in favor of the more promising gift. If we vary the case so that one believes that the more promising gift is very likely to please, we would have a standard adequacy pattern, though not necessarily a cogency one. Now consider a cogency pattern. Suppose that my end is overriding, say to protect my children; I would then like to have a minor premise that favors one alternative over another decisively, say by indicating a means that is necessary and sufficient to achieve my end. If I find one, my practical argument would be cogent. In a situation of forced choice, however, say between paying ransom and sending in the police, one might have to act on a slim difference, for instance between the option of paying ransom and calling in the police. A cautious reasoner might then infer a weak prima facie conclusion, say that prima facie (or other things equal) one should call in the police. This would preserve validity, and one would have a cogent argument for a weak conclusion. Others might infer an unqualified conclusion, knowing there is no choice and that one must act; here inductive assessment of the argument would be most appropriate, largely because both the content of the reasoning and the agent's apparent aims in doing it yield no ground for expecting that there is or should be an attempt at validity. One might still be able to construct an argument with a standard adequacy pattern.

There are, then, at least five kinds of pattern – and many distinct subcases – which the logical assessment of practical reasoning should address: necessity and optimality patterns, minimal and standard adequacy patterns, and cogency patterns. Where the underlying argument is appropriately assessed as valid or invalid, the task may be fairly straightforward, as with a necessity pattern; but it may also involve difficult questions about what kinds of ends and means warrant various sorts of practical judgments. In the case of an underlying argument appropriately assessed inductively, there is no question of the conclusion's following from the premises; the logical question is how much support the premises give to the conclusion. The answer will rarely if ever be quantitative, and it may be difficult to determine.

As with theoretical reasoning, we sometimes let the context determine whether to call an argument that is inductively satisfactory, yet has a conclusion not entailed by its premises, deductively invalid, and, correspondingly, whether to use inductive or deductive standards in assessing the reasoning process as a whole. In the former case, a deductively invalid argument may be inductively good enough to warrant our regarding the reasoning it underlies as adequate overall. After all, one may be amply justified, by inductively strong premises, in judging that, say, one should, all things considered, agree to chair a committee. Fortunately, the

classification into deductive and inductive is not crucial for applying the notions I have introduced; for the categories are not
defined in terms of that distinction, and indeed some of them,
such as that of cogent arguments, cut across it.
This section has stressed broadly logical appraisal of practical
arguments. The corresponding problem concerning practical
reasoning *processes* – the problem of their overall appraisal – is
how much justification *S*'s *believing* the premises gives to *S*'s
believing the conclusion, where the minimal requirement is that
the premise beliefs render *S* at least as justified in his believing
the conclusion as he would be in believing its negation. Appraising
the overall reasoning process requires using inferential as well as
logical criteria. Here my main point has already been suggested:
it is that however good the argument underlying one's reasoning,
the reasoning process is not successful overall if it does not meet
an appropriate inferential standard. Above all, if it is merely a
rationalization, and one holds the conclusion on some basis other
than the premises, then the reasoning fails to produce knowledge,
or justified belief, of that conclusion. One might still know or
justifiably believe it, but not *through* the reasoning. This brings
us to the issue of epistemic criteria, which is the topic of the next
section.

III The defeasibility of practical reasoning

If we consider examples carefully and bear in mind the frequency
with which competing ends and contrasting beliefs affect our
thinking, it becomes plain that practical reasoning of a kind that
is normally satisfactory may often be *defeasible*. By this I mean
roughly that even when one's reasoning expresses a good underlying argument, one may fail to be justified *on balance* in holding
the conclusion. This point is epistemic; it applies not to practical
arguments, whose logical status as abstract structures is invariant,
but to reasoning processes, which, even with the same content (or
at least the same kind of content), can yield different degrees of
justification in different circumstances. The defeasibility of practical reasoning, then, is determined by both inferential and other
epistemic criteria. This section describes it in outline; it will be

examined further in relation to epistemic criteria for the premises and conclusions of practical reasoning.

Defeasibility may be exhibited by practical reasoning whose underlying argument is valid as well as by its inductive counterparts. Even in the (deductive) case of an optimality pattern, at least some of one's justification for believing one's premises may fail to be *transmitted* to one's believing the conclusion. One instance occurs where no justification is transmitted because one believes the conclusion *for* an inadequate reason rather than on the basis of the premises. In the other cases, even if one's justification is entirely transmitted, it may not be sufficient to outweigh all the considerations counting against one's conclusion. It is not that one's justification is *eliminated*. One does not lose it, and it still counts in one's favor; it simply fails to outweigh other considerations that may emerge or lie in the background. Specifically, it may be either *overridden* by considerations making some alternative preferable, or *undermined* by factors that reduce it to a level such that one is no longer justified on balance in holding the conclusion.[3]

Consider, for instance, the justification of S's concluding practical judgment that he should chair the committee. This justification might be overridden by his realizing that it would be better to urge Ann to chair it. The justification might be undermined where, though S gets no counterevidence, such as evidence favoring a different kind of service instead, he discovers reason to doubt whether his judgment is warranted by his reasons, say to doubt the adequacy of the grounds for thinking he is competent to chair the committee. Both kinds of factors might be known to S – presumably tacitly – at the time S draws the conclusion; they may also come to mind just as, in a self-critical mood, he is drawing his conclusion; and they may come to light thereafter and do their undermining work then. Indeed, a self-critical agent may often seek such factors before acting on practical inferences.

One's justification for holding a practical conclusion is especially likely to be defeated where – as is common in practice – the conclusion is not qualified by 'prima facie' or 'other things equal' or some comparable cautionary notion. One may, after all, have overlooked a superior means, such as a third gift far more likely to please than the two that one considered. One may have failed to take account of other things one wants, say to avoid evoking

Assessment

jealousy in someone else who will envy the gift. One may also have good reason to believe one ought not to desire the end, or ought not to believe the minor premise.

These points about the justificatory protection afforded by qualifying one's concluding judgment do not imply that if one draws only a prima facie conclusion, one's justification for believing the qualified proposition (and for judging it to be true) may not *itself* be defeated. The protection falls far short of invulnerability. Drawing a conclusion which allows that if other things are not equal then, on balance, I should not *A*, does not prevent my being mistaken in believing the apparently weak proposition that, prima facie, I should *A*. The difference is between defeat of the obligation expressed *in* the judgment – which the prima facie qualification provides for – and defeat of the justification *of* the judgment itself – which it does not provide for. Both kinds of defeat are possible for a single judgment. Nonetheless, prima facie conclusions, on any of the plausible interpretations of 'prima facie', require less for their justification than their unqualified counterparts. There are still other kinds of factors that defeat *S*'s (overall) justification for believing the conclusion; but some of them, like some already cited, raise issues best considered in relation to the status of *S*'s beliefs of the premises. That is the main subject of the next section.

IV   Epistemic criteria

The purely logical assessment of reasoning is indifferent both to the truth or falsity of its premises and to the agent's justification for believing them. The overall appraisal of reasoning is not; and this section will be concerned mainly with the epistemic assessment of practical reasoning, including the relations among the truth or falsity of its constituents and *S*'s justification for believing them. I shall assume that justification in the relevant sense counts toward knowledge, and is at least for that reason epistemic; but whatever knowledge requires beyond justification and truth will not be my concern. Epistemic assessment of reasoning overlaps inferential assessment, since one factor in *S*'s justification for believing the conclusion is the inferential relation this belief bears

153

to the premises. But there are many other aspects of epistemic assessment.

Consider first the premises. There are complicated factors that affect assessment of them. Notice first that these premises may of course be mistaken without the argument's ceasing to be practical. Moreover, since one may rationally believe certain false propositions, the falsity of a premise is not sufficient to render *S* unwarranted in drawing the conclusion. If we call a practical argument that is valid and has true premises *sound*, we may then say that unsound practical reasoning may nevertheless confer justification on the agent's believing its conclusion, where this implies, minimally, greater warrant for believing it than for withholding belief from it. For *S* may have excellent grounds for believing the premises (and conclusion) even if they are false. Even if the argument is invalid, it may instantiate one or another adequacy pattern and be inductively strong. Moreover, *S*'s having sufficient warrant to *take* it to be valid may (given justified beliefs of the premises) justify *S* in believing its conclusion. There may be only a very limited range of cases in which such a logical error concerning a practical argument can have the required degree of warrant (or at least of excusability), but there apparently are some. If my premises are true and I justifiably believe them, then if I am mistaken in thinking the argument valid only because I miss a very abstruse source of invalidity, perhaps I can still justifiably believe – though to be sure I could not know – the conclusion.

We have, then, three dimensions of assessment for practical reasoning. The first, the *argumental dimension*, concerns the associated argument, viewed logically in terms of its validity or inductive strength, and viewed materially in terms of the truth and falsity of the propositions constituting it. The second, the *inferential dimension* – which is governed by both psychological and epistemic criteria – concerns the agent's justification for inferring the conclusion and for believing it *in virtue of* the premises; roughly, the question is how much justification the reasoning process itself gives to the agent's belief of the conclusion – typically by transmitting justification from beliefs of the premises to a belief of the conclusion. The third, the *epistemic dimension*, concerns the overall justification of the agent's beliefs of each of these propositions (or, if the reasoning is suppositional, the justification *for* believing them, roughly in the sense that if *S* believed them *for* the reasons constituting this justification, the resulting beliefs would be justified). In a given piece of reasoning, these dimensions may vary independently. For instance, certain reasonings offered in rationalizing an error may be logically and materially adequate, yet inferentially and epistemically defective. Imagine that *S*'s reasoning is sound, but he does not justifiably believe the premises, and his belief of the conclusion – that *he should A* – is not *based* on his inferring it from them. *S* might for all that justifiably believe the conclusion on some other basis; but the reasoning would still be both inferentially and epistemically defective.

One would hope that one's practical reasoning is adequate in all three dimensions. When it is sound (or at least has true premises and is inductively strong) *and*, on balance, one justifiably believes its premises and, on that basis, also justifiably and on balance believes its conclusion, I shall call it *cogent*. This overall notion of cogent reasoning is quite rich. Such reasoning instantiates some cogency pattern, has true premises one justifiably believes, and yields one's believing the conclusion on the basis of those premises. The reasoning is logically, materially, epistemically, and inferentially adequate. Section I indicates how, in general terms, practical reasoning of various sorts may satisfy the logical requirements, and some of the inferential requirements, for cogency. The satisfaction of the (material) truth requirements needs no special comment, except that I am of course presupposing that practical judgments, even when moral, are true or false.[4] It is the (epistemic) requirements for justifiably believing the individual propositions that now need special attention.

Consider the major premise first. We have already seen in discussing logical criteria that there is a kind of tradeoff: the stronger one's premises (in content), especially in representing one's goal as overriding, the better the prospect of validity, particularly if one's conclusion is prima facie; yet the stronger the premises are, the less likely it is that we justifiably believe them. If *S*'s major premise says only that he wants to accomplish something, or simply that he has a prima facie obligation to do something, then (if *S* is a normal person operating under normal conditions) it is not likely that he is unjustified in believing the premise. One might even think that *S* *cannot* be unjustified in believing that he wants something. But I doubt this, and it is surely false if one's premise is to the effect that one wants something more than anything else one believes to be relevant in the situation.[5] Nevertheless, clearly we are often justified in believing that we want something, or that we have a prima facie obligation to do a certain deed. In some cases we are also justified in believing that something is currently our overriding end. If, regarding the coming weekend when I am free, I have promised to check up on your empty flat on Saturday, then when my free Saturday comes I would normally be amply justified in believing that on balance I must go and check.

But things are often not so straightforward. In many cases, I would not have a practical problem if it were easy to see what my overriding end is, or what, on balance, is my overriding obligation. I may be comparing recreational prospects, so the question is mainly what I most want (or should want in the light of my basic desires). A week in the country would be relaxing, but might be too slow; a week in a favorite city would be too expensive; and there may be several other options. If I decide that all things considered, the country would be best, I might be neglecting other prospects, or wrongly appraising my own reactions to the envisaged situation itself. The mere possibility of a mistake does not undermine my justification for settling on the country, but the point is that there is room for an avoidable and unjustified mistake here. This point can also be illustrated with respect to obligations, as where one must devote time and resources to one child as opposed to another, or to a parent rather than a spouse. It is easy to go astray in such cases and unwarrantedly conclude one's reasoning. And just as we sometimes correct an earlier stance, or retrospectively admit an unwarranted view, regarding what we wanted on balance, we may also revise our views on what we are obligated to do.

The cases just described suggest that the major premise in question is itself derived from a prior piece of practical reasoning. That is often how we arrive at a major premise. But even if I arrive at a goal for my holiday by making an unreflective choice, the same points apply. An unjustified belief that on balance I should vacation in the country is perhaps easier to see to be unwarranted if traced to prior reasoning than if I casually form it after hearing someone say that the fall foliage is beautiful. It may be more reprehensible if it is grounded in prior reasoning, since

I would then have both taken some time to consider the matter and failed to meet a fully adequate standard in arriving at my conclusion. But the belief can be unjustified for the same sorts of reasons even if formed as a spontaneous expression of momentary preference. There are at least three basic sorts of reasons that explain why such beliefs fail to be justified. First, I may be mistaken about the intrinsic character of the end, say about how enjoyable a week in the country will be. Second, I may overlook how my realizing the end would affect other things I want, such as to give the family a good vacation. Third, I may overlook consequences of realizing it for my hypothetical desires, as where it has effects that I *would* want to avoid if I thought about them, say making me reclusive. It is not that I *already* want to avoid becoming reclusive; I may have no thoughts or desires to this effect at all.[6]

It is one thing to point out basic kinds of mistakes that can be made in holding the major premise; it is another to give criteria for unjustifiably making them. There is no simple formula here, and a case can be made for any of a number of standards that range from demanding to permissive. Plainly, there is a tendency to insist that, as a reasonable person would, one meet a higher standard where more is at stake, say a change of job as opposed to a choice of holiday setting. Moreover, if the major premise does not represent the end as overriding, then the risk of mistake is reduced. However, if the reasoning is undertaken in the normal way in the course of answering a practical question, then even if the *words* I use, or would use if I expressed the reasoning, do not indicate an overriding end, the *belief* I actually express by the words may commit me to such an end. I may say simply 'I believe I'd better concentrate on the older child's problems today' to express the difficulty of being certain what I should, on balance, do. But in the circumstances my belief may well be that so doing is my overall obligation. The proposition that it is my overall obligation is thus a good candidate for my major premise. Similar points apply to the use of expressions like 'I want', 'my aim', and 'I really should', as employed in expressing practical reasoning. Their common modesty of tone may obscure their frequent unconditionality of intended content.

In assessing the agent's justification for the minor premise, the task is simpler where it represents *A*-ing as necessary for the end.

In that case the question is S's justification in believing that a certain instrumental or constitutive relation holds. But we commonly conclude practical reasoning in favor of actions that we do not take to be necessary conditions for realizing our end, but only regard as something like our best bet, or good, or adequate, for achieving this end. In the latter case, in which we do not take the means to be necessary for the end, there are at least three criteria. They parallel those cited for the major premise: S may overlook a relevant feature of the action, say its unpleasantness; S may fail to see one or more relevant consequences of it, such as its eliminating the chance of realizing some other, already wanted end; and S may neglect a consequence the action has for something he *would* want on reflection. The general point is that where S does not take the action to be necessary for the end, and particularly where he believes that it is not necessary, the question of its suitability is *comparative*. This holds whether or not S actually makes a comparison. Hence, from errors of either commission or omission, S may unjustifiably believe that the action is, say, a good way to realize the end. It may be comparatively a poor way, and so in a sense may not be good at all *as* a way; and S may then fail to be justified in his belief of the minor premise.

It may happen, however, and is likely to happen in cases of cautious reasoning, that the minor premise is only to the effect that the action is *sufficient* for the end. This is consistent with the action's being inferior even to readily available alternatives. On the other hand, it may be fairly easy to be justified in one's belief that a means is sufficient, provided one may presuppose necessary background conditions which can reasonably be taken for granted: one's continued physical integrity, the presence of oxygen, the normality of others' behavior, and so on. Here we cannot fault the agent's justification in believing the minor premise; but we might well be warranted in saying that he fails to be justified in believing the conclusion. Again, it is important whether the conclusion unqualifiedly favors the action. If so, then if S has unjustifiably overlooked an alternative preferable to A-ing, he is not warranted in holding the conclusion. But if the conclusion is qualified, say by 'prima facie', then, even in the case of an over-looked preferable alternative, he might justifiably believe it. There is a danger of taking false comfort in this, however. For one thing, while we can act on a prima facie judgment,[7] it is not full-bloodedly practical. Moreover, other things equal, action based on practical reasoning is better supported by the content of that reasoning, and better justified by virtue of issuing from the reasoning, if the concluding judgment favors the action on balance, for instance represents it as such that one should, all things considered, do it.

We come now to the question of the agent's justification, on the basis of accepting the premises, for believing the conclusion. I have already stressed, as an inferential criterion for good practical reasoning, that the reasoning, as opposed to the corresponding argument, is good only if the agent believes the conclusion on the basis of believing the premises. To be sure, S may believe it on another basis as well, including different practical reasoning for the same conclusion. Here as elsewhere there may be *justificatory overdetermination*, since both reasonings may independently warrant the conclusion. My point is that if the reasoning is good, then believing the premises should be both a *sufficient* rational basis *for* one's believing the conclusion and a sufficient psychological basis *of* one's believing it.

Suppose, however, that S's believing the premises is not sufficient to justify S's believing the conclusion, but still exercises some influence on that belief. This might occur where S believes the conclusion on the basis of two independent practical reasonings *jointly* sufficient to produce his belief. We then get a number of cases. For instance, the two reasonings might or might not be individually necessary for his believing the conclusion; and, in various ways, one piece of reasoning could be more influential than the other in producing or sustaining the belief of the conclusion. Here I suggest that, other things equal, S's believing the conclusion of one such piece of reasoning is justified in proportion to two factors. One is the degree of influence of that reasoning as a basis of the belief, roughly, the extent of its causal support of it: weak support would be illustrated by the reasoning's merely inclining S to hold the belief, strong support by its fully explaining why he does hold it. The second factor is the degree to which S's premises justify the conclusion, roughly, how good a ground they provide for one to believe it. The latter variable concerns the quality of his justificatory basis; the former concerns the extent to which S's concluding judgment *rests* on that basis and can thereby derive justification from it.

The case is quite parallel, I think, to theoretical justification, say for believing a scientific hypothesis on the basis of inference to the best explanation. In each case, the degree of one's justification in believing the conclusion varies with both the degree of the belief's inferential dependence on one's premise beliefs and the quality of the evidence they express. Granted, as the number of reasonings for the same conclusion mounts up, the 'proportion' of one's justification for it received from each of them diminishes, even if their absolute 'quantity' of evidential support for the conclusion is equal. But there need not be, and in practice there apparently never is, a point at which one reaches either justificatory saturation or maximal belief strength.

One further distinction is needed in this section. Once we realize that the belief expressed in the concluding judgment of practical reasoning, say that one should vacation in the country, may be based on other factors than *S*'s beliefs of the premises, we can see that the belief's overall justification may largely derive from other sources. Where all of these sources are beliefs which themselves express premises in practical reasonings for the relevant conclusion, then provided they collectively justify that conclusion, we may say that *S*'s holding it is *justified by his practical reasoning*. It may not, however, be justified by any one *instance* of this practical reasoning, since no single piece of such reasoning need be sufficient for *S*'s justification. To be sure, *S* could combine the distinct practical arguments in question, as one can theoretical arguments. *S* would then have a single argument whose major premise expresses the several goals to which the action in question is a means, say the goals of relaxing, reading, fishing, and so on. That shows *why* it is plausible to say that the conclusion in favor of *A*-ing is justified by practical reasoning in general even if no single inference of *S*'s justifies it; it is reconstructively justified by a single piece of practical reasoning to which *S* is at least prima facie committed, one whose premises are the conjunction of the entire set of the premises of the various arguments *S* instantiates for the conclusion.

Notice, however, that human psychology being as it is, one may actually go through a sequence of practical reasonings, each giving some support to one's *A*-ing, and then conclude in favor of *A*-ing without *deliberative composition* of all the considerations into one complicated premise. The relevant conjunction might even be too involved to entertain. It also might be psychologically unsuitable to serve as a single premise: a tediously long list of desiderata may, if entertained at once, strike one as a confusing hodgepodge. To be sure, S might still believe that in virtue of the list as a whole he *has* good reason to A, and might thereby judge that he should. But this is a different (and rather odd) case. It is not judging in favor of A on the basis of a conjunctive good *reason*; it is judging on the basis of the conviction that the conjunction *expresses* a good reason. S would act, moreover, not for the conjunctive reason, but in order to do what he has adequate reason to do. Fortunately, neither the motivational power, nor the justificatory force, of the separate premises in relation to the single conclusion they support requires their incorporation in a single piece of practical reasoning. Indeed, if they are sufficiently numerous, such deliberative composition might reduce their psychological influence and perhaps even their justificatory force.

To meet the specifically epistemic conditions for cogent practical reasoning, then, S must at least justifiably believe both premises, and must conclude, on the basis of them, with a practical judgment which they warrant. This may indeed be a sufficient condition, with two provisos: first, that the justification in both cases is justification on balance, and in that way undefeated; and second, that cogency is not a kind of absolute indefeasibility, such as Cartesian certainty, but simply the sort of warrant in a piece of reasoning which, given true premises, normally yields knowledge of the conclusion. If the condition is not sufficient for cogency, that could be because S might justifiably but mistakenly *take* the premises not to warrant the conclusion, yet draw it anyway, say where it is something he very much wants to believe and he draws it from a kind of weakness of will. There is some unclarity over whether such warranted but mistaken condemnations of one's own reasoning must vitiate one's justification for believing one's conclusion. I fear that they would, but otherwise the stated conditions seem necessary and sufficient for fulfilling the basic epistemic conditions on cogent practical reasoning. There are, however, many problems in determining just when the various kinds of premises that can occur in practical reasoning are justifiably believed by the agent. The question of when such premises justify a practical conclusion, especially an unqualified one, is also difficult. But these problems are not peculiar to practical reasoning, and we have in any case indicated what sorts of difficulties they present and some proposals for their resolution.

V Rationality and relativity

In discussing the assessment of practical reasoning, I have spoken as if such appraisal were culturally neutral. I believe that the logical criteria are. To be sure, in the case of inductive criteria, it may be more plausible to doubt whether there are cross-culturally sound standards than in the deductive case. In any event, it is the epistemic criteria that should concern us most here. May we really speak as if there are objective, cross-culturally sound criteria for the justification of beliefs, particularly beliefs about what constitutes one's overriding end, where this can include moral considerations? This is a large issue which, fortunately, the purposes of this book allow us to keep largely in the background.

If one thinks that epistemic criteria are in some sense relative to culture, subjective outlook, or whatever, one can still employ the account of the assessment of practical reasoning given here. One need only embed the relevant criteria in the specific framework to which one thinks them relative. For instance, if having a moral obligation is determined simply by the demands of the culture in which it arises, then the relevant cultural criteria for moral obligation can be used both in assessing S's belief that he has a moral obligation and in appraising the degree of support this premise gives to an unqualified moral conclusion he draws. The *framework* of assessment developed above will apply, but the specific *criteria* used in it will vary across cultures.

In saying that the epistemic criteria of appraisal suggested above can be accommodated to a kind of relativity, I am *not* talking about relativity in the sense illustrated by my obligation to check up on a friend's flat being relative to my promising to do so, or by my duty to recommend students being relative to my role as teacher, as opposed to being, say, intrinsic to my condition as a rational person, like a Kantian duty of self-improvement. That quite familiar kind of relativity is *relativity of content*. The central idea is uncontroversial: relativism as an affirmation of this phenomenon, *contentual relativism*, is simply the (widely recognized) view that *what* we are obligated to do, the content of our obligations, depends on, and is in that sense relative to, such factors as our previous behavior, our circumstances – cultural as well as interpersonal – and our opportunities and limitations. What is at issue concerning the justification of practical judgments is quite different. It is *relativity of status*, and its affirmation is *epistemic relativism*, the view that what justifies a moral (or other normative) judgment – even when circumstantial variables are taken into account – is relative to, in the sense that it depends on, such variable factors as culture. Thus, even when the conditions to which the content of my obligation is relative are specified – say, a prior promise and an ability to carry it out – it cannot be unqualifiedly true that I am justified in my belief that I ought to fulfill my obligation. I am justified only within my cultural setting. Indeed, my justification *is* cultural, as opposed to universal, though, by virtue of its subject matter or at least its function, it may be moral in the same sense of 'moral' that applies to justification rooted in the same way in a different culture. On this view, there are different notions of justification applicable in different cultures, or at least in different frames of reference, whether the principle of distinction is cultural or of some other kind. The different notions are analogous, but not governed by the same criteria.[8]

Epistemic relativism may be combined with the ontological view that it cannot even be unqualifiedly *true* that I ought (morally) to do something. I consider the latter view less plausible; but perhaps it too can be largely accommodated by the framework of this book, by reinterpreting the schemata for practical reasoning accordingly and suitably relativizing the criteria for its appraisal. For so far as I can tell, all the plausible frameworks for the representation and assessment of practical reasoning will employ both the kinds of schemata I have set out and criteria of the main *sorts* I have introduced: logical, material, inferential, and epistemic. This applies particularly to its means-end structure and its appraisal as adequate or inadequate in terms of the agent's beliefs about, roughly, the value of the relevant end and the suitability of the envisaged means. The main difference would be that, on the non-cognitivist view I have in mind, normative conclusions cannot be supported by their grounds in a sense implying their *truth*. But they might still be supported in a way implying that it is reasonable to endorse them and act accordingly; and the criteria for such support might be quite similar to their counter-parts in my cognitivist account of what justifies practical judgments.

VI *The special role of moral reasons*

There remains one question of assessment that is quite neutral with respect to the issue of epistemic relativism. It concerns the content of practical judgment. If, with Kant, we regard moral judgments as, when properly grounded, deriving from reason and expressing its full legislative authority, then it will be natural to hold that an unqualified moral judgment is always overriding. It need not be motivationally overriding, as we have seen in discussing Kant's resources for dealing with weakness of will, though it must, for Kant, have at least substantial motivating power, since if reason cannot motivate in some significant way, it cannot be fully practical. It is the normative status of moral judgment which I want to consider now. Normatively, a Kantian framework implies a preponderant role for moral judgment: moral judgment is normatively overriding, in the sense that it provides both the strongest kind of justification for action and in fact a kind even stronger than any combination of other sorts, such as pragmatic and aesthetic justification. Call this the Kantian *moral priority thesis*.[9] My question here is whether an account of practical reasoning should presuppose this thesis, or indeed *any* priority relations among kinds of reasons and judgments. I shall make just two points here.

First, the question of normative priority relations belongs to the theory of practical reason, not specifically to the theory of practical *reasoning*; and the parallel question of *motivational priority* belongs to the theory of motivation. Kant was especially con-cerned with practical reason. Both the normative and the motiva-tional domains are relevant to understanding practical reasoning, and both are therefore discussed at a number of points in this book. But our account of what constitutes practical reasoning is properly neutral with respect to the moral priority thesis. If that thesis is true, this bears on what *S* is normatively committed to in drawing his conclusion. But it does not necessarily affect what that conclusion *is*, and the truth of the thesis is consistent with *S*'s

taking the thesis to be false. If it is true, however, it bears impor-
tantly on the epistemic assessment of reasoning. This brings me
to my second point.

Supposing the moral priority thesis is true, if I justifiably and
truly judge that my overall moral obligation is to check up on
my friend's flat, then I have an objective and overriding moral
obligation to do it. Imagine, however, that I also justifiably believe
that there is an overarching rational point of view which takes
priority even over the moral point of view. In that case, I could
be justified, if mistaken, in believing that my overall obligation
lies elsewhere; for my deepest rationally held views and aims
might demand believing this. Perhaps, then, despite the truth of
the priority thesis and my objective moral obligation to do the
promised job, I could still fail to meet the epistemic conditions
for justifiably holding the conclusion that I ought to do the job;
for I would justifiably though mistakenly believe, of my actually
sufficient moral grounds expressed in the premises, that they do
not entail an overriding conclusion. The point is that what justifies
my belief of my conclusion is determined by what I justifiably
believe, or am justified *in* believing, and not entirely by what is
objectively the case, including a perhaps a priori – though far
from self-evident – principle like the priority thesis.[10]

For the same reasons, on the basis of the agent's justified
beliefs, he could be warranted in drawing the moral conclusion
that he should do the job, even if the grounds his premises provide
him are weaker than would be required to warrant his believing
a conclusion that *he* takes to be overriding. Hence, he might
justifiably take himself to have a moral obligation, without being
justified in believing that it is overriding – even if it is. Thus, even
if the moral priority thesis is true, it need not bind every rational
agent to give priority to moral obligations over all others; its truth
would imply at most that it would commit ideally rational agents
to this position. To be sure, the imagined agent would normally
take his moral conclusion to be binding, provided he did not have
good justification for believing it overridden; the point is simply
that even if the priority thesis is true, its acceptance is not a
condition for rational agents' either countenancing or acting on
moral obligations.

The crucial items to be assessed in the epistemic appraisal of
practical reasoning are the premises and conclusion the agent

actually believes, together with other relevant propositions he might be expected to believe or consider, including alternative premises or conclusions. But we are not logically omniscient; hence, there can *be* propositions – such as that on balance we should keep a promise – which, though entailed by what we believe, we nonetheless do not believe, and should not be expected to believe under the circumstances. It would thus be a mistake to assess our practical reasoning on the assumption that anything we are logically committed to is always relevant to appraising that reasoning. In this sense, then, I am construing the appraisal of practical reasoning as, epistemically, *agent relative*; for it is relative to the agent's epistemic situation. In one's concrete situation, one might believe propositions that adequately support a moral priority thesis but, because one cannot (without special help) see that they do, one might not be bound to accept the thesis or take it as a constraint on one's reasoning.

This approach is consistent with granting that there may be an objectively correct normative priority thesis which ideally should be reflected in assessments of practical conclusions. Suppose an agent takes a prudential ground to be overriding, thinking, in an egoistic moment, that self-interested reasons are the only ones that matter. If moral reasons in fact override prudential ones, this would be a mistake; and if we accept their priority, we are likely to question the justification as well as the truth of the agent's concluding judgment, for example that he should put his career ahead of his obligation to his parents. Nonetheless, in an adequately reflective agent the judgment, even if mistaken, could be sufficiently well-grounded to be justified. The epistemic assessment of practical reasoning, then, should be based on what the agent concludes in the light of his reasons, together with what it is reasonable to expect him to believe given his total situation. If the reasoning runs contrary to a correct priority thesis, as where considerations of prudence are wrongly taken to override moral ones, it is not fully cogent. But it may for all that express a reasonable answer, given the agent's information and capacities, to a practical question; and certainly so conceiving it will yield a better sense of how a rational agent answers a practical question, and of how practical reasoning guides action, than expecting practical judgments to reflect correctly whatever normative priority relations there may be. We can explicate what it is for practical reasoning to be minimally adequate without committing ourselves on what kind of reasons, if any, are ultimately overriding.

We have seen, then, three interrelated dimensions of assessment for practical reasoning and four kinds of criteria. The first dimension is argumental: it concerns the corresponding argument conceived abstractly, and we have noted several patterns of argument, representing necessity, optimality, two kinds of adequacy, and cogency. The argument corresponding to practical reasoning may be appraised both by logical criteria, whether deductive or, in a broad sense, inductive, and by material criteria, which concern the truth or falsity of the constituent propositions. Second, assessment occurs in the inferential dimension: the reasoning process itself may be appraised by inferential criteria. These concern both the conditions for justifiably *drawing* the inference and the requirements for justifiably holding the conclusion in virtue of believing the premises. And third, there is the epistemic dimension: the agent's beliefs of the premises and conclusions may be appraised by epistemic criteria that may or may not concern the reasoning process or corresponding argument. These criteria concern both what (if anything) justifies the agent's beliefs and what might defeat that justification. These epistemic criteria leave open whether any of the beliefs are inferentially justified, through either practical or theoretical reasoning. Ideally, good practical reasoning expresses a valid underlying argument with premises that are true and justifiably believed and with a conclusion which is both justifiably inferred from them and justifiably held on the basis of them. This ideal may actually be fulfilled, or approximated, quite often. When an agent acts on the basis of practical reasoning that fulfills or approximates this ideal, the action will tend to be rational. But it need not be, and the conditions under which it is or is not are of great interest. They will be the main focus of the next chapter.

CHAPTER 8

Practical Reasoning
and Rational Action

The assessment of practical reasoning concerns standards for practical arguments in the abstract and, even more, for the process of justifiably concluding upon an action in virtue of one's beliefs of the premises of the argument. But practical reasoning is important in part because of its bearing on rational *action*, conceived as conduct distinct from any practical judgment that guides it. That bearing is the subject of this chapter. I begin by locating rational action in relation to practical reasoning. I then proceed to explicate how practical reasoning is important for those rational actions affected by it, and I conclude with some related points about rational action itself.

I Practical reasoning, rational action, and rationalization

If inferentialism is mistaken for the sorts of reasons I have given, and hence not all intentional actions are based on practical reasoning, then surely not all rational actions are so based either. This conclusion is in any case independently plausible. Normal conduct is often marked, for instance, by rational goal-seeking actions that are either automatic or spontaneously performed immediately when the agent sees an opportunity. We act automatically, yet rationally, in speaking, in gaming, in driving, and in doing myriad routine tasks. In speaking, we automatically adjust our volume to compensate for surrounding noise. In driving, we habitually stop for red lights. On country walks, we spontaneously pick flowers and pause to hear birds. On the other hand, much of our rational action is based on practical reasoning. This is particularly likely if such action emerges from deliberation. But it is also quite possible where we simply consider what to do, note a means to doing it, and, on that basis, quickly decide to take that means.

How is a rational action based on practical reasoning? It is not enough that it be rational action of the *kind* favored by the conclusion, even if it occurs immediately after the conclusion is drawn. For the action might still be only behavior in accordance with the reasoning. Nor is it enough that the action be caused by the reasoning or even by the motivational and cognitive elements it embodies. For the causal relation may be of the wrong sort, as where it leads to the right action by accident. For instance, if I conclude that I should break into a conversation with a visible gesture, I may be caused, by my aroused desire to speak and my belief that I must break in to do so, to let my briefcase slam shut and, as a result, to make a startled gesture just at the time I judged I should gesture. Here I have done the right thing at the right time, but neither on the basis of my reasoning nor even intentionally. What the case suggests is that action based on practical reasoning, and certainly rational action so based, must be performed *for* a reason expressed in that reasoning, roughly, in order to realize the want represented in (or suitably underlying) the major premise. My gesture in reaction to the slamming of the briefcase may not be made *for* a reason at all, though there is a reason *why* I make it. It is certainly not made for my original reason. It is an *effect* of that reason and accords with my practical judgment; but unlike an action performed for that reason, it is not a *response* to the reason.

The proposed condition – being performed for a reason express-ed in the premises – is, however, only a necessary one. If that were not so, then acting on the basis of practical reasoning would collapse into simply acting for a reason. It would thereby include automatic and spontaneous intentional actions that are not reasoned at all. A functional account of practical reasoning might allow this assimilation of action based on practical reasoning to action for a reason; but I have argued against this, and I believe it would be false economy. On my view, practical reasoning is an inferential process. If this is so, then the additional condition we need is an element of the sort discussed under the heading of the dynamics of practical reasoning. Above all, there must be an appropriate causal connection between *events* constituent in the reasoning and the action. There are at least two basic cases in which an action is based on practical reasoning.

First, it may be sufficient, for an action's being based on practical reasoning, that the concluding element, the making of a practical judgment, trigger the action (in the normal way illustrated in chapter 6). Second, it may also be sufficient that the making of that judgment *dispose* S to do the thing in question and that S then do it *as* an actualization of this disposition, provided the disposition is suitably sustained by the making of the judgment, for instance traceable to it rather than to a different judgment supporting the same action. Imagine, for instance, that I judge that I should gesture when the speaker reaches the end of a sentence, and, on the basis of my holding this judgment, my realizing that this time has come elicits my action. I am then *carrying out* my practical judgment.

As this case suggests, there must be an unbroken causal line from the judging to the action. If, for instance, I had forgotten my judgment, yet later I again judged that I should make the gesture, then in making that gesture I would not be acting on the basis of the *original* practical reasoning. This holds even if the same wants and beliefs produced the second judging by analogous practical reasoning, again giving rise to a judgment that I should gesture when the speaker reaches the end of a sentence. The causal line from my original judgment to my disposition to act accordingly has been broken by my forgetting that judgment, and my action is traceable – in the relevant sense implying a causal connection – only to the later judgment. It is possible, of course, for an action to be based on two or more practical reasonings, provided it is appropriately traceable to each. But as a particular event, an action based on practical reasoning is grounded in a particular reasoning process only if it is linked, in the way just illustrated, to that particular process. Linkage to a reasoning process of the same *type* is not enough.

There is apparently at least one more condition that can connect an action for a reason to practical reasoning which expresses the reason, and here we may have some cases significantly different from the two previously noted kinds of action based on practical reasoning. I have already mentioned (in chapter 6) the causal role a practical judgment may play as a directive force. Suppose that either the practical judgment or the affirmation of one of the premises plays such a causal directive role and thereby guides the action in one of three common ways: first, where one reminds oneself that one has judged (or one believingly repeats the judgment) that one must do this, say write a letter of solicitation; second, where one stands in a similar relation to one's affirmation of the minor premise, say in recalling one's having determined that the action is sufficient for one's end; and third, where one bears a similar relation to the major, as in encouraging oneself by recalling that the goal it expresses is highly desirable. Notice that it is not sufficient that the propositional *objects* in question come to mind: that would at most imply guidance by the relevant want and belief and would not distinguish the guidance involved in simply acting for a reason from that which occurs in actions for a reason which are *also* based on practical reasoning. On the approach taken here, practical reasoning is viewed as a real psychological process; its effects must therefore be tied to events constitutive of that process.

Regarding the connection between rational action and practical reasoning, I contend that an action is rational by virtue of practical reasoning corresponding to it only if the action is based on that reasoning. This thesis – which I shall call the *causal correspondence view* – is not universally accepted. It has been maintained, for example, that 'the action is rational when it fits the specification in the outright evaluative conclusion,'[1] where this means roughly that it is the kind in favor of which the agent has concluded the reasoning. This view is rarely defended, and may have been defended in depth only in its epistemic counterpart concerning justified belief (and knowledge).[2] I shall not argue against it in detail here. Instead, I want to distinguish between normal and *rationalizational practical reasoning*. I believe that in the light of that distinction, the causal correspondence view will seem considerably more plausible than its rivals.

Whatever else one says about rationalization, at least of concrete actions, it contrasts with explanation of them (in the success sense of 'explain', not in the mere attempt sense). With this in mind, I suggest that we may conceive a rationalization, by S, of his A-ing, as a purported account of his A-ing, given by him, which (a) offers one or more reasons for his A-ing, (b) represents his A-ing as at least prima facie rational given the reason(s), and (c) does not explain why he A-ed.[3] Three clarifications should be added here. First, 'purported account' is intended broadly, but the common cases are attempted explanations and attempted justifications. Moreover, in my use, 'rationalization' need not be disapprobative, as it usually is in the Freudian sense. I include cases in which, for instance, one quite properly rationalizes an intuitive decision by reconstructively citing *good* reasons there were for it which one could have adduced had one needed them. Third, the formulation is meant to suggest that rationalizations are normally – and often self-defensively – *motivated behavior*. A rationalization need not, however, be intended as such or even given for any self-protective purpose. The conditions for rationalization can be satisfied, for instance, by a purported account which *S* does not give in order to represent the action as rational. *S* may, for example, simply forget his real reason for doing something and cite another perfectly ordinary one he had for it. Surely one can, under various circumstances, produce an *unintentional rationalization*.

One further complication must be addressed before we discuss rationalization as manifested in practical reasoning. How should we construe cases in which *S* offers an account of his *A*-ing by appeal to several reasons, where some are reasons for which he has acted – actuating reasonings, we might say – and some are merely reasons he had for acting? Surely *S* is to some extent rationalizing. He is, after all, committing himself to at least a partial account of his action by his appeal to the reason(s) he merely had. I call such mixed accounts *partial rationalizations*, since they are in part rationalizations and in part (successful) explanations. This is not to imply that they only *partly rationalize* or *partly explain*. They might adduce a reason *S* merely had which is nonetheless sufficiently cogent to rationalize the action fully, i.e., roughly, to make it appear fully rational; and they might also cite a reason for which he acted, sufficiently powerful in producing his action to provide a full explanation for it. Here we must be careful, however: given overdetermination, what fully explains, or fully rationalizes, may not yield the whole explanation, or whole available rationalization. Other factors may also be sufficient to explain or to rationalize the action. The full explainers or rationalizers are thus still *incomplete*: while they do not merely partially explain or partially rationalize, they are only *part of what explains* or *part of what rationalizes*.

172

We can illustrate both how rationalization can enter into practical reasoning and why actions are not rational merely by virtue of accord with rationalizational practical reasoning, if we take an example in which practical reasoning is self-deceptive. There are various ways in which self-deception may produce rationalizational practical reasoning. There are two main cases. In both, rationalization can help to screen off self-deception from consciousness, as where *S* rationalizes a deed he is ashamed of, such as slighting a rival in a self-deceptive effort to make himself seem meritorious. In one kind of rationalizational practical reasoning, the reasoning rationalizes a practical judgment; in the other it rationalizes an action. The former kind was discussed in chapter 7 in relation to appraisal of the *reasoning*.

To illustrate how practical reasoning may be a mere rationalization of an action that accords with it, imagine that Susan judges, on the basis of practical reasoning, that she should send congratulations to a friend just honored. Suppose, however, that she envies the friend and is averse to sending congratulations. Self-deception might keep her from being conscious of the envy and lead to incontinent failure to act on her practical judgment.[4] It could be, however, that she also realizes that she must seem appreciative. Suppose it is this self-interested desire that actually produces her sending the congratulations. If, as she sends off the note, she recalls the original practical reasoning – a recollection that would help to veil her self-deception about her own envy – this reasoning would be rationalizational with respect to the action.

An action may, then, be both self-deceptively motivated and supportable by practical reasoning to which the agent does or can appeal as a rationalization. Can the action still be rational? We need not conclude that the action's being self-deceptive automatically precludes its rationality;[5] for it may be performed for a perfectly legitimate, if embarrassing, reason of self-interest. But if it is rational, surely that is by virtue of this reason and not through its coincidence with the (non-causative) practical reasoning. To parody Kant, an action not done *from* reason has no rational worth.

To be sure, an action that accords with (good) practical reasoning is, in the light of that reasoning, a rational *kind* of thing to do. But if the action – the concrete doing of the thing favored by practical judgment – is itself rational, it derives its actual rationality from the generative want and belief (or at least from a sustaining set of them, if this is different from the set originally producing the action, as it may be in the case of actions whose performance takes enough time to allow their initiation for one reason and their continuation for another). So far as practical reasoning is relevant, it is the reasoning corresponding to the *underlying* practical argument that carries the justificatory weight. This is the argument corresponding to the generative (or sustaining) want and belief. It is not just any argument the agent has expressed in practical reasoning that favors the action. As we have seen, some practical reasoning may serve mainly as a smoke screen that obscures what really does move *S* to action. The action rationalizable by appeal to such reasoning and, in our example, is in fact rationalized by *S* through a self-deceptive appeal to it. But *rationalizability does not imply rationality*. What makes the action rational is the explaining reasons: those that are, as it were, its psychological premises as well as normatively sufficient grounds for it.

Granted, there are times when either *S*'s making a practical judgment or *S*'s performing an action is explainable *in part* by appeal to one set of factors and in part by appeal to another, say a moral desire and one of self-interest, each desire combined with a belief that the action will realize it. If the rationalizing elements are a partial explanation of the relevant judgment or action, but are not sufficient to explain them, then we have a partial rationalization. In one case, the action is rationalized by the practical reasoning favoring it; in another, the judgment concluding that reasoning is rationalized by the beliefs of its premises. If the rationalizing factors are necessary (even if not sufficient) elements in a correct explanation of the item, then the reasoning (or beliefs of the premises) may be as much an explanation as a rationalization; for although the reasoning contains rationalizing elements, they are also indispensable to its success as an explanation. What rationalizes may not *merely* do so; it may in some cases also explain. Explanatory and (merely) rationalizing elements can be mixed in a variety of ways. Some cases defy easy classification and make the assessment of the rationality of the action quite complicated. This section indicates the kinds of variables crucial in such assessment. The next section will develop further the importance of causal connections in appraising actions.

II   *Reasoned action and acting for reasons*

An action that accords with practical reasoning is rational in virtue of that reasoning only if the action is based on the reasoning. Otherwise, while it may be rational *for S* to perform the action, the action is not – so far as *that* reasoning goes, at least – a reasoned action. Moreover, apart from other motivation, it is not *rationally performed*, just as an action that is moral for *S*, say the fulfillment of a promise, need not be morally, as opposed to prudentially or accidentally, performed. We have also seen that an action is based on practical reasoning only if it is performed for a reason embodied in that reasoning. But what are the sufficient conditions for the rationality of action so based?

In answering this, I want first to guard against intellectualizing rational action. There is even more temptation to do this than to intellectualize intentional actions, as, in some forms, inferentialism does by grounding them all in practical reasoning. Let me first illustrate how, even when conditions seem unfavorable to rational action, for instance where *S* is acting self-deceptively, rationality need not be vitiated.

Suppose that Steve, a single parent, unconsciously wants to avoid facing his dreaded loneliness upon his last child's leaving home. This leads him to consider various ways of occupying himself, since he believes (perhaps also unconsciously) that doing so will help him deal with the dreaded prospect. As he thinks about what to do when the child leaves, it occurs to him that visiting friends abroad would occupy him, and he concludes that he should visit them, self-deceptively telling some relatives (and himself) that he is eagerly looking forward to his long-delayed holiday abroad. The reasoning may be considered self-deceptive because the motivating want, to occupy himself, is grounded directly in his unconscious desire to avoid facing the expected loneliness, which is in turn part of his self-deception with respect to the child's departure. Broadly speaking, he is reasoning in the service of his self-deception and thereby keeping from consciousness his dreaded forthcoming loneliness. Still, if Steve now makes the visit, on the basis of this reasoning, say in responding to its conclusion and on the basis of the motivation and cognition expressed in its premises, is there any reason to think he acts irrationally? I believe not. He may be dealing with his problem both adequately and indeed as well as he would if he squarely faced it.

To be sure, if Steve's self-deception were causing him to overlook a better alternative, or if his wanting to occupy himself were itself irrational, that would be another matter. But if we assume, plausibly, that the visiting is his best way to occupy himself and that his wanting to do so is rational, why not suppose his action is rational? It is true that his wanting to avoid thinking of his impending loneliness underlies his wanting to occupy himself; but that want is not irrational, it is simply unpleasant to entertain. Moreover, other factors make it reasonable to want to occupy oneself: factors affecting anyone who faces a change to a less full life. So here, I think, we have a case where self-deceptive practical reasoning is not the tail that wags the dog. It apparently serves a useful, rational purpose in S's psychic economy, and may in fact do so as well as the non-self-deceptive alternatives.

It is interesting to compare Steve's case with that of Sandra, who does the same thing on the basis of precisely parallel practical reasoning, but wholly without self-deception or unconscious reasons. Would she be acting *more* rationally? There is an inclination to say so. But that may be due to her apparently greater rationality as an *agent*. Moreover, certainly she is likely to be able to *justify* her action better, since, unlike him, she can readily trace it deeper in her hierarchy of rational desires, whereas he must lift the veil of his self-deception before he can see the real basis of his action. Other things equal, then, she has better *second-order justification* than he, or at least readier access to a good second-order justification for believing her action to be rational, than he has for believing his to be rational. We might say that, as a result, her action also has greater *reflective rationality* than his, in the sense that hers is, or at least can be, grounded in fuller reflection, or (assuming that his unconscious want figures only below the surface of his reflection) at least in reflection that includes the actuating reason.

We should grant the importance of these contrasts between the overall positions of Sandra and Steve as rational agents. But it does not follow that her action itself is *more rational* than his in the primary, unqualified sense. I am not sure that it is, since I am inclined to understand rationality here as a matter of the sorts of reasons that actually explain the action in relation to S's overall

176

situation, including, for example, *S*'s readiness to change course if new information favors it. In this, action is like belief: normally, the rationality of a belief is chiefly a matter of factors in which it is grounded, not of *S*'s ability to marshal such factors in defending it. Such elements as unconscious perceptual cues, which one cannot, without special reflection, know one is using, may ground rational belief even if one is no more able to appeal to them in justifying the belief than Steve is to invoke his underlying desire in justifying his going abroad. One can justifiably believe that a voice is tense without being in a position to say any more by way of justification than that one hears its tenseness. To be sure, we may often have a more articulate grasp of the grounds of our rational action than of the grounds of our justified perceptual belief. But the supporting work of our grounds does not depend on our capacity to articulate them or to specify *how* they support our beliefs or actions – certainly not on a capacity to do so without careful self-study.

I suggest, then, that what carries the greatest weight in determining whether an action is rational is the justification, conceived as a kind of rational support, which it derives from the reason(s) for which it is performed. This does not imply that practical reasoning is unimportant in judging rational action. Practical reasoning remains a major route to acting for a reason. Indeed, it is our most explicit route: when we take it, we tend to be more aware of our reasons, and of their influence on us, than when we act for a reason without it; and when, in retrospective explanation or justification, we cannot appeal to practical reasoning at least reconstructively, we may rightly wonder precisely why we did the thing in question.

It may also be true that, other things equal, an action based on practical reasoning is more rational than one simply based on the relevant want and belief. Perhaps the often critical process of drawing a conclusion in favor of an action gives a better ground for performing it than one would otherwise have; it certainly focuses our ground in a way it need not be focused for us if we act on it automatically. Moreover, since the making of this judgment itself, as well as other events constituent in the reasoning, may play a triggering and guiding role with respect to the action, the action has a causal connection to the reasoning as well as to the crucial want and belief. Finally, the practical judgment may have a *normative* content, say that one morally must perform the action, which implies a belief that one need not have simply in acting for the corresponding reason. If, in order to fulfill an obligation, I do something I have promised to do, say help a colleague move books to another office, I take it to have that normative ground: being a fulfillment of my obligation. But if this action were a matter of habitual proper conduct and not based on practical reasoning, I might not actually hold – though I might be disposed to form – the belief that I must do it. When one acts on the basis of such moral practical reasoning, the reasoning itself is part of both the psychological and normative foundation of the action. These points may help to explain why Kant seems to take as his paradigms of moral actions those arising from practical reasoning, indeed reasoning whose force is vividly before us because it is part of what helps us resist contrary inclination. A reasoned action performed for an adequate reason is more than an expression of rational motivation and cognition; it is the climax of a rational process.

III   Aristotelian, Humean, and Kantian views
of rational action

Section II argued that the sufficient conditions for rational action include its being based on *adequate* reasons, even if not on practical reasoning. In exploring what sorts of reasons these are, we would do well to return briefly to Aristotle, Hume, and Kant and to compare their views both with what may be the most commonly held current standard of rational action, the maximization of expected utility conception, and with my own view. Since I am considering them mainly for limited comparative purposes, and am presupposing the points made in chapters 1, 2, and 3, my sketch will be very brief.

In approaching their conceptions of rational action, it is safe to make one general assumption: that for all of them rational action is such in part because it is linked, by what I have called a purposive chain, to an intrinsic, and in that sense basic, end of the agent. They differ in their conceptions of such a chain, though all of them seem to countenance non-instrumental means-end connections. But each views rational action as fitting this basic pattern, and their reasons for doing so seem to derive from the plausible – and historically fundamental – notion of both practical reasoning and rational action as having a means-end structure. If this assumption is correct, then we may hope to arrive at a broad characterization of their conceptions of rational action in part by looking to their notions of the *ends* it must serve.

Aristotle clearly takes happiness (flourishing, in a certain sense) to be both our actual final end and appropriate for this role: appropriate at least in fulfilling our proper function in the teleological order of nature. Happiness is, then, both the motivational and the normative foundation of our actions: any path from an intentional action to its ultimate motivation will reach an intrinsic desire which is, in the broad sense appropriate to happiness as an activity concept, a desire for happiness, though the concept of happiness, as opposed to that of some activity constitutive of it, need not figure in the object of the desire; and any complete justification of an intentional action will trace it, by way of the agent's beliefs, to some contribution to happiness. Not just any belief will do, of course: 'That we must act according to right reason is generally conceded and may be assumed as the basis of our discussion' (*NE*: 1103b31–2).[6] There is no formula for so acting, however: 'there are no fixed data in matters concerning actions and questions of what is beneficial . . .' (1104a3–4). What it is to act according to right reason is closely tied to the notion of virtue, which in turn is understood in relation to the person of practical wisdom as exemplar: 'virtue or excellence . . . consists in the mean relative to us, a mean which is defined by a rational principle, such as a man of practical wisdom would use to determine it' (1106b36– 1107a2).[7] Roughly, then, rational action must ultimately subserve the end of happiness in a way that accords with right reason: reason as integrated with practical wisdom (perhaps indeed equivalent to it). It is true that Aristotle is easily read as interpreting happiness intellectualistically, but there are passages in which he appears to take only the highest happiness, and not happiness in general, to consist in intellectual activity. In any case, his overall eudaemonistic conception of rational action is what I am emphasizing. Within this framework, one can diversify the basic varieties of rational action in accordance with one's account of what constitutes happiness.

In Hume, rational action is instrumentally conceived: it is action with an appropriate purposive link to one or more basic desires. But while we find, as in Aristotle, motivational foundations – which in many parts of Hume seem to be composed wholly of hedonic desires – we do not find normative foundations. Hume does not hold that it is rational to desire even pleasure or the absence of pain; rather, those desires are presupposed in characterizing rational action, for which – with certain qualifications – he might have preferred the term 'reasonable'. Moreover, there are no constraints (or at least no a priori constraints) on *what* we may desire for pleasure or on any intrinsic desires: desires admit of rationality only instrumentally, as where their objects are one's best means to one's intrinsically wanted ends. Unlike Aristotle, for instance, Hume provides no way of conceiving the pleasures of intellectual activity as a better end than those of intoxication.[8] Reason can show us what will give us pleasure, and it may condemn, as irrational, actions foolishly believed to lead to pleasure, or misbegotten because they lead to less than one might readily have obtained. But reason provides no basis for the view that we ought to want any given kind of thing for its own sake. This still leaves room for a critical use of the Humean notion of rational action, however. For what we do in the service of our intrinsic desires may be irrational owing to mistakes about its tendency to satisfy them, even if they themselves are not appraisable as rational or irrational. No desires are intrinsically rational; desires are at best natural. But our basic desires are the masters action does and ought only to serve. Its rationality is functionally conceived in terms of how well it fulfills this task.

For Kant, rational action (or at least objectively rational action) must at once accord with rational norms and be appropriately motivated by them. The moral case, which he treats as the most shining example of rational action, illustrates that Kant not only postulated normative foundations of rational action, but also gave those foundations both a priori status and motivational power. Practical reason is autonomous: it enables us to see what we ought to do; and it motivates us, by virtue of our grasping categorical imperatives, to act accordingly, even if we have no independent desire to do so. The view leaves room for non-moral rational ends, since Kant apparently countenanced non-moral intrinsic goods, such as intellectual and aesthetic ones. Again, we have the notion of rational action as traceable, by a purposive chain, to basic ends. But the ends need not involve desire – at least not for anything independent of them, as opposed to a desire to do one's duty, conceived as grounded *in* the judgment that it is our duty and not as an independent force that moves us to be moral. This intrinsic motivating power of moral judgment is a special case, indeed the central Kantian case, of practical reason as motivationally practical. Not all our desires are normatively grounded, of course. We have natural inclinations, including desires directed towards happiness. But even these do not automatically generate rational action: given the priority of moral reasons over other kinds, action in the service of natural inclinations must be morally permissible in order to be rational. By contrast with Hume, then, Kant imposes normative constraints on how a psychologically basic end can generate rational action. Moral ends are not the only suitable ones, even though they are normatively paramount; but clearly Kant is Aristotelian in regarding only some potential objects of intrinsic desire as appropriate to supply normative foundations of action, and even these things need not all be indefeasibly good.[9]

All three of these views are plausible, and all remain influential. But of the three, only Hume's position seems close to the maximization of expected utility view of rational action. For that view puts no constraints on the sources of utility – roughly, of desirability – whereas Aristotle and Kant do not allow just any desires (or motivational values) of the agent to play this role. Even Hume, however, might insist on revising the view to incorporate, as it usually does not,[10] the causal requirement that an action rational by virtue of maximizing expected utility be *based on* the cognition and motivation yielding the utility and probability values.[11] He might also hold, for reasons suggested in chapter 2, that the rationality of action may be affected by certain hypothetical desires (a point that also can be incorporated into a maximization of expected utility framework). Given these qualifications, however, much of what Hume says in laying out his conception of rational action can be expressed in, or at least reconstructed in, the maximization of expected utility framework. My conception is very different, and, as the next section will show, closer to Aristotle's and Kant's.

IV   *An epistemic conception of rational action*

On my view of rational action, the maximization of expected utility framework is deficient for many of the reasons one might formulate from either an Aristotelian or a Kantian point of view. For one thing, while it is at least in the spirit of instrumentalism to recognize that an intrinsic desire can be irrational because its object is impossible to realize, the instrumentalist view wrongly supposes that there are no substantive criteria for the rationality of intrinsic desires. Moreover, I hold that it may be rational to do something which, while quite satisfactory, does not *maximize* one's expected utility. One may, for instance, unreflectively but rationally take a readily available means to an end, thinking simply that it will easily realize the end, and having no *beliefs* about either its probability of attaining it or about the specific probabilities of its various outcomes.[12] Finally, I believe that Kant may well have been right in thinking that certain standards of rational action are knowable a priori, though here I would give happiness a larger role than Kant does as an intrinsically valuable end. Though I will not argue the point here, I suggest that it may be an a priori constitutive principle of practical reason that it is rational to want one's happiness, construed in an Aristotelian fashion, for its own sake.[13] Even if there are no such a priori principles, however, there are other ways of establishing constraints on the rationality of intrinsic desires, such as Brandt's procedure of exposing them in an appropriate way to facts and logic: using theoretical reason, as it were, to establish the foundations of practical reasoning.[14]

Given what I take to be the unity of practical and theoretical reasoning, I find it natural to employ a concept of rationality in general, and of rational action in particular, that reflects this unity. On this view rationality is *well-groundedness*. This conception is quite general; it applies not only to all the propositional attitudes, but also to actions, whose rationality derives from their relation to propositional attitudes, most notably believing and wanting. As applied to actions, the basic idea is this: rational actions are grounded in the right kind of way in the right kind of reason. The right kind of way is being performed *for* the reason(s) in question; the right kind of reason is (undefeated) *rational* motivation, guided by (undefeated) rational belief. Defeaters of the rationality of wants include conflicting wants of equal strength and rationality; defeaters of the rationality of beliefs include both one's awareness of counterevidence and one's having reason to doubt the plausibility of one's grounds. Being undefeated does not require indefeasibility. An action may be rational on the basis of a ground even if it is not impossible that anything defeat the rationality of that ground, or of grounds of that kind. It may yet be true that some grounds for action are indefeasible, as Aristotle and Kant apparently thought; but this view is not essential to my position.

What in particular is it rational to want intrinsically? Here are some central cases. One's own happiness is a paradigm of something it is rational to want intrinsically. But rational motivation need not be limited to such wants: it may well be, as Kant seems to have believed, that it is also rational to want others' happiness for its own sake. Perhaps it is also rational to want, for its own sake, the flourishing of philosophy, science, and all the arts. In countenancing this diversity of possible intrinsic goods, my view is apparently more pluralistic than Aristotle's, though clearly he took the constituents of happiness to be so various that what is put forward with the sound of a eudaemonistic monism may be better regarded as a hierarchical pluralism with intellectual activity at its pinnacle. Moreover, I agree with Aristotle and Kant that some of the things it is rational to want for their own sake may be rationally considered better than others, though I leave open (as at least Aristotle apparently did not in the case of happiness) whether there are some ends that *cannot* (or cannot rationally) be wanted instrumentally. There are surely some ends, however, including one's own happiness, that are not naturally wanted for the sake of something further.

Let me simply illustrate the well-groundedness conception as applied to actions. Some rational actions are well-grounded *directly*, i.e., they are performed in order to realize a basic rational end, say for the pleasures of intellectual activity (rather as certain non-inferential beliefs are well-grounded in, say, perceptual experience). Others are well-grounded *indirectly*, by virtue of resting on at least one basic rational end through at least one purposive chain (rather as certain inferential beliefs are well-grounded in justified non-inferential ones). There may or may not be actual practical reasoning as a mediator in the grounding relation, but since the connecting links are means-end relations, practical reasoning is always reconstructively available to the agent as a device for tracing a rational action to its ultimate motivational ground. There are also epistemic requirements on well-groundedness. If the crucial instrumental beliefs, such as the belief that intellectual conversation will promote one's happiness, are unjustified, this tends to undermine the rationality of the action in question. I say 'tends to' because there are complications. For instance, one might justifiably believe, of such an unjustified belief, that it *is* justified, and acting on it might then be rational. As this suggests, some rational actions may be better grounded, and thus more rational, than others.

Action based on practical reasoning need not be rational; but clearly, rational actions, conceived as well-grounded, are of a kind that always can be so based (at least if they are performed for a further end). The constraints on what constitute rational grounds set the standards for assessing the motivation expressed in the major premise; the constraints on what constitute justified means-end beliefs determine the standards for assessing the cognition expressed in the minor. The process of practical reasoning, moreover, can be seen in this framework to be a route to *discovery*, not just to retrospective explanation or justification, or to self-encouragement. For in setting oneself an end and seeking a means, one often discovers – by reflection or association or luck or whatever – a good means to that end.

We can see, then, that it is natural for a rational agent to engage in practical reasoning to answer a practical question. The concluding practical judgment is justified provided it is well-grounded in the agent's acceptance of the premises. Such grounding implies that the agent justifiably believes the conclusion on the basis of justifiably believing the premises. If, in addition, they are correct and the underlying argument is valid, or of sufficient inductive strength, the reasoning is cogent. If the end and connecting belief they express are well-grounded, and the agent acts for that reason, i.e., in order to achieve that end, the action is prima facie rational. It is more rational in proportion to *how* well grounded the underlying motivation and cognition are and how thoroughly it is based upon them. It can be seen to be rational in the light of this underlying motivation and cognition. But if the action is actually based on practical reasoning expressing the underlying end and belief, then its rationality is, in addition, inferential, focused, and supported by practical judgment. The action fully realizes the corresponding practical argument and thereby responds to the practical problem at hand. If the reasoning is successful, then the response is a rational approach to the practical problem. If the problem remains intractable, the *agent* is not successful. But if the action is optimally well-grounded, then failure here is not his fault. The action is fully grounded in practical reason.

Conclusion

Practical reasoning is a major element in human life. We do it in dealing with all manner of problems that require action. We appeal to it in setting out our reasons for acting. We look to it for understanding of intentional action in general, including even incontinent action. It gives us, in many cases, a partial account of what mediates between our reasons and our actions based on them. It provides a structure in which actions can be seen to be prima facie rational given the reasons for which they are performed. And partly in virtue of its parallels to theoretical reasoning, it shows us as rational beings, responsive to reasons for acting in a way that is highly analogous to our responsiveness to reasons for believing. We are influenced by both practical reasons and theoretical reasons; and while we can respond to a reason of either kind without drawing it from a process of reasoning, it is through practical and theoretical reasoning that reasons of both kinds have their most characteristic effects on our actions and beliefs.

All of these points apply to practical reasoning as Aristotle understood it. He conceived it as pervasive, inferential, explanatory, causative, justificatory, and broadly logical. If he did not take it to underlie every action for a reason, he at least saw all such action, and probably all voluntary action, as understandable in terms of what, in the light of the means-end structure of intentional action, the agent's practical reasoning was or might have been. Like the structure of our action itself, practical reasoning is to be appraised in relation to happiness as our proper and final end. Here Aristotle is thoroughly foundationalist, motivationally, behaviorally, and normatively: for every intentional action, there is a purposive chain connecting it with an intrinsic desire that is in some way directed towards happiness; and any complete justification of an intentional action will link it, through the agent's beliefs, to some envisaged contribution to happiness. Practical reasoning may accompany any link, or every link, in such a chain; and if, as is often true, the chain is deliberative, its concluding segment will typically be constituted by practical reasoning that issues in action.

So far as we can discern Hume's conception of practical reasoning, it is like Aristotle's in taking such reasoning to have a means-end structure and to be capable of playing the same range of motivational roles Aristotle apparently attributed to it. But there is a vast difference in their conceptions of practical reason, and hence of the assessment of both practical reasoning and action itself. Hume shares only some of Aristotle's foundationalism. For Hume, the role of reason in relation to action seems wholly instrumental: its role is simply to subordinate actions to basic desires, though not necessarily in a manner that contributes to their overall satisfaction in the way required for maximization of expected utility. We find, as in Aristotle, motivational foundations; we do not find normative foundations. Reason can show us how to obtain pleasure, but it provides no basis for criticizing actions as performed for an unreasonable basic end. Practical reasoning guides action relative to basic – and typically hedonic – desires which, at least apart from internal inconsistency, do not admit of assessment as intrinsically rational or irrational. If in Aristotle we find a eudaemonism that is held to be a constitutive commitment of practical reason, in Hume we find what is more nearly a motivationally sovereign hedonism that places basic desires beyond the scope of rational assessment. Hume's conception of reason thus severely circumscribes its role. But the limitation should not be exaggerated: if pleasure and pain are the rulers of most of our conduct, they are blind, and reason is their only sighted servant. It can arouse them by heralding the presence of their objects, extinguish them by pronouncing those objects unobtainable, and direct them by leading their way to gratification.

For Kant, as for both Aristotle and Hume, practical reasoning has a means-end structure. But Kant differs markedly from Aristotle in taking practical reasoning to be closely governed by general principles. Moreover, unlike Aristotle, he explicitly asserts that such principles, in themselves, have strong motivational force: commitment *to* one is normally sufficient to produce action *on* it. Rational action, moreover, must not only accord with norms discoverable a priori, it must also be done *from* that commitment. This leaves ample room for practical reasoning to play a dynamic role, but Kant seems less concerned with that role than either Aristotle or Hume. Furthermore, Kant resolutely rejects externalism regarding the motivational power of reason and instrumentalism concerning rationality. Kant not only postulated normative foundations of rational action, he also gave them both a priori status and motivational power. Practical reason is autonomous: it enables us to discern our duties; it legislates principles governing their fulfillment; and it can move us to act on these principles, whether we are independently inclined to do so or not. Again, we have the notion of rational action as connected, by a purposive chain, to basic ends; but the ends may be given by practical reason alone and need not involve independent desire. If Hume's position represents the inevitable supremacy of desire in human action, Kant's view represents the rightful, and in rational agents quite possible, supremacy of reason.

The view defended in this book is in many ways Aristotelian and, beyond that, more Kantian than Humean. But I have tried to develop a more detailed account than is offered by any one of them. The overall theory of practical reasoning proposed takes practical reasoning as an inferential process with both motivational and cognitive premises. It corresponds to a practical argument, which, in turn, is a kind of argument appropriately produced in answering a practical question. Practical reasoning is indeed an inferential realization of such an argument. Such reasoning may be conceived as a response to a practical problem, and it concludes in the making of a practical judgment. In both content and causal potential, practical judgment is directive. It calls for one's doing what it favors, and one's making it disposes one to carry out that action. A practical judgment thus provides a reason for action. When practical reasoning meets the minimal standards of adequacy, the reason it provides is normative – and so a reason *for* one to act – by virtue of the content of its concluding judgment; and that reason is motivating – and thus a reason *on* which one tends to act – by virtue of the agent's accepting that judgment.

Conclusion

Agents may or may not act on their practical reasoning, whether because of inability, change of mind, incontinence, or some intervention; and an intentional action may or may not be based on such reasoning. But practical reasoning is reconstructively available to the agent for at least partial explanation, and at least prima facie justification, of any intentional action performed for a further end, and probably for any intentional action at all. This holds even when no such reasoning genetically underlies the performance of the action; the reconstructive availability of practical reasoning derives entirely from the *structure* that intentional action has regardless of its particular genesis. Not all intentional action is inferentially grounded in practical reasoning. But all such action is connected, by a purposive chain, to motivation and belief of the kind that normally do underlie practical reasoning.

Moreover, practical reasoning plays an important role in the dynamics of action. It often serves both to guide an action based on it and to strengthen the agent's motivation to perform that action. The reasoning process or some element in it may also explain both how an intention is generated and why it is executed when it is. Yet despite this guiding, motivational role, an action based on practical reasoning may exhibit weakness of will. Neither the motivation expressed in practical reasoning nor the practical judgment in which it concludes need prevail in action, or even in leading the agent to decide, or form the intention, to do the thing favored by the reasoning. Incontinence may occur when the motivation that underlies competing practical reasoning prevails instead. But a standing desire not associated with practical reasoning, or even a sheer impulse, may outweigh the original practical reasoning. Once we realize that intentional action need not arise from practical reasoning, we can see that a weak-willed action may have many kinds of origin, including many that do not require reasoning that supports the incontinent deed.

The full appraisal of practical reasoning requires logical, material, inferential, and epistemic standards. The logical and material standards concern the corresponding practical argument, conceived as an abstract propositional structure. Here we must apply both deductive and broadly inductive standards, as well as material criteria for the truth or falsity of the premises and conclusion. The inferential standards concern the reasoning process.

They chiefly express conditions for rationally inferring the conclusion from the premises, for justifiably believing it in virtue of them, and for the belief of the conclusion to be psychologically based on the beliefs of the premises. The epistemic standards concern the agent's justification in believing each constituent proposition. Appraising these propositions requires both criteria of instrumental rationality and criteria for assessing the rationality of principles, moral and other, that might underlie acceptance of the major, or indeed might be implicit in accepting it, as where adherence to a moral principle *is* one's overriding goal. The assessment of epistemic standards also raises problems of defeasibility, such as how to specify conditions under which the prima facie justification of a practical conclusion remains undefeated.

The four kinds of standards for appraising practical reasoning are each applicable to the links of a purposive chain connecting a rational action to its ultimate motivational basis. For the most part, these standards apply even if the chain is *non*-inferential and the rational action in which it terminates is thus not connected to that ground by any actual reasoning. This is in part why the reconstructive role of practical reasoning is so important in the explanation and justification of action. That role is not only fundamental in understanding the human agent, whether in relation to motivation or belief or reasoning or action itself; it also provides an explicit tool for evaluation of agents and their actions. Even without playing a part in the genesis of an action, practical reasoning can be invoked in its explanation and justification.

Rational action is often based on practical reasoning, but it need not be: it need not be reasoned at all. When it is based on practical reasoning, its rationality can be conceived in relation to its well-groundedness. It is well grounded when, broadly speaking, it is based in the right kind of way on the right kind of reason. In the light of my conception of the unity of practical and theoretical reasoning, I construe this general idea as one would in the epistemological case of rational belief. The right kind of way for a rational action to be grounded is constituted by the action's being performed *for* the reason(s) in question; the right kind of reason, adequate reason, is (undefeated) *rational* motivation guided by (undefeated) rational belief. I make no specific assumptions about what sort of motivation is rational. But I see no reason to doubt that a number of kinds of potential objects of intrinsic desire, most obviously one's own happiness, can be rationally wanted for their own sake. Regarding the guiding beliefs, they are the sorts of beliefs that could express the minor premises of practical reasoning even if the action in question does not arise from such reasoning. They represent the agent's operative conception of what means will realize the end that governs the reasoning.

Practical reasoning is a pervasive element in successful deliberation; and, frequently as an unintrusive process of reaching a decision, it guides our less reflective actions. It occurs, often in cogent forms, in our answering of practical questions. It connects both our normative and our motivating reasons with our actions. It gives rise to actions that are based on our ends and on means which it sets out for us. And it connects many of our actions with grounds in virtue of which they can be seen to be rational. Practical reasoning is an explanatory framework, a rational structure, a unifier of reason and desire, and a central manifestation of rational agency. Even if not all of our intentional actions arise from practical reasoning, we are essentially reasoning beings, and our capacity to engage in practical reasoning, and to act on the reasons it provides us, is partly constitutive of what we are.

Notes

1 Aristotle on Practical Reasoning and the Structure of Action

1 Note, however, that according to G. E. M. Anscombe ' "practical syllogism" in Greek simply means practical reasonings.' See *Intention*, 2nd edn (Ithaca, NY: Cornell University Press, 1963), p. 79.

2 David Gauthier, in *Practical Reasoning* (Oxford: Oxford University Press, 1963), apparently takes deliberation to be equivalent to practical reasoning; see, e.g., p. 25. A similar interpretation is suggested by John Cooper; see *Reason and Human Good in Aristotle* (Cambridge, Mass.: Harvard University Press, 1975), p. 70.

3 *Nicomachean Ethics*, 1112b2–20. This is from the translation by Terence Irwin (Indianapolis, Ind.: Hackett, 1985). References to the *Ethics*, hereinafter to be given in the text, will be to this translation. I will, however, follow Martin Ostwald's useful translation (Indianapolis, Ind.: Bobbs-Merrill, 1962) in one part of the passage just cited and sometimes speak, as he does, of the first link in the chain of causation and the last step in the order of discovery.

4 In Ostwald's translation (cited in note 3), for instance. See esp. 1113a1–14.

5 For a detailed development of this idea see Alan Donagan, *Choice: the Essential Element in Action* (London and New York: Routledge, 1987), esp. chs 5 and 6. Much of what Donagan says about volition and intention, however, can be detached from the kind of self-reference which, following John R. Searle, *Intentionality* (Cambridge: Cambridge University Press, 1983), esp. ch. 3, Donagan includes in his account of volition and immediate intention, e.g. the idea that in raising one's arm one chooses that one's arm go up and that its going up be explained by that very choosing. In any case, Aristotle can be read as holding a volitional account of action without committing him to such self-reference. For further discussion of a volitional approach, in both Aristotle and, especially, Aquinas, see Donagan's 'Thomas Aquinas on Human Action,' in Norman Kretzmann *et al.*, *The Cambridge History of Later Medieval Philosophy* (Cambridge: Cambridge University Press, 1981).

6 He says, e.g., that 'the last premise is a belief about something perceptible and controls action' (1147b9–10); Ostwald's translation suggests that Aristotle went even further in the direction I am suggesting: 'The final premise, consisting as it does in an opinion about an object perceived by the senses, determines our action.' See also *De Motu Animalium* 701a8–15.

7 John Cooper holds a similar view on where the practical syllogism comes in relation to deliberation, op. cit., p. 38. I do not, however, endorse his view that 'The decision is already completed before the

syllogism can get under way' (ibid.) – unless he refers only to deciding *that*, e.g. that penicillin will suffice – as opposed to decision *to*, as expressing deliberative desire.

8   David Charles's translation also supports my reading here: 'When one proposition emerges from these two (major and minor premises), it is necessary then for the soul to assert it immediately, and in cases productive of action to do it immediately. For example, if the major premise is "Taste all sweet things" and the minor is "This is sweet," it is necessary for the man who is able and not prevented straightaway *also* to do the action' (1147a26–31). Here it is a proposition that emerges from the premises – as the conclusion from them – *and* the action is represented as separate from the conclusion. See *Aristotle's Philosophy of Action* (Ithaca, NY: Cornell University Press, 1984), p. 91.

9   There are other, related forms of weakness of will, e.g. the formation of *intentions* to perform acts which are against one's better judgment and thereby themselves incontinent. For an account of weakness of will which covers a variety of cases see my 'Weakness of will and practical judgment,' *Nous* XIII (1979). For a related discussion see Alfred R. Mele, *Irrationality* (Oxford: Oxford University Press, 1987), pp. 18–20, 25–7, and 34–44.

10   See Norman O. Dahl, *Practical Reason, Aristotle, and Weakness of the Will* (Minneapolis, Minn.: University of Minnesota Press, 1984) for an account which emphasizes the importance, in Aristotle, of integration of the agent's knowledge of the minor into that agent's motivational system. See, e.g., pp. 188–204.

11   This is controversial, however. David Charles, for instance, argues that Aristotle does allow clear-eyed weakness of will, op. cit., esp. ch. 4, pp. 191–3. For some critical discussion of Charles's view see Deborah K. Modrak, 'Aristotle on reason, practical reason, and living well,' forthcoming; and for a detailed treatment of Aristotle on incontinence which, on many points, supports mine, see Alfred R. Mele, 'Aristotle on *Akrasia, Eudaemonia*, and the psychology of action,' *History of Philosophy Quarterly* 2 (1985).

12   Anscombe, op. cit., p. 60.

13   Cp. Cooper, op. cit. Perhaps because it is not clear how an action can be a conclusion, he denies that the practical syllogism is reasoning; see esp. pp. 51–5.

14   For a detailed discussion supporting the view that the conclusion of Aristotelian practical reasoning is propositional rather than actional, see Charles, op. cit., esp. pp. 90–5. Cp. Martha Nussbaum, 'Practical syllogisms and practical science,' in her *Aristotle's De Motu Animalium* (Princeton, NJ: Princeton University Press, 1978).

15   If we follow Gerasimos Santas in holding that 'Aristotle does not really distinguish a teleological explanation from a practical inference,' we can account for the plausibility of the action-as-conclusion view without taking it to be Aristotle's considered position.

The conclusion of a teleological explanation . . . is an action in a straightforward sense. . . . But in the corresponding piece of practical inference, best stated in the first person (though of course I can go through a piece of practical inference about what other people should do), 'I want to make M healthy and I can't make him healthy unless I rub him, so I will rub him,' the conclusion is, by no stretch of the imagination, an action (unless it be supposed to be some species of 'mental act' – which cannot be taken in the context to be what Aristotle has in mind – it is tasting the sweet he is talking about).

('Aristotle on practical inference, the explanation of action, and *Akrasia,' Phronesis* XIV, 2 (1969), pp. 175–6)

16   The means need not be instrumental; it may be constitutive. For discussion of this difference, see Cooper, op. cit., pp. 21–2. (Cooper attributes the distinction to L. H. G. Greenwood.)

17   See, e.g., 1139a31–3, where Aristotle says that 'the origin of an action – the source of the movement, not the action's goal – is decision, and the origin of decision is desire together with reason that aims at some goal.' But note that even if he took voluntary action as typically intentional, this passage may not apply to all intentional action. For one thing, something done on the spur of the moment can be voluntary yet not grounded in decision: 'the actions we do on the spur of the moment are said to be voluntary, but not to express decision' (1111b9–10); yet such an action would presumably be intentional. On the other hand, if it is intentional, there remains the question whether it must arise from practical reasoning. That intentional and even voluntary action does, in *some* way, arise from it is held by a number of commentators. Mele, for example, contends (referring to the *hekousion*) that 'for Aristotle, all voluntary and intentional actions have a practical conclusion as a cause.' See Alfred R. Mele, 'Aristotle on the proximate efficient cause of action,' *The Canadian Journal of Philosophy*, supp. vol. X (1984), p. 149.

18   I have argued for this in 'A theory of practical reasoning,' *American Philosophical Quarterly* 19 (1982).

19   Anscombe seems to hold the correspondence thesis, op. cit., p. 80. My reference to *at least one* piece of practical reasoning is to allow for overdetermination of the kind exhibited by *A*-ing for two independent reasons, each motivationally sufficient to lead one to *A*.

20   See, e.g., 1177a20–1177b5, for Aristotle's treatment of pleasure as intrinsic to the relevant activity in the way I have suggested.

21   Cooper, op. cit., prefers 'flourishing', which I, too, often prefer both for its apparent pluralism regarding the constituents of *eudaemonia* and for its implicit reference to activity; but there is no translation universally agreed on, and for convenience I follow Ostwald and others.

22   J. O. Urmson, for instance, speaks of 'the view, shared by both Plato and Aristotle and many since, that nobody aims at lower-order

goals without aiming at some such higher-order goal [as the good and the pleasant].' See 'The goals of action,' in A. I. Goldman and J. Kim (eds), *Values and Morals* (Dordrecht and Boston: D. Reidel, 1978), p. 141. There are certainly passages that easily give this impression, and no doubt Aristotle is committed to the view that, for a rational, reflective agent, at least, having a first-order aim implies having a second-order one. But aiming, in the usual sense implying doing something *in order to* achieve an end, is too strong a notion to describe Aristotle's minimal commitment to the motivationally fundamental role of happiness. For helpful discussion of both how the good is to be understood in Aristotle and how agents aim at it, see Nicholas P. White, 'Goodness and human aims in Aristotle's ethics,' *Studies in Philosophy and the History of Philosophy* vol. 9 (Washington: The Catholic University of America Press, 1981).

23 In 'Intending,' *The Journal of Philosophy* LXX (1973) I have argued that there is a suitably broad sense of 'want'.

2   Hume and the Instrumentalist Conception of Practical Reasoning

1 David Hume, *A Treatise of Human Nature*, ed. L. A. Selby-Bigge (Oxford: Oxford University Press, 1888), 2nd edn ed. P. H. Nidditch (1978), pp. 459–60. Cp. Aristotle's apparently externalist remark that 'Thought by itself, however, moves nothing; what moves us is thought aiming at some goal and concerned with action' (*NE* 1139a36–7). References to the *Treatise* will hereinafter be given parenthetically by page number in the text, and some spellings are modernized.

2 David Hume, *An Enquiry Concerning the Principles of Morals*, ed. P. H. Nidditch (Oxford: Oxford University Press, 1975), reprinted from 1777 edn, p. 293. In the following paragraph, too, Hume sounds hedonistic. Note also that the end he posits is apparently construed as final in Aristotle's sense.

3 Clearly, Hume is not here being skeptical. There is of course much controversy about just how skeptical he is overall.

4 One might, of course, allow normative terms in the expression of Humean practical reasoning and give the process a non-cognitivist reading on which the major premise or conclusion or both are normative and, though not true or false, do imply motivation. I believe, however, that a cognitivist interpretation yields a better overall reading of the *Treatise*.

5 This is the kind of claim that leads Philippa Foot (and others) to call Hume a subjectivist in ethics. See her 'Hume on moral judgment,' in David Pears (ed.), *David Hume* (London: Macmillan, 1963), p. 71. One might also note that the way Hume's point is put here makes

a moral judgment sound like a statement about causal relations and thus *in* the scope of reason in whatever way such judgments are. For another valuable discussion see Nicholas Sturgeon, 'Hume on reason and passion,' forthcoming.

6 Here I differ from Penelhum, who takes Hume to hold that reason 'cannot generate any [desires or aversions] on its own account.' See Terence Penelhum, *Hume* (London: Macmillan, 1975), p. 126. I would also qualify Penelhum's point that judgments generated by reason 'have no power to initiate actions' (p. 128), though most of what Penelhum says about Hume's position on reason and passion is quite consistent with my understanding of Hume. See esp. pp. 122–30.

7 My reading of Hume here differs from Barry Stroud's. He emphasizes 'prefer' and takes Hume to be speaking of a *comparative judgment*; I take Hume to be speaking of passion and to be simply making a *comparison of desire strengths*, as where we speak of preferring reading to television not because one has compared them and ranked the former higher, but because one likes or wants the former more. My reading enables Hume to avoid a problem Stroud points out (though related problems remain however we read the passage). See Barry Stroud, *Hume* (London and Boston: Routledge & Kegan Paul, 1977), p. 166.

8 Norman O. Dahl maintains that for Hume there is no practical reason. See *Practical Reason, Aristotle, and Weakness of the Will* (Minneapolis, Minn.: University of Minnesota Press, 1984), pp. 23–34.

9 See *An Enquiry*, pp. 293–4. Cp. the preceding paragraph, in which desirability also seems to have a normative force not due solely to what is actually desired for its own sake.

10 See A. J. Ayer, *Hume* (New York: Hill & Wang, 1980), p. 88.

11 My paper, 'Weakness of will and practical judgment,' *Nous* XIII (1979), distinguishes between acting against, and merely inconsistently with, practical judgment, and discusses how practical judgment may figure in the mind at the time one acts against it.

12 In a useful essay which generally supports the interpretation of Hume I have given, Michael Smith does not deal with constitutive means in interpreting Hume and also attributes to him a stronger condition than I do on the relation of an intentional action to the agent's good: that if one were to perform it, one would realize the relevant good. See 'The Humean theory of motivation,' *Mind* XCVI (1987).

13 See *An Enquiry*, p. 65, and for discussion of the way in which Hume is a volitionalist see Penelhum, op. cit., ch. 6.

14 For a valuable short treatment of a Humean instrumentalism developed in this decision-theoretic direction, see David Gauthier, 'Reason and maximization,' *The Canadian Journal of Philosophy* IV (1975).

Notes

3 Kant and the Autonomy of Practical Reason

1 *Foundations of the Metaphysics of Morals*, trans. Lewis White Beck (New York: The Liberal Arts Press, 1959), p. 9 (393 in the *Akademie* edition). References to this book will hereinafter be given parenthetically in the text, using the *Akademie* numbering.

2 I think, moreover, that the view is plausible: even if one could fail to deserve to be *given* a good will, once one has it taking it away would be wrong; nor could one now be such as not to deserve *to have it*. Kant may also have thought that good will, by itself, could not have evil effects – as opposed to, say, causing unhappiness when *combined* with misinformation. For extensive discussion of Kant's doctrine of the unqualifiedly good will, see Karl Ameriks, 'Kant on the good will,' forthcoming. For a very different interpretation, on which 'we conclude that there is nothing good in itself, that there is therefore no valid theory of the objectively good to be found,' see Robert Paul Wolff's commentary, *The Autonomy of Reason* (New York: Harper and Row, 1973), p. 132 and esp. ch. 2.

3 The term 'from' seems causal, though not in a sense implying determinism. In any case, if the term indicates an *explanatory* relation – as I believe – we can leave open in what sense Kant could allow the relevant kind of explanation to be causal. Perhaps, however, we need not read him here as taking freedom and determinism to be incompatible. For a treatment of this issue see Allen W. Wood, 'Kant's compatibilism,' in Allen W. Wood (ed.), *Self and Nature in Kant's Philosophy* (Ithaca, NY, and London: Cornell University Press, 1984). Wood says at one point, 'Kant does *not* in general hold that freedom is incompatible with causal determinism or even necessitation of the free being's actions . . . a holy will is free even though its acts are necessitated, because they are necessitated from within reason' (p. 82). For related discussion of Kant's conception of action, see Ralf Meerbote, 'Kant on the nondeterminate character of human actions,' in William L. Harper and Ralf Meerbote (eds), *Kant on Causality, Freedom, and Objectivity* (Minneapolis, Minn.: University of Minnesota Press, 1984). Meerbote ascribes to Kant an 'anomalous monism regarding actions, with the compatibilism which this view entails' (p. 140), where the monism is that of Donald Davidson, which Meerbote describes in part as the view that action-descriptions do not 'yield . . . determinability of actions in either space or time. It of course does not follow from this that actions are not in space or time, or that they cannot be inferable and spatiotemporally determinable by means of other descriptions' (p. 156). They may indeed still have causes in the sense Davidson indicated in 'Actions, reasons and causes,' *The Journal of Philosophy* LX (1963).

4 Paton does appear to think Kant is open to the objection that 'since we cannot summon up motives at will, it cannot be our duty to act on them' (H. J. Paton, *The Categorical Imperative* (London:

Hutchinson, 1946), p. 117). If there are passages inviting such an interpretation, others do not, and Kant's overall view can be kept intact without commitment to direct voluntary control of what motives we have or which we act on. Granted, Kant may take it that we can at will act on one of two *conflicting* motives that are about equally strong; but the issue here is our direct control over which of two or more *aligned* motives – motives inclining us towards the same conduct – we act on.

5 In 'Acting for reasons,' *The Philosophical Review* XCV (1986) I offer a detailed account of acting for a reason which may well fit Kant's notion. That paper also considers cases in which the agent acts mainly but not entirely for a reason. Whether Kant would allow that any motive other than duty may influence an action having moral worth I cannot discuss; but it would make sense to use such considerations to assign *degrees* of moral worth to actions.

6 There has been controversy over whether the sort of motive Kant takes to be internal to moral judgment is a kind of desire. If so, it is not inclination, but desire to do the duty in question for its own sake. As Kant said in one place, 'Certainly the will must have *motives*; but these are not particularly pre-established ends . . . they are nothing but the unconditioned law itself, and the will's receptivity to finding itself subject to it as to an unconditioned constraint is called the *moral sense*' (*Perpetual Peace and Other Essays*, trans. Ted Humphrey (Indianapolis, Ind.: Hackett, 1983), p. 67). Such motives are *grounded* in reason so as to be 'a priori desires,' as Ralf Meerbote puts it. See his 'Kant on freedom and the rational and morally good will,' in Wood, op. cit., p. 64. Cp. Stephen L. Darwall, 'Kantian practical reason defended,' *Ethics* 96 (1985), esp. p. 93.

7 In the *De Anima*, for instance, Aristotle says that

> the mind is never found producing movement without appetite (for wish is a form of appetite, and when movement is produced according to calculation it is also according to wish), but appetite can originate movement contrary to calculation, for desire is a form of appetite . . . it is the object of appetite which originates movement. . . . That then such a power in the soul as has been described, i.e., appetite, originates movement, is clear.
>
> (433a23–433b1; Oxford translation)
> Cp. *Nichomachean Ethics* 1139a36–7.

8 That reason is constitutively normative is suggested by such declarations as that a rational being 'obeys no law except that which he himself also gives' (435), and that 'Reason must regard itself as the author of its principles, independently of foreign influences' (449). On the other hand, however creative reason is in giving moral laws, their correctness is meant to be an objective matter determinable by applying the categorical imperative. For pertinent discussions of some of the main issues raised by these points, see Christine M. Korsgaard, 'Skepticism about practical reason,' *The Journal of Philos-*

ophy LXXXIII (1986) and Thomas E. Hill, Jr, 'Kant on the rationality of moral conduct,' *Pacific Philosophical Quarterly* 66 (1985).

9   Broadie has suggested that Aristotle was like Hume in giving practical reason no power to 'set the ultimate values by which we act.'
For her discussion of this see Sarah Waterlow Broadie, 'Practical
thinking in Aristotle and in Hume,' delivered at the Central Division
Meetings of the American Philosophical Association in 1986. This
point seems correct if the intent is to deny that Aristotle took practical reason to be legislatively or, especially, constitutively practical.
But if epistemic normativity is intended (as I doubt), then I believe
that Aristotle and Hume do differ.

10 *Lectures on Ethics*, trans. Louis Infield (London: Methuen, 1930,
and New York: Harper & Row, 1963) p. 1.

11 In the *Lectures* Kant speaks of logic, as providing (what I take to
be inferential) 'rules concerning the use of the understanding' (p. 2);
and in other places as well he speaks as if reasoning were an important part of theoretical philosophy.

12 Cp. Lewis White Beck, *A Commentary on Kant's Critique of Practical Reason* (Chicago: University of Chicago Press, 1960):

> He [Kant] mentions the danger of taking the words 'practical
> reason' as if the 'object' of practical reason were comparable
> to an object of theoretical reason, i.e., as an epistemological
> object and not as an object of desire or volition. We should be
> warned by this against taking 'practical reason' to denote merely
> the faculty by which we gain knowledge of right and wrong,
> though we should not forget that practical reason does have this
> cognitive function. It provides the cognitive factor in the
> guidance of action whose *dynamis* is impulse.
>
> (pp. 39–40)

13 Perhaps if a motive of duty is necessary *and* sufficient, Kant would
grant that one of inclination might play a significant *supporting* role.
Given his contrast between actions from duty and from inclination,
this is not clear. But his *overall* theory allows such a role; Kant says,
e.g., that 'a factor whose removal strengthens the effect of a moving
force must have been a hindrance; consequently, all admixture of
incentives which derive from one's own happiness are a hindrance
to the influence of the moral law on the human heart' (*Critique of
Practical Reason*, trans. Lewis White Beck (Indianapolis, Ind.:
Bobbs-Merrill, 1956), p. 160). There may be an important contrast
implicit in the passage, between a *hindrance* and a *nullifier*. The
passage also indicates that Kant is *not* taking the motivational cooperation (or presence) of incentives to count against an action's moral
worth on the ground that it prevents *knowing* the action is done
from duty. He did hold some such restriction on self-knowledge,
however; as he says in *Perpetual Peace*, 'no man can with certainty
be conscious of *having performed* his duty altogether unselfishly'
(p. 68).

14 I leave open an option Kant has been thought not to have. Arguing against Ross's claim that one can have an inclination to do something 'yet do it simply because it is our duty,' Beck contends that 'There seems an open contradiction in saying: I have two motives *A* and *B*; each would lead me to do action *C*; I do perform *C*, but I do so purely and simply from motive *A* alone. . . . Kant would say this was the merest cant' ('Sir David Ross on duty and purpose in Kant,' *Philosophy and Phenomenological Research* XVI (1955), p. 171). There is surely no obvious contradiction here, but the imagined self-congratulation *is* groundless if, as Beck suggests, it presupposes direct voluntary control over which of two aligned motives one acts on.

15 For some clarification of how action on a moral imperative actually takes place, see Barbara Herman, 'The practice of moral judgment,' *The Journal of Philosophy* LXXXV (1985) and Henry E. Allison, 'Morality and freedom: Kant's reciprocity thesis,' *The Philosophical Review* XCV (1986).

16 Kant may have viewed both the explainability and the rationality of actions in the broad framework of a kind of motivational foundationalism. He said that

> since there are free actions there must also be ends to which, as their object, these actions are directed. But among these ends there must also be some that are at the same time (that is, by their concept) duties. – For were there no such ends, then all ends would be valid for practical reason only as means to other ends; and since there can be no action without an end, a *categorical* imperative would be impossible.
>
> (*The Doctrine of Virtue*, Part II of *The Metaphysics of Morals*, trans. Mary J. Gregor (Philadelphia, Pa: University of Pennsylvania Press, 1964), p. 43)

It is true that Kant is referring to normative ends, 'objects man *ought to adopt* as ends' (p. 43); but in the same context he speaks of such ends motivationally, for instance in saying, 'An *end* is an *object* of free choice, the thought of which determines the power of choice to an action by which the object is produced' (p. 43). His view may be that when we act for a reason we have (ultimately, at least) a non-instrumental end; and when it is an end we ought to have, we act morally.

4 The Varieties and Basic Elements of Practical Reasoning

1 Here and elsewhere in this chapter I draw on my paper 'A theory of practical reasoning,' *American Philosophical Quarterly* 19 (1982).

2 G. H. von Wright, *Explanation and Understanding* (Ithaca, NY: Cornell University Press, 1971), p. 107. He recognizes that many

Notes

schemata can represent practical inference (which he apparently considers equivalent to practical reasoning – e.g. on p. 96); but this is his final formulation. (His variables have been altered to match mine.)

3 Alvin I. Goldman, *A Theory of Human Action* (Englewood Cliffs, NJ: Prentice-Hall, 1970), p. 105.

4 Cp. Aristotle's cloak example, *De Motu Animalium* 701a16–23.

5 Paul M. Churchland, 'The logical character of action-explanations,' *The Philosophical Review* 79 (1970), p. 228. For detailed critical discussion of Churchland's schema and a defense of a similar kind of schema, see Rex Martin, *Historical Explanation* (Ithaca, NY: Cornell University Press, 1977), esp. ch. 9.

6 David P. Gauthier, *Practical Reasoning* (Oxford: Oxford University Press, 1963), p. 44 (his 'x' has been replaced by 'A'). For a recent case to the effect that rationality requires only such desirability, or 'satisficing,' judgments as opposed to judgments to the effect that A-ing is one's *best* option, see Michael Slote, 'Moderation, rationality, and virtue,' the Tanner Lectures on Human Value (Stanford, 1985). D. S. Clarke, Jr also addresses this issue in detail, e.g., in *Practical Inferences* (London: Routledge & Kegan Paul, 1985), ch. 2.

7 Donald Davidson, 'How is weakness of the will possible?' in Joel Feinberg (ed.), *Moral Concepts* (London and New York: Oxford University Press, 1969), p. 110. He says of practical reasoning that its 'minimal elements . . . are these: the agent accepts some reason (or set of reasons) r, and holds that $pf(A$ is better than $B, r)$, and these constitute the reason why he judges that A is better than B' (p. 110). (Davidson's variables have been altered to match mine.)

8 Hector-Neri Castañeda, *Thinking and Doing* (Dordrecht and Boston: D. Reidel, 1975), p. 15. A special element – 'Jones to A' – is omitted from this schema for simplicity; this should not affect what I say.

9 This last item Castañeda treats as expressing volition understood to imply something like a commitment of the will; the agent is not simply expressing intention to do the thing at some time or other or, above all, just predictively asserting she will do the deed. For a more recent statement of his views, with replies to critical essays, see his 'Conditional intentions, intentional action, and Aristotelian practical syllogisms,' *Erkenntnis* 18 (1982), and his chapter, 'Human action: intention and obligation,' in James E. Tomberlin (ed.), *Agent, Language, and the Structure of the World* (Indianapolis, Ind.: Hackett, 1983).

10 Myles Brand, *Intending and Acting* (Cambridge, Mass.: MIT Press, 1984), p. 129. A similar view is expressed in Gilbert Harman, 'Practical reasoning,' *The Review of Metaphysics* 29 (1976). For a more recent statement of Harman's conception of reasoning see his *Change in View* (Cambridge, Mass.: MIT Press, 1986).

11 For instance, in 'A theory of practical reason,' *The Philosophical Review* 74 (1965), Robert Binkley holds that 'the conclusion of practi-

cal reasoning is decision' (p. 432). Anthony Kenny sees Aristotle as taking the conclusion to be, in some cases, a decision. See *Aristotle's Theory of the Will* (New Haven, Conn.: Yale University Press, 1979), esp. pp. 142–4.

12 In 'Intending,' *The Journal of Philosophy* LXX (1973), I have argued that there is such a broad, non-technical sense of 'want'; and in 'The concept of wanting,' *Philosophical Studies* 21 (1973), I explicate wanting in this sense. A (purely) *intrinsic* want for ɸ is roughly a want for it simply for its own sake; a (purely) *extrinsic* want for it is one based entirely on one's wanting something else: roughly, wanting it for a further reason, the typical case being wanting something just as a means to something else. I have offered a related account of the relevant notion of belief in 'The concept of believing,' *The Personalist* 53 (1972).

13 For a comprehensive account of social practical reasoning see Raimo Tuomela, *A Theory of Social Action* (Dordrecht and Boston: D. Reidel, 1984).

14 *Nicomachean Ethics* 1147a1–10. If the want cited is too narrow in content, it is at least plausible in the context to think that the agent is supposed to have *some* want regarding the food.

15 I do not assume that these must express the same proposition. Castañeda has plausibly argued that they would not. See, e.g., *Thinking and Doing*, pp. 158–9.

16 See, e.g., James D. Wallace, 'Practical inquiry,' *The Philosophical Review* 78 (1969), pp. 442–3; and notice von Wright's speaking of 'first-person practical syllogisms' (*The Varieties of Goodness* (London: Routledge & Kegan Paul, 1963), p. 170). Clarke, in the work cited in note 6 of this chapter, also countenances second- and third-person practical reasoning (pp. 63–7).

17 Castañeda (in *Thinking and Doing* and elsewhere) uses 'practition' for the object of a conative attitude and develops an extensive logical framework for dealing with the connections among practitions themselves and between them and propositions.

5 Practical Reasoning and Intentional Action

1 See, for instance, Donald Davidson, 'How is weakness of the will possible?' in Joel Feinberg (ed.), *Moral Concepts* (London and New York: Oxford University Press, 1969) and Gilbert Harman, 'Practical reasoning,' *Review of Metaphysics* 29 (1976), p. 451; cp. p. 442. Davidson says, e.g., that intentional actions are 'geared directly to unconditional judgments like "It would be better to do *A* than to do *B*," ' and that 'Practical reasoning does . . . often arrive at unconditional judgments that one action is better than another – otherwise there would be no such thing as acting for a reason' (p. 110). Since he regards intentional actions as performed for a reason,

and apparently holds that the latter arise only through practical reasoning, he seems committed to the view that all intentional action arises in some way from practical reasoning. Cp. pp. 79–80 of Anscombe's *Intention*, 2nd edn (Ithaca, NY: Cornell University Press, 1963) and Joseph Raz's introduction to his anthology *Practical Reasoning* (London and New York: Oxford University Press, 1978), esp. pp. 2–5.

2   A number of writers have noted that recitation is not needed for practical reasoning. Alvin I. Goldman, e.g., says, of the propositions of a typical practical inference he cites, 'I do not *recite* these propositions to myself as I assent to them.' See *A Theory of Human Action* (Englewood Cliffs, NJ: Prentice-Hall, 1970), p. 103. He does not say, however, what, short of recitation, is required for assenting.

3   Goldman would say that the want must be occurrent at the time of action; but if so, I believe this does not require more than *S*'s being appropriately aware of the relevant object, and perception seems to suffice for that in the sorts of cases at issue here.

4   I argue for this in detail in 'Belief, reason, and inference,' *Philosophical Topics* XIV, 1 (1986).

5   This is argued in my 'Acting for reasons,' *The Philosophical Review* XCV (1986). There the explaining beliefs and wants are called *reason states*. While that terminology is in most respects preferable, there is no harm in here calling the states themselves, as opposed to their objects, reasons, and such terminology is common.

6   Judith Jarvis Thomson, for instance, has said that 'It certainly *seems* as if "I want *x*" implies "I have *a* reason for trying to get *x*." ' See her review of Gauthier's *Practical Reasoning, The Journal of Philosophy* LXII (1965), p. 186. Cp. David Milligan's view that 'A *prima facie* reason consists of a feature-want together with a belief that the action being explained satisfied the feature-want' (*Reasoning and the Explanation of Actions* (Brighton, Sussex: Harvester Press, and Atlantic Highlands, NJ.: Humanities Press, 1980), p. 122). For other views concerning reasons, and much discussion of reason and desire, see E. J. Bond, *Reason and Value* (Cambridge: Cambridge University Press, 1983), esp. ch. 2; and Bernard Williams, 'Internal and external reasons,' in his *Moral Luck* (Cambridge: Cambridge University Press, 1981).

7   This and the next two paragraphs follow my 'Acting for reasons,' cited in note 5 of this chapter.

8   Here and in the next five paragraphs I draw on my 'Self-deception and practical reasoning,' *The Canadian Journal of Philosophy* XIX (1989).

9   For an account of self-deception along these lines, with a number of references to relevant literature, see my 'Self-deception, action and will,' *Erkenntnis* 18 (1982). For a different account of self-deception, though one that also avoids postulating subagents, see Alfred R. Mele, *Irrationality* (Oxford: Oxford University Press, 1987), esp. chs 9 and 10.

10 To be sure, we always act against the background of beliefs, expec-
tations, and, very commonly, dispositions to fit our intentional
actions into a pattern even if they were not performed *as* part of
one. If planned action is essentially action for which this holds, then
perhaps every intentional action, as well as all action based on
practical reasoning, is planned, or at least part of a plan. For an
extensive treatment of plans and their relation to both intentional
action and practical reasoning, see Michael E. Bratman, *Intention,
Plans, and Practical Reason* (Cambridge, Mass.: Harvard University
Press, 1987).

6 Practical Reasoning in the Dynamics of Action

1 The sort of causal account of action I find most plausible is set out
in my 'Acting for reasons,' *The Philosophical Review* XCV (1986).
For related, and in important ways similar, accounts, see Alvin I.
Goldman, *A Theory of Human Action* (Englewood Cliffs, NJ: Prentice-Hall, 1970); Raimo Tuomela, *Human Action and Its Explanation*
(Dordrecht and Boston: D. Reidel, 1977); Irving Thalberg, 'Do
our intentions cause intentional actions?' *American Philosophical
Quarterly* 21 (1984); and Myles Brand, *Intending and Acting* (Cambridge, Mass.: MIT, 1984). On the nature of intentions and their
causal relation to action, see also J. David Velleman, 'Practical
reflection,' *The Philosophical Review* XCIV (1985). For a different
conception of intending – though one that, like Velleman's, construes
it as a kind of belief – see Donald Davidson, 'Intending,' in his
Essays on Actions and Events (Oxford and New York: Oxford University Press, 1980).

2 As Hector-Neri Castañeda puts it, 'there must be some event to
at least mobilize energy already available potentially' ('Conditional
intentions, intentional actions, and Aristotelian practical syllogisms,'
Erkenntnis 18 (1982), p. 253).

3 For an account of volition and its importance for action, see Hugh
J. McCann, 'Volition and basic action,' *The Philosophical Review*,
LXXXIII (1974). Cp. Wilfrid Sellars, 'Volitions re-affirmed,' in
Myles Brand and Douglas Walton (eds), *Action Theory* (Dordrecht
and Boston: D. Reidel, 1976); Bruce Aune, *Reason and Action*
(Dordrecht and Boston: D. Reidel, 1977), esp. ch. 2; and Lawrence
Davis, *Theory of Action* (Englewood Cliffs, NJ: Prentice-Hall, 1979),
esp. pp. 15–26. For the most part, McCann characterizes volition
intrinsically. Others, including Davis, characterize it functionally.
For a volitionalist view with a careful phenomenological account
of some important volitional processes, see Carl Ginet, 'Voluntary
exertion of the body: a volitional account,' *Theory and Decision* 20
(1986).

4 In 'Acting for reasons,' cited in note 1 of this chapter, I have gone

some distance toward a detailed explication, emphasizing (among other things) that an action under the control of reason is *discriminative* and thereby responsive to *S*'s beliefs and perceptual information.

5 See, e.g., Donald Davidson, 'Actions, reasons, and causes,' *The Journal of Philosophy* LX (1963); and the works by Goldman and by Tuomela, cited in note 1 of this chapter.

6 See, e.g., Donald Davidson, 'Mental events,' in his *Essays on Actions and Events* (Oxford and New York: Oxford University Press, 1980); and Jaegwon Kim, 'Self-understanding and rationalizing explanations,' *Philosophia Naturalis* 21 (1984).

7 I have developed this in 'The concept of wanting,' *Philosophical Studies* 21 (1973) and defended and developed the account in 'Wants and intentions in the explanation of action,' *Journal for the Theory of Social Behaviour* 9 (1980).

8 See the *Treatise*, p. 419.

9 'Moral responsibility, freedom, and compulsion,' *American Philosophical Quarterly* 11 (1974). For a contrasting view see Peter van Inwagen, *An Essay on Free Will* (Oxford: Oxford University Press, 1983).

7 The Assessment of Practical Reasoning

1 For an interesting theory along these lines see Robert Binkley, 'A theory of practical reason,' *The Philosophical Review* LXXIV (1965). See also Hector-Neri Castañeda, *Thinking and Doing* (Dordrecht and Boston: D. Reidel, 1975) and, for a recent statement, his contribution to James E. Tomberlin (ed.), *Hector-Neri Castañeda* (Dordrecht and Boston: D. Reidel, 1986). Cp. Anthony Kenny, 'Practical inference,' *Analysis* 23 (1966) and R. M. Hare, *Practical Inferences* (Berkeley and Los Angeles, Ca: University of California Press, 1972).

2 Such an argument is illustrated in ch. 4, section I. The other schemata referred to in this paragraph are also illustrated there.

3 In ch. 5 of *Belief, Justification, and Knowledge* (Belmont, Ca: Wadsworth, 1988) I discuss the transmission of justification and illustrate how such transmission can fail in cases of theoretical reasoning, deductive as well as inductive.

4 I do not suppose it self-evident that moral judgments are true or false ('cognitive'); but if not, much of what I say could be preserved. For a recent presentation of non-cognitivism, see Allan Gibbard, 'A noncognitivist analysis of rationality in action,' *Social Theory and Practice* 2–3 (1983).

5 That we are neither infallible nor necessarily justified in such beliefs about ourselves is argued in my papers 'The limits of self-knowledge,' *The Canadian Journal of Philosophy* IV (1974) and 'Self-deception, action, and will,' *Erkenntnis* 18 (1982).

6   It may be objected that if I were asked whether I want to avoid being reclusive I would say I do; hence I dispositionally want this. But this confuses a *disposition to want* with a *dispositional want*. The distinction is not sharp, but it is important. In any case, my point could be put in terms of different *kinds* of wants. Development and defense of the same distinction as applied to belief is given in my 'Believing and affirming,' *Mind* XCI (1982).

7   I have quoted Davidson as taking intentional actions to be 'geared directly to unconditional judgements;' but while there is some reason to hold this I argue against it in 'Weakness of will and practical judgment,' *Nous* XIII (1979) and, by implication, in 'Acting for reasons,' *The Philosophical Review* XCV (1986).

8   For a view of practical reasoning which conceives it as more deeply grounded in a particular culture than my view suggests, see Alasdair MacIntyre, *Whose Justice? Which Rationality?* (Notre Dame, Ind.: University of Notre Dame Press, 1988).

9   That Kant held this is argued by Nelson Potter in 'The argument of Kant's *Grundlegung*,' *The Canadian Journal of Philosophy* supp. vol. 1, pt 1. As Potter puts Kant's priority thesis, 'Moral value always outweighs any other kind' (p. 75). Three of the philosophers who have discussed the moral priority thesis extensively are Kurt Baier, William K. Frankena, and Alan Gewirth. See, e.g., Frankena's *Ethics*, 2nd edn (Englewood Cliffs, NJ: Prentice-Hall, 1973) and 'The ethics of right reason,' *The Monist* 66 (1983); Baier's 'The social source of reason,' *Proceedings and Addresses of the American Philosophical Association* 51 (1978) and 'The conceptual link between morality and rationality,' *Nous* XVI (1982) (which suggests a version of the moral priority thesis); and Gewirth's *Reason and Morality* (Chicago: University of Chicago Press, 1978).

10 The general perspective expressed here is internalism about epistemic justification. For a valuable overview see William P. Alston, 'Internalism and externalism in epistemology,' *Philosophical Topics* XIV (1986); and for a different view see my *Belief, Justification, and Knowledge* (cited in note 3 of this chapter), esp. ch. 7, and my 'Justification, truth, and reliability,' *Philosophy and Phenomenological Research* LXIX (1988).

8   Practical Reasoning and Rational Action

1   D. F. Pears, *Motivated Irrationality* (Oxford: Oxford University Press, 1984), p. 121. He apparently also holds a similar non-causal view for theoretical reasoning.

2   For a plausible defense of this view see Keith Lehrer, *Knowledge* (Oxford: Oxford University Press, 1974), pp. 122–6 and Richard Foley, 'Epistemic luck and the purely epistemic,' *American Philosophical Quarterly* 21 (1984). I have replied to Lehrer in 'The causal

Notes

structure of indirect justification,' *The Journal of Philosophy* LXXX (1983) and, in part (though indirectly), to Foley in 'Rationalization and rationality,' *Synthese* 65 (1985).

3 This formulation is developed and defended in 'Rationalization and rationality,' cited in the previous note.

4 I defend this in a number of places, including 'Self-deception, action, and will,' *Erkenntnis* 18 (1982); but much of what I say about self-deception in relation to practical reasoning would hold on various other accounts of self-deception.

5 This point is argued in my 'Self-deception and rationality,' in Mike W. Martin (ed.), *Self-Deception and Self-Understanding* (Lawrence, Kans and London: University Press of Kansas, 1985).

6 In this and the next two quotations I use Ostwald's translation rather than Irwin's, but nothing I say turns on the choice.

7 Much of this interpretation of Aristotle on rational action is confirmed by points made by William K. Frankena in 'Concepts of rational action in the history of ethics,' *Social Theory and Practice* 9 (1983). See, e.g., pp. 172–4. In calling Aristotle's version of eudaemonism a form of *perfectionism*, however, Frankena may be giving it a stronger interpretation than I have, at least if the term implies that a rational action – as opposed to an *ideally* rational one – must be optimal, as opposed to being just a good means to a proper end.

8 On this point, among others, Mill apparently followed Aristotle. But Mill's epistemology was even more empiricist than Hume's, and it left Mill with little to say in defense of construing some pleasures as intrinsically better than others.

9 In the *Grundlegung* Kant says, 'Intelligence, wit, judgment, and the other talents of the mind, however they be named, or courage, resoluteness, and perseverance, as qualities of temperament, are doubtless in many respects good and desirable. But they can become extremely bad and harmful if the will . . . is not good' (393). Apparently, these are (or can be) intrinsically good, though not unconditionally good since apart from good will they can be bad. If Kant is Aristotelian here in allowing non-moral intrinsic goods, he is not *Greek*, so far as Frankena is right in saying that 'the Greeks tended to be egoists, not only in their conception of rationality, but also in the psychology and in their views about method . . .' (p. 169 of the paper cited in note 7).

10 Take, e.g., Graeme Marshall's view that 'Predicating rationality of an act says that an appropriateness relation holds between the events that constitute the agent's act on the one hand and, on the other, his reasons for acting and related beliefs and his sensory information about the acting situation' ('Action on the rationality principle,' *Australasian Journal of Philosophy* 59 (1981), pp. 58–9). The example on p. 59 confirms that non-causal appropriateness is intended.

11 Hume says in Part II, Section I of the *Treatise*, e.g., that 'when we praise any actions . . . these actions are considered as signs; and the ultimate object of our praise and approbation is the motive, that

207

produc'd them' (477). While the subject in the passage is moral praise, the main idea seems to be that actions are viewed as *signs* of such underlying motivation. It would be at least puzzling if Hume did not take assessments of rationality in a similar causal fashion.

12 I have given a detailed account of some of my objections to the maximization of expected utility view of rational action in 'An epistemic conception of rationality,' *Social Theory and Practice* 9 (1983) and 'Action theory as a resource for decision theory,' *Theory and Decision* 20 (1986).

13 This possibility is discussed in 'An epistemic conception of rationality,' cited in the previous note; and the possibility of the relevant kinds of principles being a priori is clarified and defended in my 'Justification, truth, and reliability,' *Philosophy and Phenomenological Research* LXIX (1988). For a very different conception of rational action see Bernard Williams, *Moral Luck* (Cambridge: Cambridge University Press, 1981), esp. ch. 8, on internal and external reasons.

14 See R. B. Brandt, *A Theory of the Good and the Right* (Oxford: Oxford University Press, 1979). In 'An epistemic conception of rationality' I construe Brandt's view of rational desire as a *procedural foundationalism*, since it conceives rational action as resting on procedurally adequate desires, but imposes no substantive constraints on their content (it might also be called a procedurally constrained instrumentalism if one wants to emphasize the importance of means-ends relations in its account of rational action). This view is also critically appraised in the paper. Cp. John Rawls' view of rational action in *A Theory of Justice* (Cambridge, Mass.: Harvard University Press, 1971), which is in most respects close to the maximization of expected utility conception; see, e.g., pp. 142–50. But note that Rawls does make one apparently substantive assumption that seems applicable to the rationality of basic ends: that rational persons do not suffer from envy; see, e.g., pp. 530–4.

Index

accessibility 33
action: automatic 109, 115, 119, 168–9; based on practical reasoning 6, 108, 118, 133, 170–1; based on reasons 116; basic 30; -as-conclusion (of practical reasoning) 24–8, 93–4, 118; deliberate 47, 108–9; deterministically produced 127; dynamics of 7–8, 126–41; explanation of 7, 28–33, 126; for a reason 2, 6–7, 37–8, 57–8, 78–9, 106–7, 169, 175–8, 188; from duty 60–8; genetic basis of 114–16, 127; incontinent *see* incontinent action; indirect eudaemonistic grounding of 34; intelligibility of 7, 116–17; intentional 28, 37, 41, 47, 57, 65, 108–25, 189; motivationally rational 80; nomic connection with reasons 134; rational 2, 8, 37–8, 59, 79–80, 168–85, 190; rationally performed 175; reasoned 47, 123–5, 175–8; redescriptive understanding of 126; sustaining basis of 114; telically rational 80; traceable to practical reasoning 114–16; voluntary 28, 139
adequacy pattern of practical reasoning 148–50

agent-relative appraisal of practical reasoning 166
Allison, Henry E. 200
Alston, William P. 206
Ameriks, Karl 197
Anscombe, G. E. M. 24, 192, 194, 203
argument, practical *see* practical argument
Aristotle 13–38, 70–1, 74, 142, 179–83, 186–7; deliberation 14–16; explanation of action 28–32; practical syllogism 17–19; structure of action 32–6; unity of practical and theoretical reasoning 24–8; weakness of will 19–24, 26, 28
assessment of practical reasoning 142–67, 189; criteria 143–55, epistemic 153–62, inferential 143–51, 189–90, logical 143–51, 189, material 155, 189; dimensions of 154–5, argumental 154, epistemic 154–5, 190, inferential 154; relativity of 162–64
attending to a practical judgment 137
Aune, Bruce 204
autonomy of practical reason 80, 188
axiological foundationalism 36
Ayer, A. J. 196

Index

Index

premises of practical reasoning;
minor premise *see* premises of
practical reasoning
ends 14, 29–33, 178–84; final 30,
33, 35, 179; intrinsic 32, 178;
subsidiary 14–15, 33; *see also*
wants
enthymematic reasoning 46, 91
epistemic relativism 163–4
eudaemonism 36, 187; indirect
eudaemonistic grounding 34
events 29, 126–33, 169–70
exploratory practical reasoning 98
externalism 71, 104

final end 30, 33, 35, 179
Foley, Richard 206–7
Foot, Philippa 195–6
foundationalism: axiological 36;
behavioral 114; motivational
35–6, 43
Frankena, William K. 206–7
freedom 139–41
functionalism 58
functionalist view of practical
reasoning 88–9, 112

Gauthier, David 192, 196, 201
generation of passion by reason
49–50; identificational 49–50;
instrumental 50
genetic hedonism 41–2
genetically pervasive practical
reasoning 123
genetically practical reasoning
77–8
Gewirth, Alan 206
Gibbard, Allan 205
Ginet, Carl 204
Goldman, Alvin I. 201, 203–5
good, the 35
good will, Kantian 60–3
guidance by belief: of action 133;
of practical reasoning 110–11

happiness 30–7, 41, 67–8, 179,
181–3
Hare, R. M. 205

Harman, Gilbert 201
hedonism 187; genetic 41–2;
psychological 41; valuational
41, 53
Herman, Barbara 200
Hill, Thomas E., Jr 198–9
Hume, David 39–59, 179–81,
187–8; instrumental role of
reason 39–43; moral judgment
48–50; passion 40–3, 49, 52–5;
practical judgment 55–6;
rational action 48–51;
reasoning in genesis of action
43–8; weakness of will 51–6

incontinent action 7, 19–24, 37,
51–6, 72–6, 79, 118–19, 122–3,
189; dynamics of 135–9;
insufficient integration 23–4;
failure of volitional integration
22–3, 138; obscured knowledge
22–3, 138; purely passional 119;
weakness of will vs. weakness
in the will 73–4
incontinent belief 25
indirect eudaemonistic grounding
34
inference, means-end 39–43
inferential chain 33
inferentialism 108–19, 127, 130,
168; linear 114; and realization
of practical arguments 118;
restricted linear 115–16
inferentially realized practical
argument 118
instrumentalism 50–6, 58–9, 182;
broad 53–4; categorical 53;
inferential instrumentalist
account 47; mixed hypothetical
53; narrow 53–4; simple
instrumentalist account 47
integration: insufficient 54;
volitional 73
intention, descriptive primacy of
64–5
intentional actions *see* actions,
intentional
internalism 52–5, 68–72, 80, 104;

211

Index

Index

Santas, Gerasimos 193–4
schemata of practical reasoning
86–102; necessary condition
86–7, 92, 147; rule 86, 88, 92;
simplest basic 99–101; sufficient
condition 86–8, 92, 101;
sufficient reason 86
Searle, John R. 192
second-order justification 176
self-deception 120–3, 175–6
self-deceptive practical reasoning
121–2, 173
self-indulgence 75–6
Sellars, Wilfred 204
Slote, Michael 201
Smith, Michael 196
social practical reasoning 101
Stroud, Barry 196
Sturgeon, Nicholas 196
subsidiary end 14–15
sufficient condition schemata of
practical reasoning 86–8, 92,
101
sufficient reason schemata of
practical reasoning 86
suppositional practical reasoning
96–7; cognitively 97;
motivationally 96–7; wholly 97
syllogism, practical *see* practical
syllogism

Thalberg, Irving 204
theoretical basis relation 34
theoretical reasoning vs. practical
reasoning *see* unity of practical
and theoretical reasoning
Thomson, Judith Jarvis 203
tokenings 91–3, 101–2, 109–10
Tuomela, Raimo 202, 204–5

unconsciousness of practical
reasoning 119–23; awareness
sense 119; recognitional sense
119–20, 123
underlying argument 145
unity of practical and theoretical
reasoning 1, 8–9, 24–8, 58–9,
76–8, 80, 85, 102–6
Urmson, J. O. 194–5
utility, maximization of expected
58, 178–82

valuational hedonism 41, 53
van Inwagen, Peter 205
Velleman, J. David 204
volition 16–17, 128
volitional integration 73
von Wright, G. H. 200–2

Wallace, James D. 202
wants 36, 82–3, 92, 95–6, 112, 132,
155–7; on balance 97, 135–6;
rationality of 182–3; *see also*
ends
weakness in the will 73–4
weakness of will *see* incontinent
action
what to do vs. what it is that one
should do 103
White, Nicholas P. 195
will, weakness of *see* incontinent
action
Williams, Bernard 203, 208
Wolff, Robert Paul 197
Wood, Allen W. 197